EDUCATION UNDER SIX

EDUCATION UNDER SIX

DENISON DEASEY

ST. MARTIN'S PRESS   NEW YORK

Library of Congress Cataloging in Publication Data

Deasey, Denison
    Education under six.
    1. Education, Preschool – History. I. Title.
LB1140.D37   372.21'09   77–21081
ISBN 0–312–23748–0

Printed and bound in Great Britain

CONTENTS

TO DAVID BOYD

artist and humanitarian

ACKNOWLEDGEMENTS

The author owes a particular debt of gratitude to Mr G.W. Geoghegan and his staff at the University of Reading Education Library, where he began his quest, and to the Bibliothèque Centrale de l'Ensiegnement Publique, Paris, which also generously permitted me to borrow books. Other libraries whose help was most valuable included the Bodleian Library and the Institute of Education Library, Oxford; the BMA Nuffield Library, London; the British Museum Reading Room and the Colindale Newspaper Library; the Bibliothèque Historique de la Ville de Paris; the IBE Library, Geneva; the University of London's Institute of Education Library where Mr D.J. Foskett allowed me generous facilities for research; the Library of Bedford College, University of London and also the Wellcome Historical Medical Library, London.

Among persons whose help was unfailingly and cheerfully given during several years of research and preparation were: Polly Boyd and Richard Divers of London; Messrs Peter Clark, Maclaren Gordon, Jack Sydes and R.J. Southey, all of Melbourne; Mr Austen Kark, of Weybridge, England; and David and Hermia Boyd, from whose home in Vence I visited *maternelles* in the Alpes Maritimes. Two whose support and encouragement was always timed to coincide with troughs of depression and material difficulty were my friend George Bailey, journalist and writer, of West Berlin and my brother Randal Deasey of Melbourne.

Any writer on education owes more than words can describe to teachers and children who showed him the way to comprehend the link between play and work. Education is about children, and one acknowledges gratefully the welcome received at nursery schools and *maternelles* from Deptford (where the spirit of Margaret McMillan seems to linger) to the Mediterranean coast. Froebel, Montessori, and Piaget all learned from observing children; whatever is of merit in this work comes from the same source and is offered as a tribute to the children, mothers, and teachers involved in the changing world of boys and girls under six.

INTRODUCTION

We know very little about the change in society's view of childhood which took place around 1800. The name of Jean-Jacques Rousseau has usually been quoted as if he had contributed most to change, and he certainly insisted in *Émile* that children should be children before being men. But Rousseau is not a very good choice as the father of early care and education because he was a classic case of what is now recognized as the cycle of deprivation: he himself was deprived of parental care at an early age and he put away his own children to be brought up as orphans at state expense. When the ubiquitous James Boswell asked Rousseau why he never spoke of Émile's father, or the duties of a child to his parents, he answered, 'Oh! He did not have any parents; they just didn't exist'.

In Rousseau's lifetime, Jean-Frédéric Oberlin began what was probably the first organized attempt at education during the child's early years. This was in Alsace, where Oberlin arrived to take charge as pastor of a group of remote country villages. Oberlin and his helpers not only gathered children aged less than six into shelter, but worked out a method of instruction based on play and enjoyment in which older children participated as teachers' aides.

Oberlin's village centres were operating in the 1780s, but there was no sign that Western Europe was eager to follow his example, and small children were either neglected or left in the care of a neighbour, grandparent, or older sister while their mothers went out to work. The next move to help the youngest age-group was made when a Paris baby-minding centre was opened by private philanthropy in 1800. This was imitated in Germany and much discussed in England, where a lady novelist with an interest in education took up the cause during the early 1800s. It should be emphasised that these initiatives were in no way connected with the founding of public elementary education but derived from philanthropy and the Enlightment. The same sort of impulse prompted Coram to endow the first foundlings' home in London and led to the first children's hospital in Paris. Throughout our story public authorities were slow to move, and had to be pushed or shamed into action by individual reformers who came mainly from a radical Protestant background. Local authorities became involved after 1825 in France, for instance, but the state itself did not intervene until 1833. Indeed, in Germany, the Prussian government's reaction in 1851 was to ban the kindergarten as part of a socialist and atheistical plot.

France may claim Oberlin as a true precursor, but Britain's Robert Owen (1816) went far ahead of his time in planning a humane type of education for use within the factory system. Owen's New Lanark school took children of both sexes from three to ten years of age in day and evening sessions. It showed the influence of Owen's socialist outlook and also that of his millenarian followers and employees. The spiritual view of these followers of Swedenborg exalted the state of childhood and, together with Owen's plan to build a new society by improving the environment of factory-workers, created a unique atmosphere at New Lanark. Play was encouraged, and also singing, dancing, and open-air exercise. Significantly, the younger children (from three to five) were given a room of their own, thus creating a genuine infants' school.

Owen's message was taken to London, but the infant schools which proliferated in Britain during the nineteenth century were swallowed up in the growth of cheap elementary education for the poor. The essence of early childhood education as seen in Alsace and New Lanark had been freedom and enjoyment through play; Owen even proclaimed that children were not to be *annoyed with books*. When infants were incorporated in huge barrack-like rooms where hundreds of older children were drilled in the alphabet and multiplication tables all this was lost. Dr Andrew Bell and others devised the monitor system of supervision by older children, the 'gallery' benches to restrict movement, and offered a system of discipline and instruction.

This British formula for providing cheap shelter and instruction for the children of the poor in so-called infants' schools was widely imitated abroad. The French *salles d'asile* appeared in response to urban squalor in an overcrowded Paris district; infant schools began in Northern Italy, Switzerland, and Hungary. Their aim was to prepare future labourers and servants for their role in society by offering them the elements of school-learning, coupled with discipline and moral training.

The child from three to six, therefore, was obscured in a rush to find a cheap form of incarceration and instruction to replace the street corners, factories and mineshafts which seemed the alternative. With one notable exception reform and innovation did not come from the world of education, but from the indirect results of social reform in Western Europe. Consequently, we need to be aware of social attitudes towards children as they evolved in industrial Briatain and France. Liberal reformers campaigned for children's rights in France after 1870; this had a decisive impact on early childhood education. The value of nutrition was recogised by very few, although among them was Victor Hugo during his exile on Guernsey.

The great exception to drudgery and the travesty of education forced on the under-sixes in mid-century was the kindergarten of Friedrich Froebel. In Froebel, Germany gave children a man of genius, a teacher who realised that schools were moving in the wrong direction. Instead of suggesting a differing method of instruction, Froebel by-passed the classroom and discarded the architecture and furniture of the schools. He offered a completely different environment — the garden — in place of the *salle d'asile* or infants' school and appealed for play, self-activity and consideration for the child's own rate of development.

Industrial Britain swamped the Owenite achievement. Prussia also did its best to obliterate the kindergarten, but it was too late. Froebel's followers took his gospel to Britain, the Netherlands, France, North America and elsewhere. Kindergartens were at first largely confined to the middle class, but educators and philosophers took up the Froebel theory of child education and ensured that his views invaded the infants' school and the *salle d'asile*. The 'New Education' of the late nineteenth century owed much to Froebel and the French *maternelles* (which replaced the *salles d'asile*) began to stress freedom and happiness as desirable goals for early education. Book work and the so-called 'intellectual' skills became suspect and teachers were at last warned against trying to turn little children into first-graders or memory machines.

Apart from Froebel, improvement in the daily life of the under-sixes came from progressive medical research. On the German side of the Rhine, Virchow and Pettenkofer supported the proposal that children need health before education and pioneered public hygiene. Medical and dental inspection were introduced first in German and French city schools during the 1870s: the role of nutrition was admitted in the 1890s. A reduction in mortality among little children followed together with an awareness of the need for care in planning their environment.

From the medical profession, too, came the great contribution of Itard and Séguin to the education of 'idiots'. They proved conclusively (against all contemporary authority) that this was a possibility, using the physiological approach. Séguin's research was the starting point for Maria Montessori's method of early education, at the present time used in many parts of the world. It was also well known to Margaret McMillan and her sister Rachel, pioneers in health services for children and nursery-schools in England.

Séguin himself worked as a neurologist in North America after leaving France after the 1848 revolution. Yet the medical tradition based on his experiments with 'idiot' children, coupled with a biological emphasis on growth and medical studies in health and hygiene, left an enduring mark on the Western European tradition. This restrained pre-school education from following too far or too fast in the path of the new science — psychology.

Within a brief century the broad outlines of ECE were drawn and a tradition established for care and development of children from every social class. The basic principles were evolved without reference to prevailing education practice and often (as in Froebel's case) in opposition to it. Legally, the organization of education before six differed sharply in different countries. After 1870, England summoned five-year-olds to school and often their little brothers and sisters came too. In France, attendance at the *salle d'asile* and the present-day *maternelle* never became compulsory, but was always popular: there, younger children were kept quite separate from the others, even when they shared the same building.

The skein of inspiration and organization is a tangled one in the nineteenth century. In general terms, the precursors gave the signal for early education and showed it at its best in small, benevolently guided institutions like those of Owen or Oberlin. Then followed the period of mass provision when the early dream was lost and instruction by rote and drill was inflicted on thousands. Finally, advanced thinkers in the 1870s were given the herculean task of renovating the public organizations which had become comfortably set in their ways. They were helped by the Froebel tradition and its exponents, by medical progress, and by an evolution in society's view of its obligations to the very young.

It had not occurred to the nineteenth-century reformers that they were providing for less than the whole child whether they were dealing with the comfortably-off, working class, or backward groups of infants. In Britain, health and education were topics in a lively debate provoked by the McMillan sisters and others in the period before the First World War; they were aware of Continental reforms in improved nutrition, health inspection and hygiene for school children. In spite of rival claims by specialists in the medical and education worlds, a working compromise was reached by the early 1930s and the influence of psycho-analysis also began to be felt in the play method for nursery schools.

France, Belgium and the Netherlands avoided division of the early childhood provision movement by rival schools of psychology. A national way of education in the *maternelle* was formed in France, drawing more on practical innovators such as Froebel, Kergomard, Décroly and Montessori than on 'learning theory' or behaviourism. After 1950, the organization grew enormously in France, more than doubling enrolments in a decade, and the under-six phase was rightly called the genuinely reformed sector of national education.

In the United States, the picture was different and presented certain contradictions. A large kindergarten organization had arisen in the late nineteenth century, mainly functioning for children in the year preceding public school entrance. But the rise of psychology studies as a flourishing new science, coupled with the appearance of nursery schools for under-fives resulted in a divergence of styles and principles. The kindergarten continued in a progressive, neo-Froebel tradition, but nursery schools were often linked with the campus and patronized by the children of academics. They were also fee-paying institutions.

Early childhood studies were not the first concern of American psychologists in the first part of the century. Adolescence distracted attention from the creative years, and personality testing, IQ classification and career-prediction combined with the domination of behaviourism to narrow research into a preoccupation with 'learning theory'. Testing became a quasi-religion and its inadequacies — which are strikingly apparent when applied to early childhood — scarcely admitted.

Less distracting and more pervasive in their influence outside the United States were child-development studies, which focused on growth patterns and normal development. Much of the pioneer work was done by Arnold Gesell, who emphasised the biological background to his research and whose results were of interest to teachers, parents and paediatricians.

While psychology tended to divide research into rival camps, both child development and the study of play in the under-five world had beneficial outcomes in practice. In a sense, the British contribution to theory centred on play as a core activity in the nursery school. After Karl Groos revealed the significance of animal play, Swiss researchers supplied data from a working environment by Geneva's *Maison des*

Petits. Jean Piaget began his work there, and moved from examination of speech and logic patterns through symbolic play to advanced studies on cognition.

Both child development reports and Piagetian techniques have proved useful to educators in the day-to-day running of the under-five and under-six centres. This seems to suggest that the main stream of advance in early childhood education or pre-school education is still close to the European tradition of biological and neuro-physiological science, rather than to schools of psychology which have proved transient.

Around the nineteen-fifties, it became clear that new winds were blowing through the empirical jungle which psychologists had created in the previous three or four decades. Fixed-intelligence dogma was shaken by a number of investigators and there was also a swing towards interest in early childhood as a key period in preparation for life. The adolescent no longer retained his dominant role in educational research and there was a continuing effort to push back the formative years towards early infancy.

Britain's John Bowlby, working in an international field of research, showed the effects of separation from the mother on the child's affective life and some striking investigations showed the importance of sensory stimuli to early development. Psychology began to take note of neuro-physiology and bio-chemistry, while it was even suggested that links existed between memory ability and certain bio-chemicals in the human system.

Froebel had addressed himself to the mothers of Germany a hundred years before, after realizing their central role in the kindergarten scheme he had in mind. Now, after experiments like those of Skeels and Dye, the child began to be considered in relation to his emotional links with parents, teachers and siblings. The learning process could no longer be considered an isolated study of a single subject.

The 1960s saw a burst of federally-supported provision in the USA, prompted by liberal concern for disadvantaged and 'ghetto-reared' children. British parents, weary of a long wait for government assistance, began the Playgroup movement for under-fives and saw it grow rapidly in popularity and enthusiasm. France in a planned decade of modernization, founded hundreds of new *maternelles* and saw figures rise to a point where some two million children attended these centres on a voluntary basis.

All this expansion was accompanied by a profound revision of aims

and implications. Educators were forced to ask whether later success
might not have its origins in the nursery school. Might not the over-
riding financial investment in high schools and universities be — in the
long run — misplaced and even unscientific? The balance of emphasis
in nursery school or *maternelle* on social mixing and skill-learning
also drew anxious attention, and specialist teachers asked whether the
child's social instinct was to be used to prepare him for a *laissez-faire*
or socialist society?

If the sixties were termed the 'pre-school era' the seventies seem
to be marked by a surge of re-examination and reassessment. Teachers
and researchers have to absorb a large infusion of new scientific
knowledge and also look for justification of their methods in an
affluent, but self-critical society. Their conclusions will set the framework for education in the eighties and beyond.

PART 1: THE PIONEERS

1 OBERLIN AND MADAME DE PASTORET: THE VILLAGE SCHOOL AND THE *SALLE D'ASILE*

Pre-school education as an organized affair is barely two hundred years old and began, as far as we are aware, in Alsace in the east of France. Here, in an isolated rural parish called Ban de la Roche, a young Strasbourg graduate named Jean-Frédéric Oberlin (1740–1826) took up his work as Protestant minister to a group of poor communities. This was in 1767.

Oberlin was the enlightened pastor of the eighteenth century. Tolerant of other faiths, interested in social welfare, agriculture, animal husbandry and science, he transformed the economy of Ban de la Roche between 1767 and his death in 1826. While it is his educational work which concerns us, this could not have been achieved without the general improvement in living conditions in the area, whose population increased fivefold during his ministry. Here began the village schools for as many as fifty children from one or three to twelve and thirteen. They combined handicrafts with instruction and occupied little children in a way which was almost totally neglected elsewhere in Europe. Both sexes attended, and attention was given to exercise and play as well as the elements of education.

Three remarkable women helped Oberlin create the first 'nursery' schools in Europe: Madame Oberlin, who died in 1784; Sarah Banzet and Louise Scheppler. None of these claimed to have been the founder or originator of the method, but each contributed something to the final achievement. Sarah Banzet had already taught some village children how to knit and she was enrolled after Oberlin had paid her peasant father compensation for the loss of her labour. Louise Scheppler came to live at the rectory when she was only fifteen, helped in the schools and eventually managed the household for Jean-Frédéric.

Louise became the real head of the schools, travelled between villages, trained helpers (who were called *conductrices* or leaders) and educated herself from the rector's library after the children had been put to bed. She may indeed have been the true founder of the nursery school tradition for under-sixes in Europe, but she always denied that her role was more than secondary to that of the pastor.

17

When Oberlin had managed to repair the tumble-down school-house out of his own pocket, local children in a group of about fifty were gathered in circles while Louise knitted and talked; older girls took over her role as time passed, and she was able to concentrate on the younger children. There were problems of communication; children in one or two hamlets spoke no French — their teacher spoke no patois. Louise Scheppler decided to return with pictures and teach herself the name of the images in patois before the lesson. But it was by no means as easy as that, when the children had never seen a picture before — not even a rough drawing of a tree. First of all the children had to be introduced to pictures, then to spoken patois, and only then to French. Lessons were cheery affairs, with gusts of laughter when the children heard the strange French words they were supposed to use for everyday things. Oberlin carried the lesson further by making a small museum for models of farming equipment and tools which he was trying to introduce into the community; parents and children came to wonder at these and at their written names which the youngest had to interpret for their elders. Slowly the 'knitting-schools' served as elementary schools in the system of economy the pastor was constructing, and slowly the smallest learned to listen to Louise Scheppler's Bible stories, then to read the texts, and finally to instruct the others or join the knitting classes.

  In the early nineteenth century, a number of distinguished visitors travelled to Alsace to look at Oberlin's model community; several biographies were written, which concentrated mainly on his religious character and the moral reformation which the biographers claimed he had wrought in the district. The anonymous English author of the *Memoirs of John Frederic Oberlin*, published in London, emphasised the moral impulse behind the knitting schools:

Observation and experience had convinced him that, even from the very cradle, children are capable of being taught to distinguish between right and wrong, and of being trained to habits of subordination and industry, and . . . he therefore trained conductrices for each commune, engaged large rooms for them, and salaried them at his own expense. Instruction, in these schools, was mingled with amusement; and whilst enough of discipline was introduced to instil habits of subjection, a degree of liberty was allowed, which left the infant mind full power of expansion, and information was conveyed which might turn to the most important use in after life. During school hours, the children were collected on forms in great circles. Two women were employed, the one to direct the handicrafts, the other to instruct and entertain them.[1]

The picture is an idyllic one, and only marred by the observation that, while this was going on, the smaller children aged two or three were made to sit quietly by . . . Knowing how restless and noisy little children can be, one cannot resist speculating on how this was done. Probably it is fair to guess that they were rather bemused than bored by what was happening, for apparently Oberlin's method was based on real things, there was no fixed time-table, and the women gave no set lessons. Oberlin himself described how the sessions were conducted:

The teachers showed pictures from the realms of history, animals, and plants, on which I had written the names in French and in patois . . . They read them aloud first in patois, and then they said them in French and the class repeated the sounds. Afterwards they amused them with physical exercises, games which loosened their limbs and benefited their bodies while also improving health and showing them how to play sociably without arguments . . . all the lessons were like a game, a continual amusement . . .[2]

As the community prospered, these little schools multiplied, and a number of young *conductrices* had to be trained for the five village centres. First Sarah Banzet, then Madame Oberlin, died and left Louise Scheppler and her rector to carry on the good work. At the burial service for Sarah, Oberlin pronounced his faith in the importance of early education: 'In Childhood years, the heart is tender and pliable; what we sow in these years will never be uprooted.' Fifteen years later the work was menaced by the French Revolution and Oberlin was hauled before a local tribunal; as a man of God he was suspect to the revolutionaries who had arrested many of his Strasbourg friends. But he had a reputation for tolerance and his scientific work stood him in good stead with the followers of reason; he was able to return to the parish and continue improving the local economy and the morals of the community, which had grown in number since his arrival.

When comparative calm returned to France, Oberlin had acquired a certain celebrity among the intellectual avant-garde; eminent societies wished to honour him for his agricultural and scientific research. He accepted the honours with good grace, but was too busy to travel to Paris to receive them. His good friend Baron de Gérando, who plays no small part in the later story of the *salle d'asile*, acted as intermediary in Paris and passed on Oberlin's excuses.

Oberlin's religious views were apparently not entirely conventional; he is said to have held peculiar views, in particular about the soul, heaven and hell. A visitor to the rectory observed that Swedenborg's *Heaven and Hell* was among the books on Oberlin's shelves and deduced that he had been influenced by the founder of the 'New Church'. If this were so, it would be significant for the origins of early education, because two out of three pioneers of infant schools in England (Buchanan and Wilderspin) were also members of this sect. But there is not sufficient evidence to show that Oberlin was more than an admirer of Swedenborg's writing.

It is hard to understand why Oberlin's schools were not imitated in other parts of France. He had acquired an international reputation; his work was described in several languages; his friend de Gérando was an active campaigner for elementary education in Parisian circles. Remarkable as they were, the 'knitting schools' were an isolated venture, antedating organized efforts for little children by many years. It was a curious coincidence that the French *salles d'asile* only began in the year of Jean-Frédéric's death.

Under the *ancien régime*, the Church had born the responsibility for village schools and in a period when the grasp of central government was lax there was little supervision of standards. Like the 'dame' schools which existed in both England and Germany, French village schools were limited by their budgets, public indifference and the quality of their teachers. Threats and smacks kept order while each child was called to the front to recite his texts and rhymes by heart — or face the consequences. Of a method of rearing based on a child's natural interest in things about him we have no record before Oberlin or Pestalozzi (who was not really concerned with very young children).

Had Oberlin's method been adopted in Paris after the Bourbon Restoration in 1815 our story would have been simpler — an unbroken line of development extending from Alsace westwards. But this was not the case — private philanthropy flickered like patches of St Elmo's fire across Napoleonic Europe, but there was no connected blaze. Small schools or care-centres showed the way, and were taken up in Paris, Germany, and England. What had started in Alsace was taken from Paris to London (and New Lanark) and then by a quirk of history re-exported from London back to Paris in 1825. It all took place in a time of general apathy towards the fate of small children or their education.

The Salle d'Asile

Madame de Pastoret opened an *asile* or refuge for the infants of
working mothers not far from the church of St Philippe du Roule in
Paris as early as 1800. It caught the eye of several journalists and
was written up in the reviews of the time; the young Irish novelist
Maria Edgeworth visited it during the Peace of Amiens and wrote a
fictional account in her novel *Madame de Fleury*. In Westphalia,
Princess Pauline of Lippe took up the idea after reading about the
Paris venture and after publication of the Edgeworth novel it was
much discussed in Britain. Indeed, it may have been one inspiration
behind Robert Owen's work for young children at New Lanark and
the Westminster infant 'asylums' in London. Madame de Pastoret's
asile was the model for care-centres and crèches which appeared in
Western Europe as the century proceeded. Links between cause and
effect are tenuous at this stage, and it is only at rare points (such as
Ban de la Roche) that we can distinguish the enlightened view of early
childhood care: the true centres were those which banished restraint,
fear and instruction from the daily life of small children. Madame de
Pastoret's *asile* holds an important place in the story because it
concentrated on the very small child — the under-threes.

Baron de Gérando, philosopher and social reformer, was friendly
with both Oberlin and Madame de Pastoret. In 1825, after campaigning for the cause of elementary education for some years, he visited
London and brought back favourable news of the infant schools in
Westminster and elsewhere. Madame de Pastoret, undaunted by her
twenty years' struggle, was ready to support another venture; moreover,
a young lawyer and public man with a gift for organization called
Jean-Denis Cochin rallied to the cause and helped to found a new type
of centre called the *salle d'asile*. Here children under six were to be
sheltered in large numbers from the dangers of the streets, disease and
starvation.

Cochin was quick to see how English ideas could be adapted to the
French situation, visited England himself, and encouraged Madame
Frédéric Millet to do the same before opening a training school — the
first — in the Rue Saint Hippolyte. As mayor of Paris's twelfth district
in 1826, he was soon involved with aid programmes for poor children
in his quarter and he collected them for shelter in two rented rooms
near the Gobelins. This soon proved inadequate, and he built at his
own expense an independent *salle d'asile* designed to receive no less
than one thousand children; on the first day it enrolled four hundred
and numbers subsequently increased.

The first *asiles*, therefore, which were destined to become the
foundation stone of a whole system of pre-primary school education
in France, were built in response to a social need. Children arrived at
any time from 6 a.m. onwards, listened to some sort of lesson until
midday and again between 2 and 4 p.m. There was instruction in moral
duties and simple lessons in spelling and writing for large classes where
all ages between two and six were mixed in an amorphous mass of
children. The gallery system was adopted from English example:
a series of raised benches in tiers at the end of a large room which the
children entered and left at the blast of a whistle. Often the rules
insisted that hands were kept folded in view of the master or held
behind backs; the toddlers dozed off as the session went on and
slumped on the benches or the shoulder of their neighbour.

The large rectangular room was usually (but not always) heated
by a stove on which the midday soup simmered during morning
lessons. Children sat on a series of elevated benches with girls on one
side, boys on the other, and many visitors found much satisfaction in
the discipline which marked the 'mutual' system of instruction
borrowed from England. One who was not so impressed was Count Leo
Tolstoy, visiting Marseille during the Second Empire: 'I saw,' he wrote
later in a Russian periodical, 'the *salles d'asile*, in which four year old
children, at a given whistle, like soldiers, made evolutions around the
benches, at a given command lifted and folded their hands, and with
quivering and strange voices sang laudatory hymns to God and to their
benefactors and I convinced myself that the educational institutions
of the city of Marseille were exceedingly bad.'

The physical appearance of the *asiles* was often grim and forbidding:
one can still see remnants of the barracks style in some of the older
Paris school buildings where separate staircases and entrances gave
access to a *salle d'asile* on the ground floor, a girls' elementary
school on the first floor and a boys' elementary school on the top.
The whole building is a very emporium of learning.

The *salles d'asile* were at first defined as charitable institutions for
children of both sexes where they could be given the care required
at their age (1827). They were not officially recognized until 1837,
and, indeed, from 1827 to 1829 Denis Cochin paid for the centres in
his district out of his own purse. Gradually, the councils and
communal authorities in the rural districts accepted the duty of
maintaining these shelters for the very young, but it must be
remembered that this did not occur as a consequence of public primary
education, but alongside it.

The remnants of the old village schools, fostered by parish priests under the *ancien régime* still survived, and Revolutionary or Napoleonic leaders had made stirring appeals for elementary education for all. Yet, whatever the figures quoted at the time, it is now conceded that almost no primary school system existed at all.[3] De Gérando and some others began a society to urge the cause of elementary education in 1820, but there was little public interest, and the State did not become involved until the laws of 1833 (the so-called Guizot Law) and 1844. After Guizot, communes with more than six thousand people were supposed to maintain a proper elementary school, but the state lacked power to enforce the measure throughout France.

Although the charitable *salles d'asile* were not perfect, they undoubtedly helped to reduce the urban misery of children under six. They multiplied rapidly, as did their English counterparts, the infant schools. There were 24 in Paris and 102 in all France by 1836: at mid-century 160,244 children were enrolled and the figure rose to 432,141 by 1867. They particularly helped the struggling working mother and her offspring who enjoyed a few years of somewhat rough care and dreary instruction before coming of age for the new elementary schools.

Had the Oberlin type of school — small, personal and community-oriented — been adapted to conditions in the towns, the *salles d'asile* would have been one of the educational wonders of the age. But the communes were not ready to foot the bill for expensive new schools and training-centres. The whole principle of elementary education was still being urged on a reluctant public. Yet the *salle d'asile* achieved a great deal: it offered a structure for future reform, it cared for a large number of little children, and it created a tradition which was separate from elementary education. This last was a vital factor in enabling the later *maternelle* to evolve (after 1879) towards an existence of its own, untrammelled by the method or administration of the higher school-system.

Conditions were far from satisfactory in the early days of the *asile*. Inspectors wrote of overcrowded galleries, of 'outer offices' (lavatories) blocked up and a danger to health, of the dreadful whistle and clapper procedure for class movements and even for blowing noses in unison. A contemporary manual warned directors not to overdo the comfort of their charges, and reminded teachers that the children were working-class members of society. 'Let nothing be lacking for their health, but nothing added which could be termed a luxury, or even an extra comfort, in the case of children whose whole life will be spent in conditions of privation.' (1851)

Denis Cochin not only launched the *salles d'asile* on their way; he also found time to write a textbook for teachers which contained much that was progressive in the 1830s. 'Children,' he wrote, 'should live their day as much as possible outside in the fresh air . . . their heads should be left uncovered except when some ailment requires otherwise.'[4]

Attention, for Cochin, was not something which could be produced to order by authority's wish. 'Nor can either rewards or punishments bring it to life; it is something which comes spontaneously, supported by curiosity and the desire for knowledge, fortunately part of children's natural disposition. We must base their education on things which are suited to their taste and the range of their intelligence.'

In this very matter of intelligence, which has become the centre of a great debate in recent years, Cochin had an important warning to give which unfortunately went unheeded by the pedagogues of the nineteenth century: *'as to the development of intelligence, it should happen gradually while the children are playing, without continuous application.'* An observation of this sort marked Denis Cochin as a true forerunner of modern method who was, unfortunately, striving to improve the shelter-and-care centres at a time when children were considered a nuisance until they entered the factory.

Cochin's vision, like Oberlin's and Robert Owen's in Britain, looked far beyond the social (shelter and care) aspect of his task; the statement just quoted reveals his penetration of the contemporary fashion in instruction, which was based on discipline and rote-learning. Indeed, he defined the dual role of the *salles d'asile* by calling them places for child care and education − *'maisons d'hospitalité et d'éducation'*. Public authorities unfortunately did not share his vision and in 1848 the *asiles* were officially termed establishments of public instruction (*établissements d'instruction publique*). In the same way attempts to limit class sizes (such as were made in 1837) to a mere two hundred and fifty children encountered ignorant opposition and apathy. Groups as large as four hundred were recorded in later years.

That conditions and methods were not a great deal worse in the *asile* was largely due to a remarkable woman, director of the Paris training-school for lady assistants. The influence of Madame Pape-Carpentier (1815−1878) was paramount during a period when the French centres had to survive great social upheavals. She, too, wrote a handbook on method, which appeared in the year of revolutions, 1848, and whose title anticipated later developments by three decades. She called it *L'Enseignement Pratique dans les Ecoles Maternelles* and so introduced the name by which they are known today.

Madame Pape-Carpantier crusaded to improve sanitary conditions in the schools and tried to vary the system of instruction, which was too often a copy of the monitorial method used in English infant schools. She worked to introduce some class activities, advised her students to study the characters of their pupils and introduced the Pestalozzi-Mayo object lessons to Paris. Taking a familiar object from daily life, the teacher held it up for observation and listed its parts and 'qualities'. Little children would try to remember that an object was green, brittle, pungent, or even metallic. Adjectives multiplied on the working slates, as did the number of syllables to be repeated aloud. Yet there was a fundamental directness about the object method which linked the children with life outside the barrack room.

By mid-century the *salles d'asile* were firmly established in every part of France; the principle was accepted and local communes and councils were expected to provide shelter and instruction for needy children over the age of two. Observers began to note with surprise that not only indigent labourers, but skilled workmen and their wives had begun to leave their children at the *asile* for the day.[5] In method and organization these centres resembled British infant schools rather than the more progressive German kindergartens which appeared after the 1850s; brave efforts by social reformers and liberal educators were required to awaken the public to the need for better schools. The rights of the child in society had to be accepted slowly at a time when society itself was in turmoil, and it so happened that many of the leaders in the fight for a more enlightened early education phase were themselves in opposition to the Second Empire of Napoleon III. We have to turn away from the school-world to life outside its dull walls in order to see how change came about in France: so great was the effect of this change when it did arrive that it created the first national system of pre-school education based on thoroughly progressive principles – the *écoles maternelles*.

The Child in Society: c. 1848–1870

Industrialization did not devastate French life as quickly or brutally as it had done in England, and the boom period for French capitalism did not come until after 1870. But from the child's point of view, distress and disease awaited his growing years, even if he were lucky enough to be born a member of the bourgeois class. Overcrowding in the big cities combined with an as yet only rudimentary respect for hygiene to foster diphtheria, cholera and other infectious diseases. Child mortality was high in France, as it was elsewhere, until the twentieth century. The death of children was so commonplace that it was accepted with resignation.

It is interesting to take 1848 as an observation point because so many names which enter our record later were involved in the year of revolutions and many thereafter became opponents of a society which showed glaring contrasts between wealth and poverty. De Tocqueville found society 'split in two' in Paris after the 1848 revolution, and many liberal reformers went into opposition or even contemplated abandoning Europe altogether. Rudolf Virchow, who later did so much for health inspection and school hygiene, was opposed to the established order in Germany and many of his fellow scientists emigrated to North America. Edouard Séguin, who had successfully shown that 'idiots' could be educated and revolutionized the treatment of the mentally retarded, left for North America. In the years which followed, Victor Hugo and many intellectuals, including Buisson (see Chapter 4) went into exile. Even to the unworldly Froebel, crossing the German countryside in that summer of 1848, it was clear that something was stirring in the air and indeed his kindergarten movement, too, was to suffer in the repression after 1848.

The liberal reformers in education, literature and the sciences, who held the future of early childhood education in their hands, were therefore forced to await better times to put their ideas into practice. By the forties there were infant schools in Britain, and Continental imitations in Lombardy, Switzerland, and Germany as well as the *salles d'asile*. Concentrating on 'moral' training, their hygiene and method left much to be desired, and had to await the triumph of reform before they were cleansed and separated from the drudgery of elementary school instruction.

In rural France, children were treated with the customary alternation of affection and brutality. Rural communities were slow to discover the advantages in marching the little ones off to the village for care and custody. It was often a trek of one or two miles, local councils were not pleased with the idea of spending more money on schools and there were sufficient old women to mind the children and farm-buildings in winter, or take the goats and cows out in fine weather. Even when education became free and compulsory there was so much school dodging that it proved impossible to police the act. Older children had their uses in agriculture; small children were not much more trouble than the hens.

The general attitude of the French towards their children is an enticing subject which still awaits an author. We are learning a lot about child-rearing in the sixteenth and seventeenth century from the new historians of childhood after Raymond Aries, notably David Hunt, whose *Parents and Children in History*[6] tells us a lot about the seventeenth-century family and the stern upbringing of Louis XIII, who was regularly beaten by the servants on his father's instructions, no doubt in order to improve his development. The French were then, says Hunt, reputedly the best 'whackers' in Europe.

Nineteenth-century circumstances probably added to the general misery of childhood rather than reducing it. The number of natural children in the working class was 'startling' in 1862, partly because of the number of formalities required by the Church of a couple who wanted to marry. In an attempt to adjust the situation a Catholic Society in Lille managed to legitimize a thousand children between 1854 and 1860 by facilitating marriage among factory workers. Child (especially infant) mortality was by our standards astonishingly high and the horrors of baby farming, alcoholism and child labour all existed in France. But, unfortunately, there is nothing historically unique about the mistreatment of infants, as Hunt discovered when studying the seventeenth-century pattern.

> Infants are still starved, beaten, and sexually abused in our own day. More important, where the grosser forms of physical mistreatment have been eliminated, an equally frightening psychological cruelty can be found. Such case histories, and no doubt the unwritten histories of many children who never come to the attention of clinicians, indicate that styles of parenthood of our society have been remarkably unaffected by that cultural revolution which, we tell ourselves, has brought about a fundamental transformation in methods of childrearing.

The Second Empire

During the reign of Napoleon III travellers brought back horrifying descriptions of the condition of the poor in England's cities, though these failed to stimulate action for social reform. Charles Dickens, whose works were translated into French, was fêted on his several visits to Paris, and percipient critics like Taine pointed out that Dickens's social message had almost no counterpart in contemporary French literature. Balzac, Stendhal and George Sand were all more interested in their art than in mankind; their writing possessed none of Dickens's power of arousing the reader's pity for suffering humanity.

An exception was Hugo, leader of the artists-in-exile, who denounced the misery of the have-nots in Imperial France. At his home in

Guernsey, Hauteville House, he invited some forty poor children to a meal every fortnight,[7] and later every week. The money for this he set aside from the sale of some sketches to a publisher and by these means he launched his private school-lunch movement in 1862.

For teachers who had remained in France during the 1860s, low wages and insecurity of tenure contributed to their dissatisfaction and anxiety. In the parishes, a lady-teacher was almost the slave of the local authority, and could be dismissed at the wish of curé or parents without much difficulty. For those who kept their schools, an average wage for six hours' teaching was about ninepence a day. There were few training colleges, and little promotion. Eminent intellectuals of the stature of Edgar Quinet and Michelet lost their posts when they offended the hierarchy and many members of the teaching fraternity resigned and tried to find other ways of making ends meet. But opposition to the regime grew with the rise of secularism. Out of hearing of the police, a small band of progressives planned radical changes in education, and legislation to protect children from exploitation in industry.

Among the small group of reformers who banded together to improve conditions for children were some dynamic individuals in Paris. Madame Pauline Kergomard (see Chapter 4) with other women who were sickened by what they saw about them, began a society to rescue children from beggary and maltreatment, called the *Sauvetage de l'Enfance*. When she encountered stupidity and opposition, she observed with typical courage that the essential thing was to start the work and get something done . . . other people would always follow the example afterwards. ('N'importe – commençons, l'on nous suivra, vous verrez!')

A select few rose in the Assembly after 1871 to plead for the rights of children, and, eventually, as Pauline Kergomard had predicted, they were followed by the majority. A doctor from the Lozère with extensive experience of city hospitals, Théo Roussel, led the fight for protective legislation. He was largely responsible for the laws of 1874 controlling 'baby farming' and for inaugurating a whole chain of legislation to protect the children of alcoholics and other unfit parents. Overshadowed in the history books by the Dreyfus affair, the case of the Grégoire parents in the 1890s roused public opinion sufficiently to pass a new law empowering authorities to take children into care. Relics and traditions of the *ancien régime* which had given fathers almost Roman power over their children, were gradually overcome and replaced by legislation based on the rights of children.

The struggle, however, was long and bitter against the dead weight of conservative custom in French society.

After the philanthropic societies and the valiant work of Roussel came belated legislation to control child labour. Work was forbidden for the under-thirteens (school leaving age) in 1892; a series of subsequent measures restricted the type of task given to a minor in factories and stipulated maximum weights he could be told to carry. By 1900, a law was passed limiting the working day to ten hours for sixteen- to eighteen-year-olds. The rights of children were a long way from recognition, but the minimum rights of young labourers were admitted. Even so, Rousseauan idealism was more a feature of French literature than a fact in adult attitudes to children. In bourgeois homes the fortunate few were petted and spoiled, to the annoyance of eminent authorities on child-rearing by 'modern' methods, who recommended severity.

As late as the 1890s, Compayré was still warning parents of the evil inherent in child character, and of innate anti-social instincts. Although a Catholic bishop, Mgr Dupanloup went so far as to defend the rights of children even against their parents, the psychologist Perez postulated three basic emotions of childhood: fear, anger, and jealousy. He compared children (not very favourably) with animals and the metaphor was frequently repeated. There was even a widespread adult suspicion that over-indulgence and over-attention early in life would form a race of seven-year-olds to strut about the home like little despots. To spare the rod and spoil the child was a precept probably more widely understood in France than the inscriptions on the town halls of the new republic: 'liberty, equality, brotherhood'.

Education Reform and Anti-Clericalism

When, smarting under the indignity of defeat in the Franco-Prussian War, the French dismissed the Imperial Regime without regrets, they looked for other scapegoats. The German victory was due to superior morale and discipline in the army, it was said, and this in turn derived from the German elementary school. The German primary teachers had won the victory at Sedan, and if France could provide an elementary school system for its children, the next conflict would end differently.

The republicans who dominated the scene after 1871 were willing to take advantage of the myth for their own purposes, which included long-term plans for educational change. A vague general belief in education as one of the factors in social and economic progress had

been accompanied by plans for fundamental reforms which traced
back to Guizot's law of 1833. The grip of the Church on education
would be broken, and the rudiments of education offered free of
charge to every French child aged between six and thirteen in new
schools where they could be taught pride of country and faith in the
new republic. For Jules Ferry,[8] Paul Bert and their supporters in the
Assembly, education was of primary importance in establishing the
principles of the new state.

At a time when the population remained fairly static, a huge
building programme was set in motion throughout France; over
thirty-five thousand new schools were built between 1876 and 1898.
'With a sort of missionary fervour', wrote the author of a recent
study, 'thousands of instituteurs carried learning to the dullest,
loneliest, communes in France.'[9] Training schools for women teachers
were promised for every department in France, and the final onslaught
of the anti-clericals began against religious orders, church schools and
religious instruction. Paul Bert announced, 'We shall make war on
the good Lord, and we shall succeed. We must laicize France.
Among ourselves, Voltaire's great peals of laughter have long ago
swept away superstition. Our religion will be . . . a patriotism that is
ardent, intransigent, capable of every daring deed, ready for every
sacrifice . . . Science lights our path and guides us; love of our father-
land inspires us; we shall be the victors.'[10] It is a crucial passage,
because it proclaims the basis of a new educational morality in science
and love of country. Man's efforts were to be directed towards
improving his present state on earth under the Third Republic.

Moderates like the historian Ernest Lavisse pleaded that the lay,
secular outlook in the new education system did not imply that man's
right 'to dream about and search for' the Almighty was now denied;
but, the Society of Jesus (Jesuits) was dissolved and religious instruction forbidden in schools in 1886. Paul Bert lived just long enough to
see the success of the campaign against the 'good Lord' before dying
of dysentery, like many less famous Frenchmen, in Indo-China.

Children under six were not forgotten in all these ambitious plans
for education and Jules Ferry reminded prefects of the need to build
salles d'asile, or when this proved impractical, to install infant classes
in the projected new *écoles primaires*. So began the *classes enfantines*.
The name *école maternelle* was finally chosen for the new centres and
a committee of Ferry and his advisers chose a brilliant personality for
appointment to the inspectorate, Pauline Kergomard.

In a later chapter we shall see how the highly-original *école maternelle* was developed, creating a system of infant centres free from the tyranny of instruction. But Third Republic achievements owed something to Germany and Friedrich Froebel's kindergarten idea, too, and it is now to Germany we must turn to search for the origin of our modern nursery schools.

What France had done in the century after Oberlin was to bring to general acceptance the view that local authorities were responsible for care and education of the very young. Buildings, staffing, and methods left much to be desired but there was an independent tradition which survived attempts to incorporate the *salles d'asile* into the education ladder. Attendance was voluntary and both sexes mixed freely at this level in a manner unknown elsewhere in the French education system. Inspiration may have been lacking in the *salles d'asile*, but they represented the first Government-sponsored system of centres for the under-sixes in Western Europe to develop its own training schools and tradition.

2 FRIEDRICH FROEBEL AND THE KINDERGARTEN

Germany at the end of the eighteenth century was still a jigsaw of petty states. Although there was a common written language, well-off or cultivated Germans preferred to speak French, the language of culture. For young Germans seeking independence from France in all spheres and striving towards their own national identity, this was a time of intellectual challenge. The result was an unprecedented flowering of German culture, with a rejection of old values and the triumph of Romantic spontaneity and simplicity over what Novalis termed the 'cold dead Spitzbergen of reason'. Not the least, though possibly one of the most neglected, in this movement of innovation was Friedrich Froebel (1782–1852) who, by applying to education these new-found values, changed its course.

Froebel was still a student when the first known attempt to care for little children in Germany had been launched in Westphalia. There, Princess Pauline of Lippe was inspired to do something for small children after reading about the work of aristocratic ladies in Paris under the patronage of Josephine Bonaparte. In an article written for a journal in Detmold, which has been preserved, Princess Pauline described the care-centres for the children of working-mothers which 'Madame Bonaparte and a number of aristocratic and refined gentle-women' had begun.[1] She went on:

> I have pleasure in announcing that an experiment will be made in the summer months, during the busy harvest-time, and in a place which is very dear to me, where the name Nursery Institution [*Pfleganstalt*] indicates what is proposed. Every mother will give notice the day before, and the following morning, before her outdoor work begins, she will with peace of mind and confidence bring her children, and fetch them home again in the evening. The little ones will pass the time playing, always under supervision, but without restraint, in the garden if the weather permits, or else in the hall of the hospital which has not yet been brought into use. They will be washed and tidied on arrival, and, if necessary, clothed for the day in tunics and clean underclothing made in the orphanage and in the industrial school; and they will be fed and

generally looked after. Their diet will consist chiefly of milk foods, and we shall endeavour to give them occupation suitable to their ages . . . We should appoint as assistants the older girls from the orphanage and the industrial school during the period when they were approaching the time of confirmation and of leaving school, and thus afford them practical training as children's nurses.
The very competent matron of the orphanage and the industrial school would also undertake the supervision, and everything else would follow of itself, so easily and naturally, once the institute [*Anstalt*] is set going.

The institute, which was known as the 'Paulinenanstalt', was still in existence in the nineteen-thirties. Whether it helped, as the editor of the Detmold journal hoped, 'towards making the lower classes of inhabitants of the town more gentle and more humane' we cannot say, but Pauline von Lippe Detmold was certainly one of the few who cared for children at that time.

German Reform and the Rights of Children

Other rulers in different German states pressed the almost unheard-of cause of children's welfare after Pauline of Lippe. Bavaria deserves a special mention, as it followed the example of France's *Code Pénal* and introduced a minimum age for punishment in 1813. The Queen of Württemberg took leadership of a welfare society for children in 1816. The Grand Duke of Baden began a rescue home for deserted and neglected children in 1820 and Falk, the friend of Goethe and Herder, gathered together the waifs of Weimar and founded the Lutherhof there.

In Basle, following a severe famine in 1817, certain women's societies established infant care centres (*Kleinkinderbewahranstalten*) of working parents. Other German towns followed suit. The great Protestant social reformer Wichern founded a home in Hamburg for orphaned and difficult boys; the home, called *das rauhe Haus* witnessed the first attempt at responsibility-sharing and family groupings inside separate houses. Wichern made his famous appeal for an inland mission to Germany in 1848, a year after Karl Marx's *Communist Manifesto*, whose influence it hoped to counteract.[2]

Froebel

Friedrich Froebel was born in 1782, the youngest child of a Protestant clergyman in Thuringia. He lost his mother before he was one year old and felt the sufferings of a lonely childhood.

His first attempt at university study at Jena came to an end when he became what in our time would be called a 'drop-out'. He then tried, amongst other things, tutoring – which took him to see Pestalozzi at Yverdon – but finally returned to university, first at Göttingen and then at Berlin to study science and mineralogy.

Froebel interrupted his quest for self-education in 1813, by joining the 'Free Corps' as a volunteer to fight for Germany in the War of Liberation and it was only when Europe was on the verge of a lasting peace that he opened a school in his native Thuringia, at Keilhau. This became the real centre of his life, although he was forever moving about in Germany and Switzerland, commencing new projects, recruiting supporters or – all too rarely – raising funds. Friends and relations came to join him at Keilhau, including two comrades from the short campaign in the Free Corps, Middendorff and Langethal. There he wrote his book on 'The Education of Man'[3] which mingled philosophic speculation on the nature of things with research into the functions of a teacher and relationships between teacher and child.

Children found Froebel delightful company and his deep knowledge of the German folktale and gift for story-telling made the time pass quickly for his pupils.[4] He loved music and traditional dances, knew how to invent activities which amused and taught the class at the same time, and spoke at the child's level as only a born teacher could. But in the company of adults his intellectual dissatisfaction, combined with a certain obstinacy about the rightness of his own educational ideas probably made it difficult to converse with him. After all, he was moving in a different direction from the firmly-entrenched professional teachers of Prussia and Thuringia, and they could not help but feel it.

During the summer and autumn holidays Froebel, accompanied by one or other of his fellow-teachers, would set off on foot to visit other German states, bent on raising money and moral support for his project. The Keilhau travellers were a striking sight, for they chose to dress in a style which was then out of fashion in Germany, a sort of *altdeutsch* folklore garb, which aroused the amusement of strangers.

One of these excursions in 1828 took them to Göttingen, where an encounter with the philosopher Krause had a profound influence on Froebel's life and thought. Krause expounded a system of infant education conceived by Comenius, the seventeenth-century Czech educator and divine, and it may have been then that Froebel began to cogitate about education for children under six.[5]

Jan Amos Comenius (1592–1670) was an international figure who travelled all over Europe in the disturbed period of the religious wars. A Protestant, member of the Moravian Brethren, he had an encyclopaedic mind, which ranged across the sciences, education, language teaching, religion and ethics. When Krause was explaining Comenius's *Informatorium* or 'School of Infancy',[6] he probably emphasised for Froebel the concept of growth in teaching and in human development, and the paramount importance laid by Comenius on the period from birth to six years, when the 'roots of all arts and sciences, though we seldom do anything about it, begin at this tender age'. The Czech had set down a lot of shrewd observation of early childhood in his treatise, noticing how learning occurred spontaneously and imperceptibly as it were in play, how important were toys, with which children could exercise their bodies and satisfy an urge to construct little houses and other marvels.

In 1830, Froebel whose marriage to Wilhelmine Hoffmeister in 1818 remained childless, had the privilege of observing the arrival of a baby and its behaviour during the first few months of life. A son was born to his old war-time comrade and teaching colleague at Keilhau, Middendorff. Eagerly the two middle-aged pedagogues leaned over the cradle, watching and commenting to each other on what was happening from day to day. Always a keen observer since his geological studies in Berlin, Froebel began to note, gesture by gesture, the significant changes in the life of that new small being at Keilhau. The result was the *Summary of the story of a child's development during the first period of life*, one of the first studies of early child development, and, it may well be, the beginning of Froebel's orientation towards the world of very young children.

From then until his death in 1852, the master was almost constantly on the move. He spent a number of years in Switzerland setting up and running several schools including Burgdorf with its innovatory open-air gymnasium.[7]

Froebel was then on the eve of his revelations about early childhood education. In 1837, well over fifty years of age, he began work on the gifts and occupations, and opened a new school for the very young at Blankenburg.[8] He began publication of a Sunday magazine, opened two more schools, in Dresden and Frankfurt, and founded a joint-stock company to manage the kindergarten project. All this was not achieved alone. But for a private staff of well-wishers and activists and his second wife, Luise Levin, Froebel's many projects would have been nothing more than the gestures of an ageing dilettante.

While on summer holiday in 1849, Madame von Bülow,[9] an aristocratic German lady, came across a remarkable personage followed by a trail of village children. He was tall, with long grey hair, quaintly dressed, and he was leading his followers up a path to a little green space where he began to show them games and songs. The patience and affection with which he ran this unorthodox class moved Madame von Bülow to the heart and, recalling the incident thirty years later in her memoirs, she realized that this meeting (for she introduced herself) had shown her her life's work. She became the master's most dedicated disciple and propagandist, and lost no time in setting to work.

By a strange coincidence, one of the most influential pedagogues in Berlin, Diesterweg,[10] was spending some time in the village of Piebenstein that same summer; he had of course heard about Froebel from his collagues, but nothing to the advantage of the Thuringian innovator, whom he believed to be a crank. Madame von Bülow, who must have been a woman of persistence and personal charm, overcame Diesterweg's objections and took him to the cottage where Froebel was teaching the village urchins. The two visitors entered unnoticed and Diesterweg stayed long enough to change his opinion of the kindergarten method. He became an important ally in Berlin where he ran an influential training school, and worked for liberal principles in education.

Froebel's last years were clouded by opposition from the authorities and by severe financial problems; but with vision and dynamic persistence he had opened kindergarten schools and lecture courses in distant parts of Germany and refused to let material difficulties prevent him from visiting them each year. Ten kindergartens had opened their doors in a single year, 1847, and Froebel felt it was his duty to demonstrate his ideas to the local teachers and parents as well as to gather financial support wherever it was available.

So much time and energy were consumed in travelling and lecturing, that the master's literary work had to be fitted into any unoccupied moments during the day or night. One New Year's Eve towards the end of his life, after the celebrations were over and his friends and relations had retired to bed, Froebel went to the rooms where, at that time, he lived alone, drew out pens and paper, and wrote his long letter *To Womankind* until dawn broke.

Much of his thinking was set down in letters and in contributions to different journals; his reflections on the kindergarten were written for his 'Sunday Journal' between 1838 and 1840, and the quaint and delightful Mother and Child Songs (*Mutter und Köse Lieder*) appeared in the course of 1843.

Froebel's Principles and 'Self Activity'

When Prussia proscribed the kindergarten in 1851 it did so for all the wrong reasons, labelling it as 'atheistical' which, when we remember Froebel's reverence for the divine element in nature, is quite absurd. The ban was also, apparently, based on some confusion between Friedrich and one of his nephews who had a reputation for radicalism; it was a typical bureaucratic muddle which could not be admitted without the State losing face. Nevertheless, there is something appropriate in Prussia's action, as if in some obscure way the officials realized that this was a revolutionary departure in education.

What Froebel had done, quite simply, was to by-pass the whole traditional trappings of schooling and what was called education. He had done what modern educators are struggling to do in such innovations as the 'Open Plan' primary school: he had broken with the furniture, architecture and physical conventions of the school in Europe. While infants were still confined to the gallery or the screwed-down desk, Froebel invented the garden-room, where children placed chairs in a circle or sat in a circle on the floor, and most activities in good weather took place in a garden-space.

The foundation of Froebel's thought was the unity (both divine and human) and wholeness,[11] which were the dominant concepts in German thought from Goethe onwards. (It had affected even the theory of reading-instruction by introducing the whole-word and whole-phrase principle.) Extending this principle, Froebel aimed at a harmonious development of the whole person in his kindergarten world.

His faith in the divine element supported Froebel's confidence in the way children develop when left without interference from their elders and was the source of his most original proposals. 'Man's nature is good', he decided, 'and so are his qualities and tendencies.' He was nevertheless aware of the bad side of child behaviour, which, in his opinion, was due to a disturbed relationship between the true, original nature of a child and the distorted world of his environment.

On the issue of freedom, he qualified his suggestions by saying that a boy does need to be guided and trained for something. Without rational guidance, childish activity degenerates into aimless play instead of preparing for those tasks of life for which it is destined.[12] But the real purpose, as in all true education, is to help a process which comes from within the child, not to superimpose adult schemes upon his personality. Froebel, remarked a twentieth-century commentator, had grasped more clearly than Pestalozzi the vital principle that 'all true development, and consequently all true education, is a self-directive process – that purpose is the key-note of human culture and advance'. This alone makes Froebel one of the princes of education, with an enduring place in the history of thought.[13]

His was the search for a philosophic basis to education, to discover the symbolic nature of things. Mathematics was not a matter of learning to do sums, but was rather a study of truth and order, one method of approaching the law and unity which is a manifestation of Divinity itself. He felt obliged to set down his thoughts in acceptable academic form, attributing his discoveries to universal laws which he thought were obvious to everyone. His law of opposites, law of development and interconnection, and the part-whole principle run through his writings. These and the biological principle of 'preformation' which he often quoted, were then in general acceptance. Froebel's emphasis on historical development has been traced to trends of thought in German universities at the time: no scholar has yet belied his originality in cutting a new path through the trappings of conventional pedagogy. Neither Rousseau, Goethe, nor Pestalozzi could lay claim to an act of inspiration which by-passed the classroom. In a sense, Froebel was among the first of the 'de-schoolers'.

As a writer, Froebel seems to reflect and discourse without inhibition, and much of his work was digressive and obscure. In the nineteenth century his works were supposed to be studied as a whole, and heavy passages of obscure style and symbolism were treated as scripture. Only recently in English have intelligent selections been made which show how much true glitter was there among the dross.[14]

His psychological views were governed by the concept of innate ideas, of a slumbering being within the child who should unfold like a plant to make the complete adult. His principles were erroneous, but they were the starting point for his valuable discussion of child development, the origin of most modern theory. In his later writings, contributed to journals in order to explain the kindergarten, he returned continually to this theme: 'The plays are in themselves a whole, and, indeed, a whole the parts of which develop from one another, and . . . so also is the development of the child himself felt and perceived, and therefore striven for by himself as well as by his observant nurse, as a whole constantly unfolding from itself; hence it receives further nurture.'[15] He is implying here the sense of purpose behind learning, and later in the same section he returns to this idea with one of his most significant statements: 'Children till now were too little employed, or not judiciously — that is to say, not self-actively enough.'

The slight awkwardness in English is not felt in the German original: '*nicht selbst und freithätig genug*,' and the idea has gained strength from educational practice in our time. If we gather even a few fragments of Froebel's philosophy of education together, and compare them with the German school environment in his time, where teachers were told that 'the method of instruction must endeavour first and foremost to train the memory . . .' we can form some idea of his genius. 'Play is the highest level of child development. It is the spontaneous expression of thought and feeling — an expression which his inner life requires' or 'The ability of a human being is to grow in felicity to his full power and to achieve his destiny depends solely on a proper understanding of him in childhood.'

Froebel's Gifts and Aids

After an educational exhibition in London in the 1850s, an article written by Henry Morley appeared in Dickens's journal, *Household Words*. It is an excellent description of the first set of kindergarten material and equipment devised to accelerate education without books. The gifts and aids have now disappeared from nurseries and kindergarten and been replaced by a wide variety of factory-built occupations for under-sixes; these are all, however, based on the discoveries of practical innovators like Piaget, Montessori, Séguin and Froebel himself. Henry Morley here describes the archetype: of particular interest is the way in which Froebel's unity in diversity is achieved through the play-things. Feeling and vision are linked with song, story, historical background chats, mathematics, and practical creation. Through it all runs the thread of symbolism which obsessed Froebel and which research by contemporary scholars like Piaget has shown to be a core feature of early childhood play.

A box containing six soft balls, differing in colour, is given to the child. It is Froebel's 'first gift'. Long before it can speak the infant can hold one of these little balls in its fingers, become familiar with its spherical shape and its colour. It stands still, it springs, it rolls. As the child grows, he can roll it and run after it, watch it with sharp eyes, and compare the different colours, prick up his ears at the songs connected with his various games with it, use it as a bond of 'playfellowship' with other children, practise with it first efforts at self-denial and so forth.

One ball is suspended by a string, it jumps, it rolls, here, there, over, up; turns left, turns right, ding-dong, tip-tap, falls, spins; fifty ideas may be connected with it. The six balls, three of the primary colours, three of the secondary, may be built up in a pyramid; they may be set rolling, and used in combination in a great many ways giving sufficient exercise to the young minds that have all knowledge and experience before them.

Froebel's 'second gift' is a small box containing a ball, cube, and roller (the last two perforated), with a stick and string. With these forms of the cube, sphere and cylinder, there is a great deal to be done and learned. They can be played with at first according to the child's own humour: will run, jump, represent carts, or anything. The ancient Egyptians, in their young days as a nation, piled three cubes on one another and called them the three Graces. A child will, in the same way, see fishes in stones and be content to put a cylinder upon a cube and say that is papa on horseback. Of this element of ready fancy in all childish sport Froebel took full advantage. The ball, cube, and cylinder may be spun, swung, rolled, and balanced in so many ways as to display practically all their properties. The cube, spun upon the stick piercing it through opposite edges, will look like a circle, and so forth. As the child grows older, each of the forms may be examined definitely, and he may learn from observation to describe it. The ball may be rolled down an inclined plane and the acceleration of its speed observed. Most of the elementary laws of mechanics may be made practically obvious to the child's understanding.

The 'third gift' is the cube divided once in every direction. By the time the child gets this to play with he is three years old — of age ripe for admission to the Infant Garden, which is intended for children between three and seven years old. Instruction — always by means of play — is given for only two or three hours of the day and should set each child, if reasonably helped at home, in the right train of education for the remainder of its time.

An Infant Garden must be held in a large room with plenty of clear space for play, and connected with a garden into which the children may adjourn whenever weather will permit. The garden is meant chiefly to assure, more perfectly, the association of wholesome bodily exercise with mental activity. If climate but permitted, Froebel would have all young children taught entirely in the pure, fresh air while frolicking in sunshine among flowers. The garden, too, should be their own; every child the master or mistress of a plot in it, sowing seeds and watching day by day the growth of plants, instructed playfully and simply in the meaning of what is observed. When weather forbids use of the garden, there is the great, airy room which should contain cupboards, with a place for every child's toys and implements; so that a habit of the strictest neatness may be properly maintained. Up to the age of seven there is to be no book work and no ink work.

The third gift — the cube divided once in every direction — enables the child to begin the work of construction in accordance with its own ideas, and insensibly brings the ideas into the control of a sense of harmony and fitness. The cube divided into eight parts will make many things; and, while the child is at work helped by quiet suggestion now and then, the teacher talks of what he is about, asks many questions, answers more, mixes up little songs and stories with the play. Pillars, ruined castles, triumphal arches, city gates, bridges, crosses, towers, all can be completed to the perfect saisfaction of a child, with the eight little cubes.

Then follows the 'fourth gift', a cube divided into planes cut lengthways. With a liberal supply of such cubes, it is easy to make clear to the children the elements of arithmetic. Not only can the elementary rules of addition, subtraction, multiplication and division be mastered, children can become thoroughly at home in the principle of fractions, in multiplying and dividing them — as real things; in time it will become easy enough to let written figures represent them — to go through the rule of three, square root, and cube root — and in the process insensibly the groundwork of geometry.

Froebel's 'fifth gift', a cube divided into twenty-seven equal cubes, and three of these further divided into halves, three into quarters, brings with it the teaching of a great deal of geometry, and much help to the lessons in number.

The 'sixth gift' is a cube so divided as to extend still farther the child's power of combining and discussing it. When its resources are exhausted and combined with those of the 'seventh gift' (a box containing every form supplied in the preceding series), the little pupil — seven-years-old — has had his inventive and artistic powers exercised, and his mind stored with facts that have been absolutely comprehended. He has acquired also a sense of pleasure in the occupation of his mind.

But he has not been trained in this way only. There are pieces of wood which can be made into letters, small sticks which make straight lines, patterns, pictures. With the help of peas softened in water, sticks may be joined together, letters, skeletons of cubes, crosses,

Figure 1: Froebel's Fifth Gift

FORMS OF LIFE.

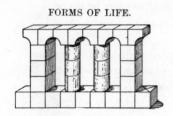

Ruins of a Cloister.

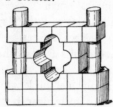

A Portion of a Wall.

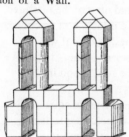

Ancient City Gate.

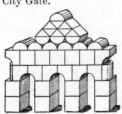

Royal Archway.

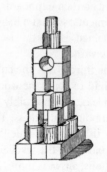

Monument.

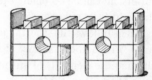

Gate of a Fortress.

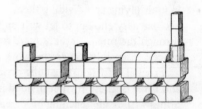

Railroad Train on Bridge.

Railroad Station.

prisms may be built; houses, towers, churches constructed, firm enough to be carried about . . . plaiting, cutting, pricking of plain or coloured paper leads to symmetrical patterns 'of exceeding beauty'. Then there are games by which elementary astronomy, and others laws of Nature, can be made familiar.

Froebel discourages the cramping of an infant's hand upon a pen, but his slate ruled into little squares, or paper prepared in the same way, is used by him for easy training in the elements of drawing. Modelling in wet clay is one of the most important occupations of the children who have reached about the sixth year, and is used as much as possible, not merely to encourage imitation, but to give some play to the creative power. *Finally*, there is the best possible use made of the paint-box, and children engaged upon the colouring of pictures and the arrangement of nose-gays are further taught to enjoy, not merely what is bright, but also what is harmonious and beautiful.[16]

These 'gifts', which Froebel and his disciples carried with them on their journeys in little boxes, were not the result of meditating on great first principles in the universe — Froebel's favourite style of reflection. Although he claimed to have little sympathy with inductive method, many of them were worked out from observation after showing them to children and seeing how they played with the simplest forms. (The *Mutter und Köse* songs, too, began from life, when Froebel was watching a mother carrying her baby about in the farmyard at Keilhau, imitating farm sounds and movements.) Far from insisting on his material being repeatedly used in the same way, he laid down that 'the best kindergarten games are the result of following the children's lead'.[17]

The paradox of Froebel lies in the comparative obscurity of his life and work, and the world-wide success of his plan for a child's garden for the early years. Even now, if one searches the bulky histories of German education, there is little recognition of his achievement to be found. The man who did more than anyone else to spur international interest in the crucial years of child development, and whose practical suggestions were incorporated in other systems which called themselves by other names than *kindergarten*, seems to have been almost forgotten. His name survives in organizations where his writings are seldom studied. But in the context of German education and child-rearing practice during the last century, his contribution was astonishingly advanced, as we can see by looking at the best-selling German morality picture-book, *Struwwelpeter* and the case of Dr Schreber.

In *Struwwelpeter*, a brightly coloured picture book which sold many editions not only in Germany, but in the English-speaking world as well, child disobedience is punished in many unpleasant fashions. The boy who sucks his thumb when Mamma is out of the house may expect a visit from 'the great, long red-legg'd scissor-man.' This terrifying personage strides across the room, catching the little fellow in the act, and – slices both his thumbs off in a trice. The child is left to show the stumps to Mamma, whose only reaction is to say: 'I told you so!' This cheerfully illustrated 'morality' book appeared in 1845, and was the work, not of some penniless (and sadistic) scribbler, but of a doctor – and mental specialist – called Hoffmann.[18]

At about the same time, that is to say when Froebel was unsuccessfully trying to raise public interest in the Kindergarten plan, another German doctor, Daniel Schreber, was writing his books on child-rearing by his own method – a combination of terror, repression, and physical restraint. Schreber said that children must sleep flat on their backs in a straight position, and devised a harness to keep the child in the right posture. He emphasised the 'medical importance' of walking and sitting straight, and invented his *Geradhalter*, an iron cross-bar to be worn at home or at school to keep the child's back straight. His *Kopfhalter* was worn as a head-brace to keep the young fellow's head from falling either forward or sideways.

Schreber was not an unimportant crank. He dressed up his 'educational' proposals in a pseudo-academic style and talked of laws of nature and morality as glibly as any philosopher of his time. On play he advised parents of the rule that only one toy should be used at a time and that 'sufficient energy' (physical or mental) should be expended on it before the child is given another. Play and toys helped to establish the rules of cleanliness, care of property, and tidiness; an immoderate indulgence in 'the pleasures of art', on the other hand, could lead the child into the dangerous area of hysteria, hypochondria, and 'fantasies'. Dr Schreber published a whole series of books between 1839 and 1862; his *Medical Indoor Gymnastics* was well received in Britain and ran into *twenty-six* editions.[19] He was dedicated to remedying the moral softness he perceived in his age, and recommended a gymnastic association to the students' societies, advising them to 'force their members to join!' He also began the well-known 'Schreber Gardens' – strips of land where city dwellers could tend the soil and grow their vegetables at the week-end. Numerous Schreber associations flourished, especially in Saxony, before World War I.

Dr Schreber's advice to the German public on how to improve the race was accordingly well received and may indeed have been more popular than Froebel's liberal proposals for the child's physical and spiritual freedom. Schreber's own family life was not so successful. One son killed himself, while the other, a distinguished judge, went off his head and spent thirteen years in mental asylums, in one of which he died.

A British psycho-analyst who recently investigated the links between Judge Schreber's obsessions and the realities of his upbringing reveals the high-minded torments Father Schreber inflicted on his children in the name of education. The process invites comparison with features in modern totalitarian child-rearing practice (as in Russia) and with the behaviourist views of B.F. Skinner.[20] That is of course, another matter, but the whole case of Dr Schreber and his teachings reveals dramatically how enlightened, in the context of mid-nineteenth-century Germany, was Friedrich Froebel.

Principles like these were made known by Froebel's disciples in their travels throughout Western Europe and the United States after his death. The influence and energy of the Ronge couple in England, Miss Elizabeth Peabody in the United States, and above all, Madame von Bülow in France and the Low Countries carried the new idea of education to the world beyond the Rhine in the 1850s and 60s. After no less than one hundred lectures, Madame von Bülow still felt she was only at the beginning of her task in Paris. But Madame Pape-Carpantier was interested, and the kindergarten was given a three-months trial under her supervision; after which it was cautiously recommended in an official report.

Calling on the historian Michelet, Madame von Bülow made an impact 'like a flash of light.' 'She told us,' wrote Michelet later, 'everything at once; her theories, her life, her simple doctrine that *the child is a creator. Help him to create, and that is all*.' Rousseau, reflected Michelet, makes Robinson Crusoe a hermit, Fournier makes use of the monkey instinct, Jocelot develops the instinct for life and discussion, but Froebel puts an end to teaching children through words alone. 'His development and training are not instilled from without, but drawn forth from the child itself, and are not arbitrary.'

Drawn forth from the child itself — *'vom Kinde aus'*. This was to become the principle of progressive educators in Europe fifty years later; the message had arrived too soon in France, and found the ground unprepared. Despite journalistic interest and offers of financial aid, the kindergarten in France never quite caught on, and Baroness von Bülow had to look to Belgium, Holland, and England for a more favourable reception.

Brussels, Ghent and Antwerp adapted the kindergarten method to combine it with their *écoles gardiennes*. The appearance of a textbook in the French language, composed with the help of Madame von Bülow and carrying her introduction, gave the movement a reference book which had been notably lacking. Published both in Brussels and Paris, the *Manuel pratique des jardins d'enfants* by Monsieur Jacobs opened thus: 'Woman's mission in life is a sacred one, because her tender care has to foster the early development of the child's faculties'. The manual went on to encourage French and Belgian teachers to experiment with the method and not to be put off by the absence of a real garden and other equipment. Some plants growing in pots might serve as a replacement, and the animals could be represented in pictures. One thing, however, could not be left unchanged by the teacher or organizers of the *salles d'asile* or *écoles gardiennes*: the steps of the iniquitous gallery had to be done away with, that 'bench of boredom and torture for young humans on whom their Creator had bestowed the need for life and occupation!'[21] Unfortunately, the English gallery system persisted for many years on the Continent and at home, until in France Pauline Kergomard launched her successful crusade against it in the reformed *école maternelle*. Once again, Froebel's message had come too soon.

Madame von Bülow returned to campaign again in Paris in 1867 with some success, and kindergartens were opened in the Rue Puebla. But any gains were wiped out by the collapse of the Second Empire and the German invasion: no German-sounding method of education could be acceptable to those who had had to endure the Siege of Paris. France remained one of the few countries where the kindergarten made little direct mark.

3 ROBERT OWEN: 'HAPPY TO OUR CLASSES'

'It must be evident to those who have been in the practice of observing children with attention, that much of good or evil is taught to or acquired by a child at a very early period of its life; that much of temper or disposition is correctly or incorrectly formed before he attains his second year; and that many of the durable impressions are made at the termination of the first twelve or even six months of his existence.' In spite of the rather cumbersome prose, the quotation from Robert Owen's *A New View of Society*[1] shows the insight which justifies us in greeting this factory owner of the early nineteenth century as one of the founders of modern pre-school education.

He penned these lines in justification of his plan to enclose a playground area outside his 'New Institution' at New Lanark in Scotland. His revolutionary idea of education included this playground as a place where the village children could go as soon as they could walk alone, and before they were old enough to enter the school itself. What was more, he intended it to be a place where they should be not virtuous, not well-behaved, not pious or attentive, but happy. Each child would be told that his task inside the playground would be twofold: he was never to injure a play-fellow but, on the contrary, 'to contribute all in his power to make them happy'.

Robert Owen (1771–1858) and his helpers began their work in 1816 in Scotland at New Lanark where Owen, a Welshman of humble origins, had come to manage a group of cotton mills in 1800. He was a self-made man, who consolidated his position by marrying the mill-owner's daughter and had sufficient energy to spare from a successful business career to concentrate on social reforms and to travel and publicize his ideas in later life. Voluble, atheistic, self-confident and philanthropic, Robert Owen believed that the cardinal evils of society were the 'necessary consequences of ignorance' and was determined not to persevere with prosperity at New Lanark unless it was also accompanied by sound education for the workers. Confident in the rational doctrines of the Enlightenment, his genius was to use money as a means to the improvement of society, and he was impatient with business partners whose narrow-mindedness stood in the way. His irreligion became notorious — as he meant it to be — and later invalidated his experiments by bringing disapproval upon his schools, but Owen continued to stump the country preaching the cause of social reform, was still in the foreground during the struggle for the Great Reform Bill and was received by royalty when he journeyed abroad in 1817 and 1818.

His autobiography, written when he was over eighty, describes his journey in a fashion which is most entertaining when we follow the accounts of what he told this duke in Germany and that scholar in France, noticing that his audience usually remained (in his words) silent in respect for the importance of the 'New Views' expounded by their visitor. In a remarkable example of hindsight Owen included a visit to Oberlin but the passage of time resulted in transferring Oberlin from Ban de la Roche (where he was throughout his working life) to Freiburg in Switzerland (where he certainly was not). Even without the geographical blunder it is unlikely that Owen would have found nothing of interest to report about Oberlin's infant schools, apart from their originator's interest in New Lanark.[2]

Owen has been described as one of those bores who are the salt of the earth, and his idiosyncrasies cannot mar his great contributions to education, not only in the schools he established for the children of his workers, but in the educational philosophy which was their incentive. When Owen spoke of the education of small children, we seem to be hearing a voice speaking from a modern lecture-hall, well-grounded in the ideas which have come to us through Oberlin, Froebel, Montessori and Piaget.[3]

Owen believed that thousands of children in Glasgow ran the risk of forming vicious habits and being condemned to poverty unless, and it was an important qualification, this ignorance and poverty was removed by a proper education. His faith in education was enthusiastic and at first he supported the methods of Bell and Lancaster, who proposed in the late 1790s mass education carried on by child monitors in a huge room, or rooms. Up to a thousand poor children could there be taught to rudiments of reading, writing, and arithmetic, henceforth to be famous in educational history as the 'three Rs'. Lancaster, a free-thinker, and Bell, a Scots clergyman, enjoyed a vogue which was only disturbed by doubts as to Lancaster's religious respectability; in the eyes of the governing class their type of system was well suited to keeping thousands of poor children in one place at one time at the cost of very little trained manpower. The rigid monitorial system with its huge impersonal rooms was absolutely unsuitable for infant schools and Robert Owen soon realised this, seeing that their 'system' made for mechanical learning, but that the pupils who emerged from this mass-production line could nevertheless have acquired the worst habits 'and have their minds rendered irrational for life'.

The monitorial system, with all its disadvantages, facilitated instructions throughout the nineteenth century, from the age of six to ten, by which time the pupils were required to take their part as apprentices in industry, factory-hands, or down the mine. Owen meanwhile had received sixty three-year-olds, forty-six four-year-olds, and fifty-nine five-year-olds (and a number of older children up to ten) into three rooms in a separate building at New Lanark. The older children were accommodated in the same building on the upper floor. Outside the building there was an enclosed area, where the younger children could play in any except the severest weather, when they retired to amuse themselves indoors.

Supervisors of the children received instructions from the mill-owner on how they were to conduct the school. No child was ever to be beaten, threatened, or abused, and the teachers were supposed to approach them pleasantly, with a kind manner and voice. The children were not to be *annoyed with books*, 'but were to be taught the uses and nature or qualities of the common things around them, by familiar conversation when the children's curiosity was excited so as to induce them to ask questions respecting them'.[4] All the children were told to make each other happy, and especially to look after the younger ones and to teach them how to be happy too. When observers were sent to inspect the school from Leeds in 1819 they described a glow of health, of innocent pleasure, and unabashed childish freedom on the faces of the Owen pupils. There was no anger, no quarrelling, and no tears were shed. The guardians of the poor at Leeds were indeed surprised at a school where neither rewards nor punishments existed, where children were told to play, and to play in the open air as much as possible, to be happy and to help each other.

Robert Owen had thus founded the first infant school in England and almost the first in Europe to be based on freedom, fresh air and play. The extent to which Oberlin's schools in the Ban de la Roche district resembled the New Lanark school in these respects is uncertain, for the two cultures, the climate, and the character of the inhabitants showed a marked difference. Owen's achievement was so much in advance of his time that one can only feel a sense of wonderment at the accuracy with which he hit on the right principles of infant health and development. It is probably best to quote the laconic tribute of Robert R. Rusk, one of the first modern authorities to rediscover Owen's work: 'The success of his plan and the future of the movement alike attest the soundness of his scheme; he anticipated by a century the present-day Nursery School movement.'[5] In the 1970s one is impelled to make the further comment that a century and a half has elapsed and reactionary views have been shaken by two major wars and wave after wave of radical or socialist change without England having been able to provide Owenite schools for the majority of the under-fives.

James Buchanan in New Lanark and London

Once his school was functioning for the benefit of his workers' children Owen turned for someone to manage it and carry out his principles. After an initial error when he chose a professional educator of the old type, who, of course, didn't have the faintest idea of what Owen was trying to do, a simple Scots weaver of thirty, named Buchanan, came to help with the school. Owen had found an assistant as gifted by nature for the work as Louise Scheppler proved in Ban de la Roche. One of Buchanan's notable assets as an infant teacher was that he was a musician, and the children were able to march to his flute, sing hymns to his accompaniment, and take simple gymnastic exercises. They sang the rules of the school and sang as they marched off on a fine day to play by the side of the river Clyde.

> 'March away, march away,
> Happy to our classes,
> There we will our lessons say,
> When we're in our places.'

sang the children as they came in from play, and even if the half rhyme displeases the refined ear, all this added to the atmosphere of cheeriness which Buchanan created with his own natural, simple-hearted personality.[6]

When Buchanan left for London, his departure undoubtedly changed the character of New Lanark. The subject is hard to discuss with accuracy because of Owen's attempts to belittle Buchanan's work later; Buchanan's descendants, on the other hand, claimed that he had no equipment to work with. 'a bare room, without even seats, much less toys, pictures, or anything else to amuse or instruct the children'. A description by Robert Dale Owen of his visit in 1824, included no mention of equipment for infant classes but he said the small children attended half-time, remained inside the school only for half a day and spent the rest of it 'in perfect freedom' outside, under the care of a young woman who had the management of no less than one hundred under-fives.

In their outdoor play the infants 'acquired healthful and hardy habits, and are, at the same time, trained to associate in a kind and friendly manner with their little companions; thus practically learning the pleasure to be derived from such conduct, in opposition to envious bickerings, or ill-natured disputes'.[7] There were apparently hoops and sticks and similar playthings in this area.

Westminster and Wilderspin

Once in London, Buchanan started a school in Westminster called the 'Free Day Infant Asylum', which in name may have owed something to the Paris shelters opened by Madame de Pastoret. Another teacher of talent and equally humble origins, Samuel Wilderspin, met Buchanan through the influence of the 'New Church' of Swedenborg which then flourished in London. Wilderspin conducted an infant school in Spitalfields, and set down his views in a book which attracted much attention when it was published in 1823: *Infant Education, or Remarks on the Importance of Educating the Infant Poor*. Wilderspin's book was widely read abroad, and accepted as a model of correct procedure.

There was for a time some controversy about Wilderspin's claims to have been the originator of infant education, a debate which has lost interest with the passage of time. Wilderspin seems to have devoted much thought to what he was doing, and to have devised a systematic method for handling the infants 'from as soon as they can walk to seven years old'. Although Oberlin preceded them in practice, and Comenius in theory, neither Owen nor James Buchanan can be denied a measure of the credit, recognizing as they did the right to freedom of the pre-school age child. Owen invested in New Lanark not only his fortune but his reputation and his talents, which were considerable. To Wilderspin we owe, however, an anecdote which brings before us a vivid portrait of what the atmosphere of a London infant class was like in the 1820s (he is describing his own experience):

As soon as the mothers had left the premises the teacher found
that he could not win the interest of babies who had never been
left alone by their mothers: they crushed around the door and
one began crying 'Mammy! Mammy!' That did it, and the rest
crowded to him, screaming as best they could. Mrs Wilderspin
tried in vain to calm them, and the noise increased to such a point
that she fled from the room, followed shortly after by Wilderspin,
who left the pupils in a dense hysterical mass, crying, yelling, and
kicking the door.

He wrote later:

I will not attempt to describe my feelings, but ruminating on what
I then considered egregious folly in supposing that any two persons
could manage so large a number of infants, I was struck by the
sight of a cap of my wife's adorned with coloured ribbon, lying
on the table; and, observing from the window a clothes-prop, it
occurred that I might put the cap upon it, return to the school;
and try the effect. The confusion when I entered was tremendous;
but, on raising the pole surmounted by the cap, all the children,
to my great satisfaction, were instantly silent; and when any hapless
wight seemed disposed to renew the noise, a few shakes of the cap
restored tranquility, and, perhaps, produced a laugh. The same thing,
however, will not do long; the charms of this *wonderful* instrument
therefore soon vanished, and there would have been a sad relapse
but for the marchings, gambols, and antics, I found it necessary
to adopt, and which, at last, brought the hour of twelve, to my
greater joy than can easily be conceived.

Wilderspin deserved full marks for keeping his head in that
situation common to every new teacher when his class begins to
disintegrate in front of his eyes; but, more than this, he went on to
reflect about the experience and use it to advantage in future teaching
practice. 'I felt that that memorable morning had not passed in vain.
I had, in fact, found the clue. It was now evident that the senses of the
children must be engaged; that the great secret of training them was
to descend to their level, and become a child; and that the error had
been to expect in infancy what is only the product of after years.'[8]
When one considers the English attitudes of the day to young
children, Owen and Buchanan were, of course, remarkable innovators.
The eighteenth-century young had been sheltered in dame schools or

charity schools, grammar schools or the newly-promoted Sunday
Schools, which enrolled no less than 850,000 children at the turn of
the century. The latter had the great advantage for hard-headed
business men of leaving the children 'free' to toil in mine or factory
for the rest of the week; only the Sabbath was for learning. In all of
these, little attention was paid to the infant age-group (the under-
sixes), and their main purpose was to teach 'the true spelling and
distinction of syllables with the points and stops'. As in France or
Germany, the method was dull, repetitious and backed by the use of
fear and constraint.

To view, as did Owen, happiness in childhood as compatible with
education was an astonishing departure from tradition. In recognizing
the importance of the environment as a means of building his new
moral world, he preceded Froebel, the 'New Education' and the
progressives by many decades. After his departure to found a back-
woods Utopia in North America (at New Harmony, Indiana) the
schools declined into 'the British and Foreign system', or, as at New
Harmony, embarked on a type of modified Pestalozzi method: the
great period of Owen's experiment was, therefore, between 1816 and
1824, when he sailed for North America. The happy child in school-
time then disappeared from England, except for fortunate exceptions,
until his reappearance in the kindergarten and reformed infant schools
at the end of the century.

The efforts of individuals like Owen, Buchanan and Wilderspin,
although they led to the establishment of a number of centres for
shelter and early education, particularly in London, could not be
called a movement; they were isolated examples for others to imitate,
and particularly impressed the founders of the Paris *salles d'asile* in
the 1820s. Childhood in nineteenth-century society was lived in
cottage, town tenement or middle-class houses, and there were sharper
differences in child-rearing between the classes than there are today.
Country children, for all that they usually were woken early, put out
in all weathers, and made to help with the farm, lived a rougher and
freer existence than those in the towns.

Nursery Life

We know more about the childhood environment of the Victorian
middle-class than we do about the others; records and memoirs have
remained to tell us about nursery and nanny, dolls and picture-books.
When people in this stratum of English society woke up to the fact
that there were tens of thousands of children outside this comfortable,

secure environment, they finally determined that the working-class needed nurseries rather than classrooms, and so grew up after a long delay the 'nursery school movement'. But for most of the century the rights of the middle-class infant and those of the poor showed little similarity.

Respectable middle-class children were segregated from the world and also from their parents by the nursery walls and intervening corridors. For their first decade they were watched over by nurse and governess, taken on special occasions to visit their parents downstairs or visited by mother or father on ritual occasions when they called at the nursery to say good night.

The child was kept very busy, learning his table-manners, obedience and respect for authority, the alphabet and numbers up to ten. Listening to moral tales read aloud by their nurses they found out which kings and queens were bad and which were good, using *Little Arthur's History of England* as their text. The nursery in those days of large families was a well-peopled school-room, almost the size of some present-day playgroups, and it was managed with a discipline based on religion, the sense of sin, 'speak when you are spoken to', and 'enjoy plain fare'. One of the interesting revelations of recent research has been the primitive diet given to children even in the great houses: curds and whey, bread and milk were victuals recommended by the standard book of home medicine published in the eighteenth century. Bread and milk (porridge in Scotland), broth in the evening, small beer or wine-and-water to restore the spirits were the usual fare, and Queen Victoria when young once refused her daily bread and milk and tearfully demanded a plate of good sausages instead. Only Queen Victoria could get away with a rebellious performance such as that. Other little boys and girls would have felt a touch of the rod or been 'sent to Coventry' for refusing the fare supplied by the Almighty in his goodness.

The nursery-room was simply, even austerely, furnished. There was a table in the warm corner where maids could chatter while they darned stockings, a larger deal table for meals, a plain white painted cupboard for toys, another for clothes, and one for the chinaware.[9] Several little beds were arranged in what was frequently the attic, and must have been a draughty place in winter. Dress itself was simple, and consisted of one warm frock with a change in the winter, and the same in the summer in lighter materials, muslin or lawn. Boys had loose jackets and long, tight trousers.

Education in even the comfortable homes was repetitious, based on

the Three Rs, and continued most of the day with a break for meals
and a walk. One little boy, who was given away by his parents from
an over-large family, recalled later that he could never recollect one
moment of (indoor) childhood in which he was not 'undergoing
education of some kind, and generally of an unwanted kind'.[10] As
mid-century was reached, however, a change in toys and technology
adaptable to learning occurred: clockwork toys and musical boxes
were joined by magnets, trains, the stereoscope which opened the
nursery doors to far countries and foreign, sunlit cities. Best of all,
the magic lantern had arrived by 1850 and children in the darkness
could see the slides tell the story of some adventurous journey to
spread the knowledge of the Bible among people in Africa or the
islands of Polynesia. Printing, too, had begun to develop methods of
colour reproduction which led to cheap story-books with coloured
plates, and titles like: *Mother Hubbard and Her Dog, The Fox and the
Goose, The Old Woman and Her Pig, Goody Two-Shoes, Mother Goose*
and *Robinson Crusoe*; all survived from the eighteenth century to
confound serious writers of religious tracts for the young.

Grimm, Aesop, and after 1846, Hans Anderson's *Wonderful Tales
for Children* (as the English translation which appeared in that year
was called) brought fairy-stories into the foreground of nursery
reading and story-telling, and were accompanied by all sorts of new
stories for boys: *Mr Midshipman Easy* by Captain Frederick Marryat
had come out in 1836 and it was soon followed by *Masterman Ready*
and *Children of the New Forest*, a first-class historical romance for
young readers. Ballantyne produced *Coral Island* in 1857, and it was
followed by Anna Sewell's *Black Beauty*, first of a long line of animal
stories in the seventies (*A Dog of Flanders*, first of the dog stories,
came out in 1872 and was a favourite of Ruskin and Cardinal Mann-
ing). *Treasure Island* appeared in a children's magazine called *Young
Folks* in 1882.[11]

The toyland of middle-class England was reigned over by the doll,
and there was none of the proliferation of animals and oddities which
trip the unwary on entering a modern child's playroom. Even Golliwog
had to wait until Miss Upton wrote her *Adventures of Two Dutch Dolls
and a Golliwog* in 1859, and Teddy Bear, that extraordinary and
lovable by-product of Theodore Roosevelt's life and times, did not
appear until 1903 at the Leipzig Toy Fair. Like the Christmas Tree
which Prince Albert had introduced to England, and the Easter Bunny,
Teddy was part of Germany's gift to Western children and shopkeepers.

The Germans, who were expert doll-makers, had worked out an

organized *system* about doll-play by mid-eighteenth century, and
mothers and nurses were advised to 'direct young minds in the right
way' lest otherwise dolls be used just for amusement and run the risk
of careless destruction. Doll games which centred on a home tableau
in the dolls' house demanded proper behaviour by the children;
meals were served by the child seated at the table to her doll guests
and etiquette observed when tea was being poured or the guests
welcomed at the door.

Such, in brief outline, was the world of the middle-class nursery.[12]
It was almost invariably described as a secure and inviolate dream-
world, in spite of austerity and discomfort. Conscious of its absence
from the lives of the poor, later reformers in England determined to
pattern new centres for little children on the nursery rather than on
the elementary school. The United Kingdom evolved her nursery-
schools, while neighbouring France evolved the 'mothering' school —
the *maternelle*.

The Rights of Children

When we come to judge the state of child-care, both for the poor and
the well-to-do, and deplore the stiff discomfort of Lancaster or
Wilderspin's galleries, we do well to remember the general brutality
of a society which transported tens of thousands of its own nationals,
including children, to the convict colonies of Australia. Many of the
young boys who were able to survive the conditions of the six-months'
journey below decks were destined for the unspeakable miseries and
torture of Point Puer and Norfolk Island, a veritable hell on earth.
Even their more fortunate brothers were put to serve on ships of the
line as trainee naval officers at eleven or twelve, or were taught their
Latin by means of the rod from the age of *four*. Like the author Samuel
Butler, they might have seen another boy in fetters, or in the school
dungeons, kept in silence with only straw and a blanket, bread and
water, and thrashed twice a week by a beadle who came in for the
purpose. Such was the punishment for attempting to run away from
school.

The state of poorer children was controlled, to some extent, by
legislation. In 1842, for instance, an act limited the hours for children
working in the mines to thirteen or fourteen a day. A child of eight,
giving evidence before a commission of enquiry told how he worked
alone as a 'trapper' in a mine. His job was to open and close one of
the doors which allowed air into the mine, and he was left alone to do
it throughout what would have been daylight hours above ground.

'I have to trap without a light,' he said, 'and I'm scared. I go at four
and sometimes half past three in the morning and come out at five
and half past in the evening. I never go to sleep. Sometimes I sing
when I've a light, but not in the dark; I daren't sing then.' His
condition in life was that of thousands, and was, if anything, better
than that of the chimney-sweeps who were sold to their masters by
parents or foster-parents who did not want them. As in the mines, the
smaller the child the better the investment. Chimney-sweeps varied in
age; some, who must have been unusually agile and hardy for their
age, were only four or five – eligible for the smallest groups in
Froebel's kindergarten or the *salles d'asile*. If a chimney was twelve
inches square their masters claimed that the children went up it with
ease, but many chimneys were narrower, sores formed on their knees
and elbows, causing excruciating pain, and only the fear of the master's
stick or a bundle of straw lit under their feet sent them on their way
to the top. Climbing the smaller flues they were told to keep their
arms above their heads – or jam in the chimney. Occasionally they
died of suffocation in the soot, or were burned to death in the flue.
There were at least a thousand such poor little devils apprenticed in
England early in the nineteenth century.[13]

Legally, the existence of children had been recognized sporadically
in England, since Henry VIII's time; a statute was then passed that
children over *five* and under fourteen 'who lived in idleness' could
be put to service lest they became beggars and undesirables. Sir
William Blackstone, the great English jurist, pointed out that by
ancient Saxon laws, twelve years was the age of discretion, and below
that age a person could not be 'guilty at will'. Yet cunning could be
present in young children out of all proportion to their age, and the
law would take this into account in ordering punishment. 'Under seven
years of age,' declared Blackstone in his *Commentaries*, 'an infant
cannot be guilty of a felony, for then felonious discretion is almost an
impossibility in nature; but at *eight years old* he may be guilty of a
felony.' Seven years was the point of division between childhood and
responsibility in mediaeval France also, at which time the young boy
'passed out of the hands of women', and went to school, was
apprenticed, or sent to serve in another household. One wonders what
tribal or later-Roman logic contrived to fix this point of departure
from an age of innocence and dependence on the woman-protector.
After that age, the supreme penalty, with many intermediate
gradations of flogging or psychological torture, could be paid by the
offending child; it is only fairly recently that parents, in Anglo-Saxon

countries at least, retain a virtual monopoly of punishment and torture of their children.[14]

Even for the well-to-do family, where parents did not need to rent out their offspring as labour, or employ them sewing in the home, affectionate relationships were remote or non-existent in many cases. Seafaring men might see their sons once or even twice a year, and child mortality made it a matter for providence whether they met them again at the end of the cruise. One of Captain Cook's voyages of discovery ended at the graveside of one of his two children. Quite apart from the standard rate of infant mortality which remained high until after the turn of the century, there was the persistent threat of diphtheria, scarlatina (30,000 deaths in 1863 alone) and phthisis, or tuberculosis. The approach of cholera from Eastern Europe was heralded by William IV in a Royal Speech to Parliament, and when it struck Britain in October 1831, it attacked the families of rich and poor alike. In this respect, it differed from typhus, known as 'the poor man's disease'. A family might consider itself fortunate if three out of five children reached the age of fifteen in Victorian England.[15]

In that age of disease and famine it would be easy to forget the brave efforts of the individuals who tried to help England's children. Dickens wrote with admiration of the teachers whom he saw at work in the Ragged Schools of London, 'the Masters are extremely quiet, honest, good men. You may suppose they are, to be there at all.' During the Crimean War, ladies like the explorer Richard Burton's future wife worked night and day to help the destitute families of absent soldiers; we can obtain some idea of the size of the task when we read that she enlisted the help of *150* girls in her welfare club. Dublin-born T.J. Barnardo began his Stepney mission for starving children in 1870 and it was later claimed that no destitute child was ever refused care in a Barnardo home.

The astonishing thing for us is probably not the immense suffering but the enormous resistance to the idea that children deserved to be treated as human-beings worthy of sympathy and respect. It was still a world in which John Bird, aged less than fourteen, was hanged in prison and where even as late as 1894 children aged ten were still in full-time employment. The notion of children's rights belonged only to a few individuals as enlightened as Owen, Dickens, or Barnardo. Yet, finally, by the 1890s, a Royal Society was formed for the protection of children from cruelty, many years after the founding of a society for prevention of cruelty to animals.

The employment of children under nine had been prohibited by the passing of the Factories Act in 1819 and older children's working hours limited to twelve a day, but child labour was highly esteemed by thrifty employers throughout the nineteenth century, and it was only gradually that the middle classes, lulled by the pleasant sounds of activity in the nursery-attic, realized what happened to children from poorer families. Part-time child labour was not made illegal for another hundred years. The Factories Act was difficult to enforce, and the evidence produced before a House of Commons Committee in 1832 indicated the presence of children of seven or eight, six, and even five in the mills and factories. The conditions under which they laboured led to permanent impairment of their health through lack of sleep and poor diet if for no other reason. A race of working-class cripples was evolved by an industrial system which eliminated most infants through early mortality in the slums. Although there were improvements after the resulting scandal, eight-year-olds were released for the market in child-life by the Factory Act of 1844, and provisions for children who worked in factories to attend school (as well) for two hours a day failed for lack of buildings. Inspection in 1864 revealed that children under eight years of age were working until ten o'clock at night, and strong opposition resisted the attempt to outlaw such crimes, for the country and the prosperity of Britain's middle classes was thought to depend on such labour. In the mines, child labour, as the Marquis of Londonderry pointed out in Parliament, was essential for the country's well-being (and especially in such mines as he owned himself). As a compromise, the law which was eventually passed prohibited children working underground at an age below ten.

But social conscience stirred itself sufficiently to introduce the idea of education for the 'lower orders' at public expense. Despite conservative opponents of expenditure on children, such as Lord Londonderry and James Graham, radical and liberal pioneers gradually won the fight for provision, even though conditions and methods in the school left a lot to be desired.

Statesmen like Lord Brougham urged that children could learn a lot before they were six, and educators such as Leonard Horner pleaded for schools where children of the working classes might improve their religious, moral and intellectual character. These new views had to be modified, of course, because of conservative fears that the poorer classes might thus become permanently discontented with their station in life. Education, as some of the founders of the French *salles d'asile* had suspected, could become a dangerous two-edged sword if it were not carefully supervised; nevertheless, some public funds were devoted to building elementary schools after 1833.

By 1845 inspectors began to report on the serious work that was being done in these primary schools for the masses. Fletcher, and his successor Bowstead, referred disparagingly to the older view that very young children should only be amused and kept from harm, albeit with a certain amount of discipline and 'moral control'. Elsewhere he wrote:

> Many institutions may now be met with which prove by the results of their teaching that the four years of a child's life preceding the age of seven are not much, if at all, less valuable in an educational point of view than the four which succeed. There are infant schools in my district in which the upper classes, consisting entirely of children under seven, read the New Testament or a simple secular book fluently and intelligently, write on a slate in a fair round hand, know many of the simpler properties and relations of numbers, set down on a slate any number under 100,000 correctly from dictation, are acquainted with the main features of the earth's surface and of English geography, have definite notions of all ordinary forms, and possess an appreciable amount of exact information on natural history and objects of general utility.

Nor was this all, for 'in addition to these mental attainments they have acquired habits of obedience, attention and observation, facility of comprehension, and a general moral culture, which distinguishes them at a glance from untrained children of the same class and age'.[16] There were positive features in these reports. Fletcher launched an attack on the 'prodigy system', whereby the child who could learn off by heart a travesty of the language of science or a desecration of that of Scripture was held up for the admiration of his slower companions, and recommendations were made by both inspectors for improving the intake of qualified and competent teachers. By 1870 the movement towards early education for the masses was in full swing, and in an estimated child population in England and Wales of 1,179,228 three to five year olds, there were 275,608 at school: almost twenty-five per cent of the total. There were also no less than 18,755 *under* three at school in 1871-2. Teachers found that, unless they admitted the 'babies' their elder brothers and sisters were kept home to mind them.[17] This proportion continued to rise, moreover, to 29 per cent ten years later, to 33 per cent in 1890 and even to 43 per cent in

1900, when there were over 615,000 children in public elementary schools, while others were of course attending private classes and kindergarten.

By establishing the school-entrance age at five years in 1870, England laid the foundations for her infant-schools of today, which bring small children to school when, in other countries they attend kindergarten-preparatory year, the *maternelle*, or are left to play in the street. During the Parliamentary debate, the Earl of Shaftesbury reminded his fellow peers in the House of Lords that the Workshop Act had been no protector for some children 'because they toiled in the houses of their parents, and the only protection which could be given them was that they should be placed under the care of the School Boards'. He tried, unsuccessfully, to lower the limit to four, using educational discipline as a means of protecting children from the poverty or greed of their own parents. In farming areas, it was pointed out during the debate, children began to have a money value 'as soon as they can shout loud enough to scare a crow'. There was no very clear awareness as to why five, rather than six, had been chosen for the Bill, and after a wavering debate the Act was passed, not to make education compulsory, but allowing School Boards to make bye-laws at their discretion requiring attendance at five.

In Robert Owen's time, the very young were grouped together from two to six years; Froebel's kindergarten welcomed children under six; there seemed no valid educational reason for the lower age limit. Gladstone had proposed the Bill; Disraeli could have forced drastic changes upon it, but he was apparently keen to get on with parliamentary business. 'The lower age-limit of five survived the Parliamentary mastication of Forster's Bill,' wrote Szreter,[18] who examined closely the debate at Westminster, 'to emerge unaltered, not out of an examination of educational desiderata but out of a clash of sound and spurious economic and humanitarian arguments.' Thus the great decisions on education may be made in a free parliament, and national honour satisfied: in a burst of patriotic rhetoric, one of the Bill's sponsors had demanded of the House: 'Englishmen and English-women, are Austrian children to be educated before English children?' Britain's Parliament had risen to the challenge.

It was then ten years before, in a 'definite though belated step forward', education between five and ten became the law of the land. Unfortunately, much of the benefit of this move had been forestalled by the iniquities of the Revised Elementary School Code, issued in 1861. The Duke of Newcastle's commission, which preceded the

Code, fairly displayed contemporary attitudes in the country gentry and town bourgeoisie who were pleased to learn that children leaving an infant school at *seven* should read, write, and 'cipher' correctly. The Revised Code (which owed nothing to Owen or Froebel, and much to traditional instruction) stated therefore, that while grants should be made to elementary schools, they should depend on the results of examining all the children (including the infants) in the three Rs. In vain more enlightened bodies such as the Home and Colonial School Society protested; for thirty years infant schools were haunted by the dreaded coming of the inspectors, a visit which hung over both pupils and teachers alike as a governmental sword of Damocles. Even though the youngest children were later excused from examination (!), this poison spread downwards through the system and wiped out the gains in freedom, play, and happiness which had been achieved after Owen. Crowded infant schools conducted on the gallery method awaited unfortunate little three, four, or five year olds in seven thousand assisted schools.

There may have been dedicated and enthusiastic teachers; equally there may have been schools which were not overcrowded, but it is difficult to find much to say for the infant schools of late nineteenth-century England. They were considered a desirable alternative to the 'close, crowded, and dirty' dame schools; they removed the children of the poor in large numbers from the dangers of the street and drudgery in the home for a few years; they offered elements of instruction in the 'three Rs' and the distinction of passing the 'standards' at the age of seven, but their conduct seems to have owed too much to Bell, Lancaster, and the 'gallery system'. As late as 1900 an observer heard a baby class repeat one sound 120 times continuously, while lessons were unbroken by a single manual occupation in many baby classes during an entire morning. One who remembered vividly his first day's schooling, in 1876, sketched the picture in later years:

My mother and I were somehow led by somebody into a classroom. It seemed an enormous apartment, and was filled with babies arranged in galleries, almost to the ceiling, as I thought — all steaming, murmurous, and palpitating with suppressed and uneasy life, in an atmosphere thick with dust and smelling acridly of chalk, varnish, and dirty clothes . . . The lady teacher asked my mother my name, and began to write it down in a large register. Before she had finished the entry, however, one of the babies at the top of

the gallery fell off his seat and rolled right down one of the gang-
ways to the floor at the bottom, raising a dreadful succession of
thuds and screams. The teacher went on writing, with just the
merest lift of the head.

'It serves you right,' she said: 'I was just watching for that to
happen. You're the worst wriggler in the class! How often have I
told you to sit still and keep your arms folded? And now, you see,
you are punished for your disobedience!'[19]

Allowing for slight literary exaggeration, the description does
illustrate the merits of the gallery system for the unfortunate young
women who were supposed to teach eighty or ninety little children
at a time in a room without equipment other than benches and steps.
If they were packed tight enough, they were unlikely to fall, and
according to most accounts, the smallest sat on the bottom steps
where they could tumble only a little way. One critic described this
sort of infant instruction as penal servitude, which exposed its raison
d'être with the long awaited arrival of the inspector who called on
individuals to read aloud from the Bible or an approved book, count
up to a hundred – if they were aged five or six – and say or sing
the multiplication table. Sick children were carried or dragged along
to school on that great day, so as not to miss the grant of six shillings
which the inspector could bestow. This state of affairs continued until
Froebel and other liberal influences penetrated English schools in the
1880s, and led to the liberal Revised Code of 1892.

The German influence of the Prince Consort made England much
more sympathetic to the foreign gospel, ready to listen to kinder-
gartners as she was to replace the old Yule Log by the Christmas Tree.
Madame von Bülow had lectured in London on her tour of the
European capitals in 1854 and Herr Hoffman had delivered lectures
on Froebel theory to the Polytechnic Institution.

A Bloomsbury kindergarten was opened by a couple called Ronge
for children of German liberal exiles and Manchester, Belfast, Dublin,
Croydon and Bedford soon acquired their own. The Froebel Society,
predecessor of the National Froebel Union and the Froebel Institute,
was founded in 1874, and training centres were established in several
cities, including the one in London which plays an important part in
teacher-training to this day.

Froebel's own writings were not available in English for several
decades after the first kindergarten had opened in Tavistock Place;
his teachings were disseminated through pamphlets in several

languages written by propagandist-educators like Baroness von Bülow.
In English Herr Ronge and his wife produced *A Practical Account of
the Kindergarten*, and there was a flood of publications in the United
States, where Miss Elizabeth Peabody had opened the pages of her
journal, called *The Kindergarten Messenger*, to the cause. Some of
these publications and translations of Froebel returned across the
Atlantic to stimulate further interest and strengthen the background
knowledge of kindergarten supporters. The kindergarten seemed to
offer a formula for early education which appealed, whatever its
faults, to the radical, intellectual sectors of the middle classes.[20]

The rigid traditional methods of education not only marred the
young lives of tens of thousands whom Froebel failed to reach. They
frequently wrought a dreadful change in kindergarten method when
adopted by the elementary schools, turning it into yet another form
of education by rote. Large groups of children sat performing 'kindergarten exercises' with blocks and beads, straining their eyes as they
threaded and wound to train their hand and eye as early as possible.

But some authorities soon became aware of the debasement in
kindergarten practice and there were circulars to warn against this.
In both the United States and England a reaction came from Froebel
scholars against the Froebelized 'learning which went directly against
the spirit of Keilhau'. Warnings were given against arbitrary selection
of 'some object such as a potato' around which 'all songs, games,
stories and gift exercises' were made to revolve. By the early 1890s
Education Department inspectors reported on the change in infant
education, admiringly telling how with their musical drills, hand
occupations, kindergarten work, games, and fairy, maypole and other
dances, infant-schools seemed to be 'almost as good as any imperfect
human institution can be'.[21]

The spirit of this 'New Education', as it came to be called, sprang
from Froebel's basic principles of child interest and natural self-
expression through play. He had shown the way to freedom from
instruction; but his work had been done in rural Thuringia. The
impelling necessity was now to find a way in which his principles could
be applied in the rapidly developing industrial cities of Britain and
Europe.

4 PAULINE KERGOMARD AND THE *MATERNELLE*

The *salles d'asile*, like the English infant schools, tended towards physical constraint and a goal of instruction; after 1870 the danger was that these traditions would be adapted for the Third Republic. Church schools and religious teaching were to be done away with, and in their place education in its narrower sense could fill the children's day. The Republic had an undoubted mission to educate girls and boys along secular lines, and if spiritual claims in child-rearing were rejected, it would have been hardly surprising if utility had won the day. If the *salles d'asile* were assimilated to the elementary school system, then alphabet, pot hooks, sums and reading books could be expected to triumph.

The extraordinary thing was, that this did not occur. Instead, France, after a struggle, produced the only system which explicitly rejected intelligence-training and the 'three Rs'. One doubts whether this could have come about without the personality of a highly unorthodox woman who totally rejected the place of instruction in the lives of the under-sixes. In part, her proposals are still followed to this day, and ensured an integral education of the whole child in France's *écoles maternelles*.

Pauline Reclus, later Pauline Duplessis-Kergomard (1838–1925), was descended from generations of Protestant farmers in the Bordeaux district.[1] Her father was an Inspector of Primary Schools, a captain in the National Guard and a monarchist. Her mother died when Pauline was only ten and her father remarried soon after. Pauline, as the youngest of seven, remained at home with her stepmother and father. But she was not happy in the new household and left to stay with an uncle. For reasons of conscience, this Protestant pastor had abandoned his parish and departed to a remote area with his wife and eleven children. Pauline's aunt eked out their small income by running a rather unorthodox school for young girls (without timetable or syllabus) and her energy and devotion to her husband's life-work could not fail to make a deep impression upon Pauline.

But before long she had to return to her father's house; her future had been decided, and she was to enter a private training school for teachers in Bordeaux.[2] Here Pauline Kergomard found her vocation, and passed her examinations with flying colours. Finding no difficulty in handling the theoretical work, she used to find time to help her less gifted friends, or, for preference, make an excursion next door to the small school attached to the institute. The difficulties encountered by some of the young teachers there did not discourage her, and she enjoyed taking their place and spending her time with real children rather than in studying theories of childhood. This was one of her endearing characteristics as *Inspectrice-Générale* many years later: she never became so involved in organization or theory (even though she wrote volumes about infant education) that she was too busy to notice the individual child or the personal problems of his teacher.

Excellent student and promising teacher though she was, she was not prepared to submit to discipline without good reason, and her principal reported her general attitude as one of marked independence. This, again, was a trait which she later, without hypocrisy, tried to apply to the treatment of school-children; writing more than twenty years later, she said:

> There is too much respect in our *écoles maternelles*, the type of discipline which gives top marks for good behaviour to the child who does nothing wrong [*qui ne fait rien*]. Myself, when I have to choose between this sort of discipline and disorder and noise, I prefer the disorder and noise a hundred times over, because at least noise and disorder means to me that they are really alive!

When Pauline had obtained her teaching certificate (known then as the *brevet de capacité*) she took up private teaching until 1861 when one of her sisters invited her to share the apartment in Paris she and her husband had taken near the Hotel de Ville. Suzanne, her eldest sister, had married Benjamin Laurand, a civil servant who had become private secretary to the celebrated Baron Haussmann, then Prefect of the Seine. Noémi, the second daughter, had married her first cousin, one of the eleven children of the Pastor of Orthez where Pauline had lodged after her mother's death. The Laurand ménage had access to the corridors of power through the Prefect's office; the Reclus were intellectuals. Elie Reclus wrote for learned periodicals and was described as an ethnologist and 'mythographer'. His position was as precarious as that of Laurand was secure: he had renounced the ministry after completing his training, and had also been implicated in a serious political affair which conspired against Napoleon III.

Thus Pauline Reclus, who continued to take private pupils and earn a reasonable living, had friends in both camps during the 1860s.

Elie Reclus was a freethinker and had served a term of exile for his politics: Benjamin Laurand was a rising official under the Second Empire. The young woman from Bordeaux was small, attractive without being pretty, full of life, charm and energy. She dressed well, loved dancing, entertainment and the world of Paris middle-class society; those who knew her best predicted that she would marry money, would in fact have to marry money, to satisfy her needs. But instead, she was drawn to a different kind of person, a Breton writer named Jules Duplessis-Kergomard.

Her husband, for they were married at the Oratory late in 1863, was a republican of 1848, some years older than she and not at all well off. He had lived in exile in Brussels but had been permitted to return in 1856. He had gone with Garibaldi to Sicily as a correspondent, and after his return became well known in minor literary circles in Paris. He was a man of impressive appearance, courteous, idealistic and well read. Unfortunately, he lost faith in his writing and himself after marrying Pauline and became practically inactive; as they had no private income, this threw the burden on his wife's shoulders. In a curious parallel with her mother's life and that of her aunt at Orthez, she was obliged to bear a family (there were two sons) and provide for them for the rest of her days. Monsieur Kergomard fell into that state known to the Greeks as *Akedia*, and was no use at all as a breadwinner.

Under the new republican regime many of the young intellectuals who were in opposition before 1870 found positions of importance. While Pauline Kergomard was engaged by the famous publishing firm of Hachette to write a series of biographies of famous men to be read by children, she met Ferdinand Buisson who asked her to contribute to his famous *Dictionnaire de Pédagogie*. The meeting was a fortunate one, for Buisson was a rising star. Inspector-General of Primary Education at that time, he became Director of Primary Education later, and was instrumental in securing her appointment by Jules Ferry, in 1879, as Delegate to the Inspectorate of the *Salles d'Asile*. (She had, at Buisson's behest, prepared herself formally for the position by sitting for the examinations preliminary to high positions in the inspectorate.) For the next twenty years her influence was paramount in reconstructing the entire system of pre-school education in France.

The *école maternelle* is not a school in the usual sense of the word. In 1882, even though the basic laws had been passed in the previous year, the atmosphere and tradition of the old *salles d'asile* dominated the scene. Everything had to be constructed anew, the spirit of what Pauline visualized as the *maternelle* imparted to the teachers, parents, and public organizations. From 1882 onwards we can follow the development of her thoughts in her articles published in the periodical *L'Ami de l'Enfance*, which she edited, in her two books and in the regulations which appeared under the official imprimatur to guide the *directrices*.

Prophetically, rather than objectively, she drew a distinction[3] between the *salle d'asile* and the *école maternelle* as follows, summing up what was for the time an extremely advanced doctrine: Children used to have to go through the *salles d'asile* no matter what the cost was to their personality, even if they emerged stunted in body and depressed in mind. The basic principle in the *maternelle* should be to model itself on the child instead of the other way round; its duty was to modify and improve itself until it became quite acceptable to him.

The child's individuality had to be respected, and any form of education which denied or ignored it was false.

> When we hand out a diet of ready-made facts to be learned by heart, and expect a child to submit to instruction which he is incapable of absorbing, we are attacking his intellectual and moral freedom. Under no circumstances should the child have to submit to instruction; education is something he himself should set in train and activate.[4]

When she commenced her campaign to re-shape the infant schools of France in a human image, the new delegate had the loyal backing of the Republican government which had established free, compulsory and secular elementary education. The new-style *maternelles* (she did not like using the word school even in the title) were to be free, voluntary, secular, and mixed: there is no segregation of the sexes at this level in France. Towns with a population above two thousand were invited to create *maternelles*, at the expense of the municipal or parish council. (Towns or villages with populations below this figure may open a *classe enfantine*, to be attached to the elementary school. There are still a large number of these in France — at the last reckoning, but their numbers, *in proportion* to those of the *maternelle* proper, are decreasing.) The state was to be responsible for training and paying the salaries of all teachers in the *écoles maternelles*.

During the 1880s and 1890s the issue of lay schools from which religious instruction was barred by law, was hotly debated in France, and organized religion did not take kindly to the new style introduced by a government of freethinkers, rationalists and positivists many of

whom were also practising Freemasons. When Pauline Kergomard
first inspected the schools for little children, she is said to have been
taken aback by the sight of infants reciting their catechisms by rote
and repeating prayers when the classroom clock struck the quarter.
Her journeys through the provinces encountered opposition and strong
criticism from the clerical press, not least in south-western France
where her family was known to have belonged to the Huguenot
persuasion since the time of the *draconnades* and even before. There
was also considerable opposition to a woman taking a position of such
eminence in public life, which increased after her election to the
highest educational body in France: the *Conseil Supérieur de l'Instruction Publique*, in 1886. The climate of opinion was such that the
co-education of infants was opposed on moral grounds and an argument
on the issue of male inspectors in girls' primary schools was wrapped
in similar spinsterish suspicion.

The Third Republic had set out to banish religion from the state
schools, but was concerned to retain a basis of moral training in
education to fill the vacuum. The sources of this lay in the social
philosophy of the French Revolution and had been formulated by
Condorcet — at least this was the belief of Pauline Kergomard's
circle. Frederick Froebel had insisted in placing the Christian faith at
the centre of his educational philosophy; this was not possible for the
pioneer of the *maternelle*, working as she was under the aegis of Ferry
and his successors in the republican majority. Her own belief was that
moral training was of importance in the *maternelle* and that this could
be based on the existence of the child's conscience. From observation
she had discovered that the child's knowledge of right and wrong
existed before the power of speech, and she used the pages of *L'Ami de
l'Enfance* to illustrate her views for the benefit of teachers.

She was determined to fight for cleanliness (*hygiène*) and health
for the children first of all. In 1880 she discovered that there was not
one Parisian *salle d'asile* which enjoyed the favour of a medical
inspection (1879 was the year when medical inspection began: it was
made obligatory in all schools eight years later). Suggestions and
recommendations for cleanliness run throughout her written advice
to schools.

Her second cardinal principle was that of liberty, which she
conceived as existing within a family; it was this principle which led to
her dramatic attacks on old-fashioned 'discipline' and her support for
disorder and noisiness as the apparent alternative. Discipline meant
routine in many schools, and routine was an enemy present in the

majority of *salles d'asile*. She had to cope with the opposition of many older teachers who had known nothing other than the policy of repression of the sort practised by the mother of Julian Vallès, who beat him once a day so that he should not be spoilt.

Paradoxically, her love of liberty led to rejection of the 'Froebelised' kindergarten which to her could never become the *French* way of doing things, since it was based in many places on slavish adherence to a routine with the gifts.

'*Une école froebelienne ne sera jamais une école vraiment française,*' she wrote in 1890 in her magazine: 'A Froebel school cannot really be a French school.' She clapped her hands when she came across some new Swiss centres where the teachers told her that they did not use a German method *or* a French method but the *human method* for their children.

It was through Madame Kergomard that the play-principle came into French *maternelles*; the kindergarten experiment which was tried out in a *salle d'asile* in 1879 did not impress enough to be adopted throughout the French system, but the best features of Froebel were assimilated. The Director of Primary Education later described her admiration for much of the Froebel faith, saying that she had 'freely admitted that she had taken from the German teacher whatever she thought would benefit us'.[5]

The old way of doing things was hard to shake. Ministers, educators, inspectors, generals and visiting princes were delighted to see one hundred children take up position on their benches and gallery steps like Prussian soldiers, without mistakes or fuss, as if they were operated by a hidden spring. To the outside observer who was not gifted with special insight, the *salles d'asile* offered an encouraging picture. 'What a calm and charming sight it is to see these happy refuges,' commented one minister.

> One hundred or one hundred and fifty children gathered around one woman, and only one, come and go, climb up and come down again, talk, count, and sing at the slightest signal, absorbing with pleasure first elements of knowledge and the germs of those moral feelings which promise to provide our country with honest citizens in the future. Seeing all these activities done cheerfully on the mere authority of word and example, without the least disturbance or noise, without a tear falling from an infant's eye, we have to admit the power of educational methods used in the salles d'asile.

When she was appointed to the inspectorate in 1879 these 'calm and charming' sights seemed to Madame Kergomard like a challenge to every instinct she possessed. Dusty halls without air or proper lighting, grey walls broken by windows which conformed to the regulation and were placed six feet above the floor so that the children would not be distracted from outside, and grubby play yards met her eye. Custom ruled that the windows were kept shut for fear that a draught might slip into the building; the unmade yards became muddy swamps after a shower of rain.

The furniture appeared to her totally unsuitable for children. Tables were too high, and were screwed to the floor; in the dining-hall there were none, and children ate off their knees; a lack of couches and stretchers meant that the smaller children dozed on the grubby floors and every workroom had the inevitable flight of steps where pupils perched for their lessons. Here a younger teacher supervised their behaviour while the principal read a lesson aloud, and many pairs of eyes looked about as if uncertain where the adults wanted them to focus; it was a curious gaze, said one observer, which seemed a mixture of vagueness and strained attention. In disgust, Pauline Kergomard wrote that *'the ideal of almost all the persons intimately or remotely interested in this sort of institution has been to make of the maternelle a school with all the disagreeable features of the school'*.

In their labour to construct a new education for a new republic, the *maternelle* committees in Paris found that almost everything had to be designed anew; patriotism was to replace religious instruction while a popular, national culture took the place of daily prayers and Bible stories. Soon after Ferry became Minister of Education, the distinguished scientist and anti-clerical deputy, Paul Bert, wrote to warn him of the gaps in French education for the young; he pointed particularly to a failure in providing music and songs.

'One of the saddest gaps in our primary teaching is the absence of singing from most schools. Both Swiss and German schools owe their superiority over ours in the matter of moral training to one thing – their songs. If the Minister agrees we would try to make a great effort to introduce singing immediately into our schools.'[6] The Minister did agree and well-known musicians were asked to draw up plans for introducing songs and musical training to the new schools.

Ministerial instructions to supply the legal background to the new order began to appear from 1881 onwards; to a large extent they govern the *maternelles* to this day. It was decided that local councils would bear the expense of buildings, furniture and teaching equipment,

while the government assumed responsibility for teachers' salaries and
the way the centres were to be run. Now officially termed *écoles
maternelles*, they were divided into two age groups, which have since
been increased to three: small, middle and older children. Attendance
was voluntary, and sexes were not to be separated at this level.

The instructions of 1882, later revised and remodelled but never
revoked, defined the purpose and method of the *maternelle*. They were
known by heart by generations of teachers and *directrices* and are
well worth considering if we are to understand the French system,
now so extensive, well-organized, and rich in technique.

> The *école maternelle* is not a school in the usual sense of the word:
> it shapes the transition from family life to school, and keeps the
> affection and softness of the family while introducing the child to
> work and school routine.[7]
>
> As a result, the lady principal should not be concerned at
> passing over to primary schools children who have made progress
> in their lessons but rather children who are ready to learn
> [*s'instruire*].
>
> Good health, hearing, sight, touch are trained by a series of
> little games and experiences; habits are begun upon which the
> school can build later; the child will have a taste for gymnastics,
> singing, drawing pictures, little recitations, an eagerness to see,
> to observe, to imitate, to question and to answer; there should
> be a certain faculty of attention, fostered by skilful management,
> confidence and good nature; finally, intelligence awakening in a
> mind which is open to good and moral impressions: — such are
> the results which should follow first years in the *Écoles
> Maternelles*. And if the child arrives at primary school with this
> sort of preparation, it *matters little whether it adds to this a few
> pages of the spelling book or not.*

Further instructions (1887) clarified the 'moral' side of *maternelle*
experience: learning to live as a social being, the child will become
aware by stages that he should love and obey his parents and
teachers. He will learn not to be selfish, brutal, or lazy and will
become daily accustomed to being both generous and gentle,
enjoying work and brotherhood; *this* is what he ought to learn before
reading and writing, but only to the extent allowed by his physical
development. In 1895 it was suggested that the first principles of
moral education should appear through conversation and poetry of a

sort 'to inspire children with a sense of devotion towards their homes, their country, and their God'. The instructions hastened to say that these principles were independent of all religious instruction.

In the guise of gymnastic exercises, physical play managed to break into the old routine, provided it took place under strict supervision,[8] and only before 9 a.m. and after 4 p.m. Schools were open from eight until six in winter and seven till seven in the summer, so that working mothers had a fair opportunity to earn the rent-money. Eager to destroy the tradition that children had to sit still in the classroom, Pauline Kergomard supported a commission of inquiry in 1889 which spoke out on the 'disastrous effects' of premature intellectual education on a child's health and physical development. Well in advance of other countries, the French report advised stopping all work which required immobility; as a result, new time-tables insisted that any 'intellectual' lessons would be separated by a song, walking, or movement of some description, and they were not to last more than twenty minutes at a time. They were to be given in the mornings, and the under-fives were to be spared attempts to teach them reading and writing: it was, wrote Pauline Kergomard in 1886, contrary to logic to teach reading to children before they knew how to speak.

Parents, local councillors and teachers were not ready to accept in a hurry the school which was not a school in the usual sense of the word. To them schools without reading and writing were not schools at all but some new intellectual fad from Paris; ambitious and ignorant parents, then as now, demanded to see some evidence of material progress and were not over-impressed by the ideal of freedom for little children who would soon have to earn their living in the self-confident bustle of French society. For Pauline Kergomard the changes did not go far enough; even the word *école* was repellent to her, and she would have liked the name *maternelle, tout court* over the doorway to the newer buildings. Inside she wished to see a large family of free infants, managed by a principal (*directrice*) who was the mother of a great number of children.

When she entered the official world, she discovered that girls entering the *salles d'asile* were given only four months' training, which was increased after 1878 to one year. After some years of effort and persuasion, Buisson and the government assimilated teachers to the primary training system, which was then growing rapidly throughout the country. It was a step forward in salary and status, giving teachers also the right to transfer to other stages of the elementary school organization if they felt misplaced. After labouring to obtain proper recognition for her teachers, Madame Kergomard now discovered that there were disadvantages in the college training procedure; the *écoles normales* seemed to be teaching a lot of intellectual theory which was against the spirit of the *maternelle*. Girls who now considered themselves almost as *professeurs* wanted to treat their little pupils as *écoliers*, school children. They quite mistakenly looked on the *maternelle* as a preparation for elementary school work.

Travelling, lecturing, visiting schools and writing, Pauline Kergomard endeavoured to ring in her changes in early childhood care. Writing her handbook for teachers, *The Child between Two and Six*, she tried to give as much practical help as possible; there is a specimen syllabus, a multitude of practical exercises and sound counsel of cleanliness and behaviour. Puzzling over the problem of managing children in a group, she wrote that she had learnt a great deal from the Paris parks, where she noticed that children played in sandpits without ever bothering to look at their nursemaids or guardians. '*L'enfant occupé se garde presque seul,*' she concluded, 'a busy child hardly needs to be supervised' — and recommended the principle to her students. As for equipment, instead of books and slates, she wanted to see materials which few had ever imagined as part of a school-building: dirt, sand, spades and buckets, rags and paper and leaves — anything out of which the child could make something and on which he could 'leave the mark of his little personality'.

The originality of all this, appearing from her pen in Paris twenty years before Montessori, Décroly, or even John Dewey, guaranteed that it would be misunderstood by many and overcome tradition only slowly. Change in education is not usually a clear matter of linear development; the *maternelles* had not abandoned the bad old ways by the end of the century, but the right way had been shown. It was in print and it was official, which meant a great deal in France; only co-operation between parents and school, teacher and inspectress was needed for the *salle d'asile* to vanish. This had to wait for the changed attitudes of the twentieth century when Madame Kergomard in retirement could see her work reach general acceptance and understanding.

5 SÉGUIN, ITARD AND MONTESSORI: THE PHYSIOLOGICAL APPROACH

While Froebel was finding a vocation in the troubled Germany of the Napoleonic years, a young Frenchman from Provence managed to avoid army service and train as a Surgeon (Third Class) in Toulon. This was Jean Itard, whose medical study of experiments in educating mentally deficient (or 'idiot') children led to great changes in early childhood and pre-school education for the normal child. Itard, and his successor Edouard Séguin, founded a tradition which drew attention to the importance of sense-training and physiology in the development of the child's all-round ability. It was their innovatory work which inspired Madame Montessori to begin practical research in Rome, and so led to a whole method of early education based on training movement and sensory perception.

Jean Itard (1775–1838) came in contact with Napoleon's celebrated physician, Larrey, in Toulon and was encouraged to do advanced research in Paris, where he specialized in care for the deaf and dumb, then a field in which France led the way.[1] Rousseau's friend and neighbour, Pereira, had been in charge of the Paris Deaf and Dumb Institute, and made progress with his highly original method for treating the inmates in the eighteenth century. Two other early nineteenth century leaders in work for little children – de Gérando in France and Aporti in Italy – were among the enlightened investigators of the problem and wrote treatises about possible solutions. Yet medical science in general lagged behind social reformers in attempting to improve the conditions of the unfortunate inmates of institutions and asylums; Itard was one of the few to show an interest in treatment of the severely retarded and mentally deficient child.

In 1798 a group of men hunting in the wilds of Central France came upon a naked lad who seemed to have grown up among the wolves and other forest animals. The boy was about twelve years of age, but spoke no word of intelligible language; taken in custody by the hunters, he later escaped and spent a hard winter out in the wild, without showing signs of exposure or suffering when he was found again. He lay flat to drink from pools and streams, preferred moving on all fours like an animal, and tore off any clothes which were given him after capture. A leading contemporary authority on natural history inspected him and announced that the lad was an imbecile. For convenience sake, he was given a name, Victor.

Victor was brought to Paris in 1799, as a curiosity who drew a lot of attention at first, when the fashionable crowd came to see him show his reactions to the wonders of the capital. They were disappointed, because Victor's reactions were limited to his responses to food, drink, and restraint. He did not suddenly recover the power of speech, and they lost interest in this 'disgusting, slovenly boy, affected with spasmodic and frequently with convulsive, motions, continually balancing himself like some animal in a menagerie; biting and scratching those who contradicted him, expressing no kind of affection for those who attended upon him; and, in short, indifferent to everybody and paying no regard to anything'. He was placed in the care of the Deaf and Dumb Institute where Jean Itard commenced his investigations and his attempts to develop the lad's personality and senses. It proved to be uphill work.

Victor's senses of touch and hearing seemed to be atrophied; his eyes lacked expression, and seldom rested on any object for long. He could not open a door, or climb on a chair to obtain food; his moods varied between melancholy depression and bursts of wild laughter; his whole existence seemed to be that of an animal. Itard refused to listen to his medical colleagues who declared the lad a hopeless idiot, and decided (intuitively rather than by scientific process) that Victor had once known certain things and skills common to a four-year-old, but had since forgotten them. The doctor set out, therefore, to revive his memory and develop his senses.

In a spirit of curiosity Itard embarked on his first successful learning experiment, when

one morning, as he was impatiently waiting for the milk, I arranged on a board which I had prepared . . . these four letters — L A I T. Madame Guérin, whom I had previously instructed, approaches, looks on the characters, and gives me afterwards a bowl full of milk, which I pretended was for my own use. I went up to Victor and gave him the four letters which I had taken from the board; I pointed to the board with one hand and with the other gave him a vessel full of milk. The letters were immediately replaced, but in an inverted order; they formed T I A L instead of L A I T. I pointed out what changes had to be made, and when he had reproduced the sign correctly, gave him the milk.

It will scarcely be believed, but after five or six such trials he had learned how to arrange the four letters and also had an idea of the relation between this alphabetical arrangement, and his need . . . that is to say, between the word and the thing. This I have a decided right to infer from what occurred eight days after this first experiment. He was seen, just before his evening excursion to the observatory, to provide himself, of his own accord, with the four letters in question; to put them in his pocket and when he arrived at Citizen Lemeri's house (where he went every day to take milk) he produced the letters and put them down on a table in the form L A I T.[2]

The story of the experiments and tasks devised by Itard in his attempt to re-educate the savage child was told in two reports which have lost none of their interest even now. Edouard Séguin, Itard's successor, observed that he did not know of anyone who would not gladly exchange all subsequent titles for the authorship of the two pamphlets on the 'Wild Boy of Aveyron'. It is a story of mingled success and failure, marked by endless patience and inventiveness on the doctor's part, helped by Madame Guérin. This remarkable woman tried to supply the tenderness which Victor had obviously lacked, and it was no easy affair with a strong boy who had fought with tooth and nail to survive in the forest.

Itard was obviously a man of considerable strength and self-control; he had to cope with fits of rage and violence which interrupted the 'lessons' and their excursions around Paris. Sometimes the methods used were severe, for Itard decided to employ Victor's emotion of fear as a lever to control anger and resistance to instruction. At the Paris Observatory, Itard noticed that the lad was afraid of heights; he accordingly used it as a threat — holding poor Victor out of a window in a tall building to reduce his urge to violence. He was locked in a closet sometimes when he failed to perform his learning tasks and after some time had passed he responded to stern or reproachful looks from the doctor by becoming penitent and sad. This technique was used when Victor escaped from custody and wandered in the forests near Paris until he was picked up by police and taken to a prison cell. Itard said no word when he went to collect the lad, but his stern silence was immediately understood. Under this type of control, the fits of rage gave way to grunting and occasional sobs when he was faced with a too-difficult task.

Itard's original list of aims had included awakening the boy's

nervous sensibility, leading him to the use of speech, attaching him
to social life, and extending his ideas. The faculty of speech defied all
Itard's ingenuity, and although Victor could obey simple instructions
and understood what was meant by some words after some months,
he never spoke an intelligible phrase. As it was, Itard's achievement
was considerable, for at the end of the first stage he could copy all
the words he knew; at the end of the second he could write them all
from memory; and at the end of the third he could write these words
to express his needs and ask for a means of satisfying them.

With the onset of adolescence and Victor's growing strength, the
authorities feared the effect of his angry fits and petulance on the
other inmates of the institute. Itard had expected an improvement
in behaviour and learning after puberty, but he was disappointed and
the unfortunate lad even attacked Madame Guérin. As there seemed
to be no further improvement in his learning capacity, he was no
longer a scientific hope; he was a curiosity and a possible danger to
other children. The authorities ordered his removal and he was sent
away with the loyal Madame Guérin to the country, where he died at
the putative age of forty. Whoever had thrown the child out in the
wilds of Aveyron succeeded finally in their object of separating
Victor from mankind.

The puzzle of Victor's origins accordingly remained unsolved, and
there was no certainty about the age at which he had been abandoned.
When found, his body was covered with scars, which were probably
due to scratches and small bites, but there was one long scar across
his throat. Had his parents tried to slash the child's throat before
abandoning him, or had he survived some frightful encounter with
wild beasts? As he recovered no early memories, there could only be
speculation about his origins and existence under such conditions.
How had he survived at all in one of the wildest and coldest districts
of France? For Itard, at all events, the study of Victor proved that
the concept of a 'Noble Savage' was nonsensical: 'Man,' he recorded,
'is inferior to a great number of animals in a pure state of nature, a
state of vacuity and barbarism, although it has been unjustly painted
in colours the most attractive.' Thus the eighteenth-century dream
was dispelled by the sordid, miserable functions of animal life which
marked Victor's stage of development.

Edouard Séguin

Itard's disappointment did not deter another French doctor from
using Itard's reports as a starting-point for further experiments which

ended in success. Edouard Séguin (1812–1880) began his work in
France in the 1830s, but as a socialist of the Saint-Simon school he
was dissatisfied with the turn of events after 1848, and chose to leave
for North America. He had a long and active career in medicine,
constantly working for improvements in the treatment of mentally-
retarded patients in asylums. A bridge between two worlds, his
importance has never received full recognition either as scientist or
educator. His work in Paris was, for example, the source of inspiration
for the first London asylum based on humane educational methods,
which opened at Highgate in 1847. From Highgate branched out the
other major centres for treatment of the insane in Britain.

Séguin's school was recognized by a French governmental
commission which investigated it in 1842, and admitted that he had
brought his (idiot) pupils to a knowledge of letters, reading, writing,
and drawing; he had also made them familiar with abstract ideas of
form, colour, density and weight. Basically, Séguin stressed the need
to develop a person's all-round ability in unity, saying 'the organs
of thought, of movement, of sensation; functions of body and soul;
handwork, intelligence and morality – education should include them
all.'

This was the fundamental principle from which Séguin proceeded
to attempt educational work with severely subnormal or 'idiot'
children, as they were called in his time. Rejecting contemporary
medical opinion, which believed that these unfortunates could not
be improved without a change or modification in organs which were
in fact 'beyond modification', the French doctor from Clamécy
opened the first school for 'idiots' in 1839.

In the Séguin School, the physiological method which he had
elaborated began by training movements and muscular activity,
bringing order and direction where there had been waste and aimless
gestures. The inertia amounting to complete absence of movement
was not, Séguin claimed, due to paralysis of the body, but rather to
what he termed the 'negative will' characterized by the words 'I will
not' – and this negative will had to be transformed into affirmation.

Equipment and methods used to oblige – rather than force – the
unwilling idiots to walk, or even to stand were ingenious. For the
pupil who would not stand erect, two narrow blocks or steps were
placed in front of him and he was raised on them, from which he
usually proceeded to fall, his fall being broken to avoid any real
damage. Then he was put back on the steps again, and after some time
it was found that the pupil began to exert strain on his leg muscles so

as *not to fall*. These exercises made it possible for him not only not to fall — which he had intended — but to stand, as the teacher intended.

When other blocks were placed in position there were signs of anxiety and bewilderment, the pupil crying but, eventually, stepping forward on to another position: walking had been achieved. In training early hand actions similar devices were used, and the pupil was arranged on a hemisphere-shape, with his hands resting on another round shape. Failure to grasp meant failure to stand, and while the teacher governed the fall by control of a body-harness the pupil was made to learn that grasping prevented falling. Those who resisted this piece of learning were put to a ladder, where the teacher's hands were held over those of the pupil to prevent a fall and the feet were pushed off the rung on which they were standing. When the turn of the hand came it wandered, moved round vaguely in the air, and had to be guided at the right moment to the rung beneath; if he did not grasp spontaneously he was assisted to grasp with the teacher's hand covering him. So, step by step, and possibly week after week, until the backward child learned to grasp at rungs for safety and move with the teacher's guidance up and down them.

The equipment was of considerable variety, and some of it sounds familiar to us now from subsequent imitations. There was a 'nail-board' (our peg-board) with holes into which the child fixed nails, afterwards removing them and beginning again; there were solid geometrical figures with slots shaped to fit them; beads, coins and pieces of cardboard to be picked up by the fingers; buttoning and lacing the threading beads for the more adroit pupils. The greatest favourites, Séguin observed, however, were objects in daily life: spade and barrow, and watering-can. It was found that idiots could be induced to imitate their mentors and when personal concentration was required, the lessons were begun in isolation and silence; the room used was neutral in light and colour. After some imitation had begun, group work ensued with up to a dozen children, in silence copying the motions of the teacher who conducted them through simple changes in posture and hand or head positions, closing 'by three cheers and three claps of the hands, for the pupils are now warmed, bright, tired, but not exhausted; final immobility'.[3]

Believing, after Pereira, that touch was the most important sense and that the others were modifications of it, Séguin concentrated in this way on manipulation, anticipating modern practice by teaching number with objects and proportions with rulers of different lengths. Reading was taught by a method evolved in New York asylums at the time, moral training was not considered an impossibility and the French innovator put great emphasis on social training and social activity. Toys should be used, he said, not for selfish individual play, but for common enjoyment and thus help to develop their capacity for social life. 'They cannot be made to play together,' he wrote, 'with or without toys, without learning and increasing their moral qualities: playing is a moral power, amusing the lowest idiot is another; our children must enjoy both.'[4]

Victor, the Aveyron 'savage', had been virtually incapable of affection for those around him, although he was pathetically dependent on Itard and his motherly helper. But Séguin's severely-retarded children were able to advance through social activity towards love, and, just as he had used the faint sparks of imitation to expand their strength and control over muscular action so he believed that they felt love from their teacher. 'To make the child feel that he is loved, and to make him eager to love in his turn, is the end of our teaching as it has been its beginning.'[5] Séguin's early years among the Saint-Simon group revealed themselves again in his valuable emphasis on the value of love in fostering growth, for the French social reformers of 1830 had eventually transformed their philosophy into a religion of love. We will see that this part of the teaching of Séguin made a particular impact on Maria Montessori and others who re-discovered his work at the turn of this century.

Maria Montessori

On the Continent the tradition of Itard and of Séguin's early work remained strong in the medical schools and institutions for treatment of insame or severely-retarded children. Access to his later research and writings was limited however by the fact that *Idiocy* had been published in America, and in English. When a young woman graduate of medicine (the first female doctor of medicine in Italy) did discover Séguin's 1866 work, it came to her with the force of revelation.

Maria Montessori (1870–1952) came from a medical background to the study of education in the eighteen-nineties. She worked through her medical course at a time when there was a growing interest in psychology in Germany, France and North America; at Rome, Giuseppe Sergi who had a powerful influence on Maria Montessori's choice of career, had founded a laboratory for experimental psychology and lectured in anthropology. After visits to the Bicêtre asylum in Paris the young graduate felt doubts about the way the ideas of Itard and Séguin were being applied; she felt that attention was focused on

a routine use of Séguin's didactic apparatus, and the real meaning of
his discoveries had been obscured.

The impulse to combine medicine and education in practice
with severely-retarded children turned Montessori away from conventional medical practice. Dissatisfied with her intellectual training
she also enrolled in Rome as a student of philosophy to find out
what principles governed the study of education. Between 1900 and
1907 she lectured at the University of Rome in 'pedagogical
anthropology', visited institutions for the severely retarded and
insane, and read and re-read Séguin until she knew his last work
almost by heart.

'The man,' she wrote later, 'who had studied abnormal children
for thirty years expressed the idea that the physiological method . . .
must come to be applied also to normal children.'

In 1907, Maria Montessori was given charge of her first group of
normal children, dwellers in a poor district of Rome, and began to
experiment with them to see if methods such as Séguin's would be
effective on children who were not retarded so much as neglected.
It was ten years since she had graduated and begun her work with
the mentally subnormal in 1896. By a curious coincidence, Dr Ovide
Décroly in Belgium had written in the previous year that he found
no differences of nature between normal and abnormal children and
that 'the same psychological laws apply — but for the latter, mental
development is generally retarded; progress is slowed down, so that in
this case one may observe stages which pass so quickly as to be invisible
in normal children.'[6]

Long before the opening of the *Casa dei Bambini* in 1906, Maria
Montessori had taught severely-retarded children how to read and
write, to the astonishment of the Roman public. She anticipated little
difficulty in applying the same principles in the *Casa dei Bambini*, and
in fact encountered none. She introduced Séguin's apparatus for
training the senses and, observing that children became absorbed in
one item, to the point of repeating an exercise with it forty or fifty
times while the next task lay idly by, she began to discard some
equipment and form ideas about constructing improved items.

Passing fingers across the letters with his eyes shut, listening to
the names of the letters, and tracing them with his index finger and
then a pencil, the Montessori pupil linked the sound of the alphabet
with touch, sight, and muscular co-ordination. He had to learn *how*
to write before writing. Madame Montessori deduced this from the
case of an 'idiot' girl of eleven who could not darn socks or sew a hem.

Here Froebel provided a cure, as the teacher remembered his mats in which strips of paper were threaded transversely in and out among vertical strips, providing movements similar to darning. The eleven-year-old, after practice on the Froebel mats, developed her movements for sewing before she encountered the particular problem of sewing; when she returned to it, there remained no difficulty.

Madame Montessori herself wrote so voluminously, that all her thoughts about child-care have not appeared in print even now. But a number of books are in existence: *The Absorbent Mind, The Montessori Method* and *The Advanced Montessori Method*, which have much to offer to the student. These describe her philosophy of childhood, although she did not write a textbook on procedure. Her work at the *Casa dei Bambini*, her lectures, and her training courses given in different capitals of the world exerted an influence far beyond infant education.

Among her reflections on the nature of childhood, she predicated five stages in growth: in the first stage (between birth and three years of age) the child goes through the Absorbent Mind and Sensitive Periods, which create emotional and intellectual growth unconsciously. This she emphasises as being an intensely creative period. During the second stage (from three to six), these unconscious ideas are being brought to conscious level. The third stage, from six to nine years of age, is one in which a model of reality has been made, and the child begins to form his academic and artistic skills. From nine to twelve, during the fourth stage, the child's personality opens towards the universe; he is learning with his conscious mind now, in ways which are strongly similar to the first, unconscious stage. Intellectual interests for an entire lifetime are now being determined.

In the fifth stage, from twelve to eighteen, he is exploring concentrated areas of interest, and choosing patterns of endeavour for his lifetime; but our culture obliges him to defer the choice.

She believed that education should be reorganized, in accordance with these stages, and that the traditional and largely meaningless ones of nursery, primary, secondary and university should be dropped. Her own work was largely centred on the first stages, from birth to six, where she insisted on an environment which should be both free and beautiful. The child in the first stage is setting his own value on his personality through independent effort. 'The child realises that he can be independent and achieve things through his own efforts. In order to reach these results it is necessary to place the child in a free environment where he can make social contacts on his own.' Then

Dr Montessori makes a characteristic observation: 'We are confronted here with a simple and important fact, which is that we find that to help the child is not what he needs. To give help to the child impedes . . . liberty is not to be free to do anything one likes, it is to be able to act without help'; her aids, or 'apparatus' as it is sometimes called, were therefore self-administering; the teacher is not fussing around the child to show him how things work,

Her main principles, in which she followed the Froebel tradition, include a belief in the goodness of child nature, the belief in spontaneity in early education (from which springs the self-education the importance of which Froebel underlined) and a general unfolding of the child's inherited powers which are helped or hindered by school experience. No less than Froebel, Montessori saw her work for children blocked and negated by politics and warfare. When the First World War broke out, twenty years later, she had just begun her lecture courses in England and America; her schools were banned by the Education Ministry of the Third Reich; when she found herself in India on a visit after the outbreak of yet another war, the possession of an Italian passport caused the British authorities to treat her as an enemy alien! On the positive side of the account, the same world disaster obliged her to remain in India for many years, where her philosophy of education acquired a multitude of disciples and has been applied in hundreds of infant schools.

Speaking in London when she was eighty-one, Maria Montessori spoke of her critics and her faith, in these terms:

> The child is not merely the beginning of a human body, not only the beginning of a human soul. The child is the point where all that man really is and is meant to be can be revealed — even easily and in a beautiful way.
>
> That is my philosophy about which people talk so much while looking at me and not at what I point out. This is my optimism which some consider so touching. This is my 'illusion' so many refuse to share. This is the greatness of my heart about which so many sentimentalities are said.
>
> This is what we must learn and penetrate, understand profoundly and when we start doing so we are nearly safe. Then we can know that mankind is not doomed. Then we discover that there is something more and something different at our disposal which we can take up and utilize! [Exclamation mark in original.]

At the time of this lecture which she expressed in typically idealist and almost mystical terms, she and her teachings had been under fire from behaviourist and Gestalt psychologists for forty years, for so long, in fact, that these schools had begun to depart from the front of the stage and to make place for other theorists. At first they had reproached her with her mid-nineteenth century roots in formal discipline and outmoded faculty psychology. Even the heritage of Séguin had been anathema to W.H. Kilpatrick of Columbia, who stated flatly that he declined to accept the sense-training, and 'the didactic apparatus we reject in like degree'.

When the Montessori schools first appeared, before the First World War, they caused a sensation by their emphasis on liberty for the individual child. Although, as we saw, there had been to English eyes a lax atmosphere in American kindergarten early in the century, other countries had not followed suit. Moreover, there had always been an explicitly-stated routine about using the Froebel Gifts in their sequence: the cubes were to be used at each session, they were never to be knocked down, each shape was to develop from the preceding shape, and so on. Maria Montessori, on the other hand, was enchanted to see one child so taken with an item of equipment that she repeated a simple movement with it for an entire session! Individual liberty was operating in such a way as to exclude from the programme the concept of collective responsibility, said some. Neither American teachers, nor their Continental counterparts in *écoles gardiennes* or *maternelles* were prepared to go as far as Montessori in encouraging child-liberty, in spite of the tradition of American society on the one hand and Pauline Kergomard's rejection of Prussian discipline on the other. It was left to the English nursery school to develop, after the McMillans and the great influence of the Montessori lecture tours and training courses, a programme of personal liberty and auto-education.

It was, however, only within the matrix of a prepared environment that Dr Montessori recommended the practice of perfect liberty, and her recommendation was founded on the view that if adults are continually checking and interfering with a child's choice they are also effectively suppressing his chance to develop his own will. On social order, she said:

> The liberty of the child should have as its *limit* the collective interest, as its *form*, what we universally consider good breeding. We must, therefore, check in the child whatever offends or annoys

others or whatever tends toward rough or ill-bred acts. But all the rest — every manifestation having a useful scope — whatever it be — and under whatever form it expresses itself, must not only be permitted but must be *observed*, by the teacher.[7]

The further impression by some educators that they were being asked to accept a system rather than some important innovations led to distrust of the Montessori teachings, a distrust reflected in the *maternelle* selection of certain aids and approaches, but explicit in the rejection of the whole 'method'. Wherever the movement went, however, it led to experimentation and enterprise. In Denmark, for example, it appeared in or about 1917 first of all, in a school for crippled children. Thereafter, a lady who had attended a course in London converted her class for feeble-minded children to the Montessori method. Training courses began in Denmark in the 1920s and were later converted into a general, two-year, course for the training of infant teachers.

The new ideas rapidly affected Geneva, where some pioneering work had been done in the *écoles enfantines*, and where Claparède and his team were based in the Institut Jean-Jacques Rousseau. In 1913, some teachers at the institute collected their own children together and began with them a 'Montessori' course. The result, in spite of the presence of Mlle Audemars, who had been trained at the London Froebel Institute (in a very different method, it must be admitted) was chaos for about a month! After that time the parents held a conference and decided to modify their methods; order was re-established and the classes grew into the well-known *Maison des Petits* which became celebrated as a centre for research and observation. Professor Bovet, who was there at the time, said that they were never able in Geneva to adopt the full orthodoxy of the Montessori method, as their plan was to guide children's development, not to indoctrinate them. Again and again we encounter this type of comment in different countries, which rejected the method as a whole. Again and again, and it is part of the paradox, we come across the same classrooms adopting parts of the Montessori plan; and blending them with other methods: 'Where are we then?' wrote Bovet about the *Maison des Petits*. 'Is it some sort of educational museum? Here are the Froebel games and occupations; but those little chairs are Montessorian, and the tables too originated from Rome, although they have been perfected since.'

An eminent English teacher wrote in praise of Montessori

equipment in those early days before it had acquired general acceptance:

> It is an invaluable asset to the Kindergarten . . . it pushes the child on to analyse the dimensions of space, to study colour systematically, to think about number, about sounds, and about words. That thought accompanies the manipulation of the material is often made evident by the children's reflections. Thus, Stanley, working with colours, was heard to say:
> 'These are all blue, but they're not the same blues. Harry, laying the Long Stair: this is long, and this is short; Miss Robertson is longer than you, and you are longer than me.
> – Agnes, at word building: these are letters; that's a word. We speak words, but we don't speak letters 'cause they don't mean things.'

France welcomed the new method from Italy, although the *maternelles* were by then established throughout the country, and did not require any new organizational stimulus: aspects of the new approach were used and incorporated into French classwork. Much of her enthusiasm and vision of the needs of the individual child struck a common chord in the heart of the *maternelle*, where cognitive development is far from being ignored. There are still a number of 'Montessori' schools in France, one of which takes children at elementary school age and although there was some criticism of a method which appeared 'too rigid', Montessori helped to impart life and hope to the admirable French organization in the 1920s.

Belgium was more critical – Belgium where Froebel's influence had penetrated deeply in the *écoles gardiennes* at the turn of the century. There it was felt that, while the Montessori system possessed undeniable virtues, there was a certain imbalance in emphasis, betrayed by the encouragement of the child's perception and cognitive ability at the expense of the affective emotional side. Moreover, teaching of basic skills came in too early in child development; much was done for the child as an individual, but socialization, *la vie collective*, and a modern child's need to 'get along' with his fellows in changing situations was largely ignored. Belgium, in any case, had a local alternative in the work of Ovide Décroly. The Netherlands welcomed Madame Montessori personally and adopted her ideas with enthusiasm in a number of schools; the international Montessori organization is now based in The Hague, and it was in Holland that Maria Montessori died, in 1952. Perhaps the most sincere compliment paid to her ideas has been the spate of imitations which have appeared commercially as 'methods' to form reading and writing skills, more or less based on Montessori techniques; even some of the most recent pre-reading programmes as used, for instance in British infant schools, owe something to Madame Montessori's inventiveness and understanding.

Montessori schools spread across linguistic boundaries with the same *élan* which marked the early growth of the kindergarten movement. Many people came to connote infant education with Montessori education. Moreover, the lectures and training courses led to reconsideration of some of the principles and practice of primary and even secondary education. To quote Montessori was a characteristic mark of the progressive in education during the 1920s and one enthusiast introduced her methods throughout his inspectorate in a London suburb.

There were influential critics, too. The psychologists found her basic thinking unorthodox and, in any case, rooted in psychological beliefs which had been current in the previous century. For those who clung to the fixed-intelligence principle, there was not much credence to be attached to the Montessori idea of the personality and mind 'unfolding' under its own forward momentum. Even comparatively recently, influential critics in the United States felt that 'nowhere did Montessori support the American's commitments to play, imagination, creativity and self-expression . . . Her claim, moreover, that children could read and write by age five went against the thrust of the American movement and conflicted with research which suggested that children so taught could be emotionally and physically harmed.'[8]

The Montessori method is essentially non-directive, in the sense that the teacher remains as much as possible in the background, ready to assist when the child has finished one task and is ready to begin the next; supporters claim that Maria Montessori obtained a lot of her ideas empirically, by watching what children themselves wanted. Piaget, reviewing the method, indicated a paradox implicit (in his view) between this claim and what Madame Montessori proceeded to do. In the matter of sensory-motor development she became the victim of the thing she feared most; she imposed on the real situation a discarded laboratory theory. Firstly, said Piaget, it is not feeling which appears in the infant's evolving perception, nor is it an isolated perception of an action. The whole of activity itself – sensory-motor intelligence or practical intelligence if you wish – appears from the very first months in child life, and intelligence is at work organizing perceptions as a function of actions.

Because of this, the combinations of intelligence play a much more important part by their dynamism than the sensations which are produced – the product. Montessori, who genuinely wished to protect child development from the clumsy interference of adults, ended by equipping her school with materials partly inspired not only by adult psychological theory, but an artificial theory at that. Under these circumstances even this much-admired equipment may become a liability in the class-room.

Montessori, Décroly and Claparède, were all trained in medical schools before they turned to psychology and education. Where they differ from other scientists, too, is in their practical contribution to education. There seems to be no such gulf between those who manage little children daily and Madame Montessori, as there is between nursery teachers and Thorndike or Piaget. One can see Décroly's influence in many centres; it has infiltrated through its practical value into the scramble of a morning session. Not so the learning theorists or the scientific doubters. Indeed, there seems to be a slight, but discernible shift in the opposite direction towards conversion of the psychologists to progressive nursery-school principles, which were previously deemed to be out of step with acceptable research. Take the case of the American, J. McV. Hunt, whose work has had a considerable impact on our views of heredity and environment.

As late as 1962, someone introduced Hunt to the work of Montessori, whom he had heard of only vaguely, and would have identified as a 'kindergartner, and an educational faddist' who had made quite a splash about the turn of the century. To his surprise, Montessori seemed to offer some proposals which were psychologically sound, despite her rejection by the old school (pre World War I) of academic authority represented by Kilpatrick in the United States. Hunt was sufficiently taken with the Italian materials and method to write an introduction to a new edition of Montessori which appeared in 1964. Without falling into the error of seeing this solitary swallow as herald of a coming summer, it is reassuring that there is a *rapprochement* possible between the two alarmingly disparate schools of thought, the one medico-methodological, the other psychological and academic. Not without significance is the increased interest in Montessori shown by American journals of higher educational study. We can now see, that the theorists of the 1900s were working within the framework of the heredity-genetic school, which was committed to reject the claim that environmental situations in the *Casa dei*

Bambini or elsewhere could aid the development of intelligence. Moreover, as some of the leaders in the kindergarten movement in the United States then lamented, respect was not given to the early childhood period as a key stage in cognitive development.[9] Much of this way of thinking has changed dramatically in the last twenty years.

Looking at Montessori's scheme Hunt came to the conclusion that it could help considerably towards solving certain motivational problems connected with 'the problem of the match' as he termed it. This matching problem related to individual expectations and abilities (on the one hand) and tasks to be performed on the other in an outside situation. The disparity, or incongruity between the two stimulates the individual to respond, to be motivated, as psychologists would say, and learning results from his mastery of the task or problem. Should the disparity seem too great, one may become fearful of the consequences and give up the attempt, but if it is at a point which may be labelled 'optimum incongruity' — the points set neither too wide nor too close, then the learner's brain equipment sparks and cognitive growth takes place. The 'problem of the match' could be encountered successfully in the Montessori learning environment, thought Hunt, and his favourable impression still stands, despite criticism he heard later about the method as a whole. If the practising psychologist can be brought to consider the work of some leading child-educators like Montessori, we may benefit by the interchange of views. It is certainly odd to reflect that there are many experts in the psychology field in the United States and else-where who have not considered her proposals.

The Montessori organization, with its authorized apparatus and approved courses, has run the risk of being isolated from the progressive movement by its own mystique. When we were making inquiries about Montessori schools, we were greeted with courtesy in several countries by committee members, but in conversation with a London headmistress we were sharply put in our place — because I had mentioned that our four-year-old had been accustomed to using some items of the Montessori apparatus in her play. 'But what makes you think that you know how to *use* these aids in the proper way? Don't you know this is a *scientific* system demanding a scientific training?' After beating a retreat it occurred to me to wonder if this rather august lady knew how many French, English, Indian, and American schools use parts of the 'scientific' apparatus in conjunction with free play or Décroly aids?

In fact, parents who are dissatisfied with the extreme 'socialization'

approach to 'early childhood education' and the apparent aimlessness
of free-play schools are turning more and more, particularly in North
America, to the Montessori way of doing things. Changes in theories
of intelligence and learning which have taken place since World War II
have led to more emphasis being placed on methods which appear to
press the claims of cognitive development programmes. That most
evaluative studies have not found any long-term gain in IQ acquired
by Montessori pupils does not put off admirers of her way of doing
things, which combines orderly behaviour with a learning curriculum.
As the world outside changes towards cacophony and disorder, the
virtues of the Italian method are set in bright relief.

Maria Montessori remains one of the most puzzling and stimulating
innovators in the history of infant education. A medical graduate rather
than a pedagogue, she originated a method which bade fair to become,
not a single example of early childhood education, but the dominating
and quasi-exclusive system. None can doubt her sincerity, but her
pronouncements were often cloaked in a half-mystical mood of
revelation and prophecy. Her method for teaching normal children
was evolved from experience with the severely retarded; yet when it
was propagated by herself on lecture visits and training courses in
foreign capitals it began to affect and invigorate, not early childhood
education alone, but primary and even secondary education.
Condemned by the educational logicians and philosophers, it gained
a prodigious following. Abandoned (as a complete method) in France
and England in the 1930s, it nevertheless can be seen in vestiges and
items of equipment or exercises in every *école maternelle* worthy of
the name. Surviving the psychologists who condemned it, the
Montessori method has begun a second surge of international life,
attracting support by its emphasis on the child's concentration on his
task without interference from the teacher, its suggested value for
cognitive development, and its cleverly designed apparatus.

'She knows everything about savage religions, Greek art, Italian
architecture, modern science, and English kindergartens, but of
children she knows little,' scoffed one of her detractors in the 1920s.
More seriously, it has been pointed out that there is a basic philo-
sophical contradiction apparent between the founder's 'primitive
naturalism' and her intuition of education as a spiritual fact.
Montessori began from scientific practice, and ended as the prophetess
of a quasi-mystical and optimistic order wherein the human being
develops his intellect and personality by his own incentive from
childhood onwards. To reject her views of the spirituality of education

is not quite so easy if one believes that this is not merely her problem, but one of the basic dilemmas mankind must face in our century.[10]

6 PIAGET AND THE THEORY OF PLAY

Qui Joue, Jure — Alain

A natural education is by practice, by doing things,
and not by instruction, the hearing how, as you may see
in the flight of a young bird.

Caldwell Cook, *The Play Way*

Nothing distinguished early childhood education from other levels of
education so much as play, and the theory of play. In a sense, the
place of play in the under-five's world has attracted almost as much
attention among Western European specialists as has psychology in
the United States. It formed the central feature of British nursery-
school practice, and helped to create a new method of therapy for
disturbed children under psycho-analysis. It has drawn together the
examinations of experts in many fields: ethologists, anthropologists
and cultural historians have undertaken a great deal of research about
play; it has thrown light on developmental stages, and is central to
the question of freedom or direction in the nursery environment. Play
for the twentieth-century European schools of research has offered
a biological and functional insight into the child's inner life which
can only help to enlarge our understanding.

The play element in human culture formerly belonged to young and
old alike, wrote Huizinga, the great Dutch historian. He considered
play to have been a central feature of Western culture before the end
of the eighteenth century, which has almost disappeared from adult
behaviour by the 1930s. There were a few survivals: the dramatic
performance within the British Houses of Parliament and some puerile
examples by the uniformed automatons who were then strutting
about the European political scene. Of quite a different type, thought
Huizinga, was the Boy Scout movement, which openly styled itself
a game, and was built on 'a deep understanding of the mind and
aptitudes of the immature'.[1]

If Huizinga was right in thinking the play-element had begun to
wane around 1800 the curious fact is that the period coincides with
the time when play made its appearance in education and became a
valuable auxiliary in early childhood centres such as Oberlin's,
Owen's or the 'play-schools' which apparently existed in Holland.

93

J.P.F. Richter, the popular German writer better known by his pen-name Jean-Paul, set down his observations on children's play in a book about education called *Levana* which appeared in 1804.

He suggested that play was of value for mental development, but not for the body, which advances without help of this sort. Play was able to develop all the powers, without imparting an undue influence to any single one. The adult should understand that when children played with things picked up here and there, such games were quite different from what the adult imagined them to be: for children there are *only* living things. For this reason, they have no need of elaborate presents such as coloured eggs, because with white eggs their fancy is at work at once, imposing the colours and designs. Coloured paintings are a waste of time; if we give the child a drawing, his imagination does the rest.

Most children's games for Richter appeared to be imitative; he conceived them as of two sorts, positive and passive. There were games which received impressions, learning and apprehending games these, and others of a different type which involved action, forming the powers of the individual.

A second classification Richter used was between theoretical games such as listening to parents (seeing themselves one moment as solitary, the next as part of a whole company), and practical play where the child uses bodily movements and acts out dramatic fancies. A third division finds the child only playing the game, and does not really act and feel it.

Richter's book insisted that play should be seen by adults as a serious activity, not just as a pastime. The consequence of *Levana* were to be felt throughout the century in Europe, and those who refused to accept the kindergarten entire, adjusted their methods to the German theory of play-education, as for example did Pauline Kergomard in Paris.

The American psychologist Hall and the German Groos, produced two widely different studies of play in the 1890s. Hall, trained in Germany, was a founder-figure of the American psychological school who initiated child-study programmes much criticized for their lack of scientific precision. Groos differed from other German psychologists in maintaining the biological foundation of mental phenomena, and it was this attitude which characterized the Swiss, Piaget, who followed in his footsteps.

Karl Groos' *Animal Play* (published in 1896) offered an interpretation which gave functional meaning to the gambolling of the primates. Play could be considered useful in both child and animal behaviour as a preparation (*pré-exercice*, in the French editions of his work) for adulthood. So play was not to be thought of horizontally, as we sometimes think of our children's happiness, but vertically, with the future in mind. The difference is a crucial one.

A young Genevan scientist, Edouard Claparède, was stimulated by *Animal Play* into further research into the educational implications of games and play. When Claparède published his work on child psychology he sought to restore the horizontal aspect to play, which he felt was important for present needs and able to provide immediate satisfaction. It was, in fact, by placating the child's needs of the moment that it prepared him for the future. Claparède, as head of the Institut Jean-Jacques Rousseau in Geneva, was a person whose authority drew attention from educators and psychologists. Groos and the Swiss school, writing at a time when renewed interest in Froebel had appeared among an enlightened few, gave the broad outline to modern psychological theory of play, enriched by further discoveries by Sigmund Freud and his followers.[2]

When the Viennese, Freud, introduced the notion of repression in early childhood, inner conflict, and re-enactment of our disturbing fantasies in play, a new phase began which led to 'play-therapy'. Play acquired a new significance when seen as the means by which a child could perform again the happenings which had affected him deeply in his emotional life; child psychologists, some of whom had undergone psycho-analysis, talked of play as a symptom of unconscious conflict. Schoolyard aggression could be interpreted as a child's method of curing some of the evil effects of his home life; dolly-spanking was closely connected with dreams of retaliating on, or suffering from, a mother's acts. Rough play could be of positive benefit to the actors, and therefore not to be repressed in the name of mere order and discipline. Indeed, the whole picture of a teacher's own attitude to discipline was re-examined, and punishments became suspect to the well-informed educator.

The Progressives: Susan Isaacs on Play

It was partly the value of play as therapy for unsettled children which attracted the progressive educators in the 1920s. In non-directive schools, such as the Malting House school in England, young pupils were believed to be learning as much by messing about in the laboratory or setting fire to things in the garden as by applying themselves to their books in the conventional manner. Susan Isaacs used her terms at Malting House to record in notebooks as much as she could observe of the significant play of pupils, and noticed that small children, like chimpanzees, know when they are watched and alter their behaviour accordingly.

> When James (3 years and three months: Mental Range 126) first came to the school, he spent a good deal of time talking to himself, talking out his phantasies as he played alone with a toy engine or motor-car. We caught remarks about 'and *this* bus goes very fast', or 'and that one got knocked over', and so on. But this was strictly soliloquy, an indulgence in private phantasy, and not collective in *any* sense. How well separated it was in the child's own mind from his real relations with people was well shown on one occasion. James was playing absorbedly in the middle of the lawn with a bath of water and several jugs, and talking to himself about what he was doing. One of the adults of the house, observing this, walked very quietly over the grass and stood close behind the child, to hear what his phantasy was. After a time, James, who had gone on as if he had noticed nothing, suddenly turned round and addressed to the grown-up a matter-of-fact remark about the water.

(In similar mood, a young chimpanzee showed less patience with his watchers, and, first threatening them with a brick obviously too large to go through the bars, waited until they were laughing at him before he dropped the brick and plastered them with sand while they were still enjoying his supposed stupidity.)

Solitary play, concluded Mrs Isaacs, when the private fantasies are acted and talked out seems to have in it a minimum of ideation and of objective reference, and to show a schizophrenic quality. But when the children are playing together, even if the play be of a simple repetitive type, in what could perhaps be called a collective fantasy, there is always some definite degree of social reference to the other children sharing in the common activity. Even if one child is imposing his will upon the others, acting the mother or father to their part as babies, yet the whole is a shared activity, in which each of the various roles supports and complements the rest, with a moment-by-moment adaptation.[3] This led Susan Isaacs to query Piaget's description of the *collective* monologue, for in company she found that her English children talked socially *to* each other, and it was when alone that they indulged in egocentric monologue. She rejected the idea of a stage of development, which might correspond to the concept of monologuism, therefore.

Apart from its value as laboratory material for her research, what was the Malting House view of the school's responsibility — if any —

towards the play of pupils, which seemed to show 'a schizophrenic quality'? An illuminating passage deals with precisely this point, and serves to define the attitude of the post-Freudian nursery school teacher towards play.

> In general we tried to use our parental powers in such a way as to reduce the children's need for them. We held one of our tasks as educators to be that of counteracting the dramatic tensions in the child's mind; and the only way to do this is to bring in the real world at every possible point. The way out from the world of phantasy is through the constant appeal to objective reality, to physical and social facts, and to interests and activities directed upon these. In the external world the dramatic inner tensions of the child's mind and the adult's are deflected and diffused. And in our school our constant aim was therefore to throw our own weight always on the side of an appeal to the world of objective fact, and to stimulate intelligent observation and judgment on the part of the children.[4]

Thus the teacher sees her role as mediant between the world of pure fantasy-play and social behaviour, conducting a sort of group-therapy among the under-sixes.

Melanie Klein

Psycho-analysts in clinical practice used play-rooms and play situations as an essential part of their technique. Some used a playroom or collection of toys to win the child's confidence and the dirty and bedraggled woolly toys which lie about in suburban health centres are a sad relic of all this. Some specialists constructed elaborate towns, villages, and landscapes, on which the child could wreak his own special form of havoc. This changed world in miniature helped the expert to interpret what were the main problems upsetting the child. Melanie Klein (1882–1960) used toys in this way to help her treat very young children; on a low table in her rooms there were small toys, men, women, animals, carts, trains and also paper, scissors and pencils. 'Even a child that is usually inhibited in its play will at least glance at the toys or touch them,' she found, and was in this way given a view of the child's complexive life.[5]

Some of Klein's cases were under five, and her descriptions of treatment throw into sometimes rather surprising relief the Freudian approach. Ruth, who was four and a quarter, resorted to acute fear

and anxiety when it was suggested she stay in the room with the
analyst alone, and for several visits a nurse had to remain with her.
Klein finally pressed the issue by asking the nurse to stay outside,
which precipitated a crisis of tears and screams. As Ruth refused to
touch the toys, the analyst took over her part, and went to the toy
table where she began to repeat Ruth's play from a previous visit.
After a time this had the hoped-for effect, and the child calmed enough
to start finding fault with the play, objecting to the position of this
or that and became quite upset about the placing of a sponge in
relation to certain figures. The analyst explained to her that the
sponge represented her father's penis in her unconscious mind which
gave Ruth apparently some relief. An under-four who, in Klein's
opinion had a strong passing homosexual attitude, was treated with
similar methods.

Such case-histories led Melanie Klein to draw conclusions about
the workings of the baby-mind, where, too, she found signs of
aggressive fantasies. In her essays collected in *Love, Hate and
Repression*[6] she wrote that the baby who was frustrated at his
mother's breast might build up fantasies that he was attacking and
biting the breast. She declared that 'the psycho-analysis of small
children, which enabled me to draw conclusions also as to the workings
of the mind at an earlier stage, has convinced me that such phantasies
are already active in babies . . . the effects of this early phantasy-life
are lasting, and profoundly influence the unconscious mind of
the grown-up person'.

Klein's work had a considerable effect in several countries; she
was exploring what was a very new field of study in her studies of small
children and the thinking process in infants. The unconscious-tension
theory was behind most interpretations until some psycho-analysts
such as Anna Freud came to admit that play did not always reveal a
child's deepest preoccupations.

Jean Chateau

Inspired guesswork by the psycho-analysts led to benefit and release
from tension in some — perhaps many — cases: there was less
confidence in this procedure in France than in Britain and the USA.
Jean Chateau, an eminent French educator, did not believe that his
child was replacing her own mother when she played at mothers,
nor that there was self-substitution when she evoked electricity, a
tree, or a fish jumping into a frying-pan. There was often formality
and ceremony in children's intent observance of the play-rules. Even

in the old games like marbles and '*chat perché*', there were gestures to be made and words to be said; the child who deviated from the proper form was reproached for it by the others.

Most curious were the 'ascetic' games which Chateau noted, when a child sees how long he can stand on one foot, stare at the sun, hold his breath, or bite his own arm until he is ready to cry out with pain. In these games the child shows self-control, and in other ways he shows his will power. (By not saying a word; not moving; not making a noise; and so on.) All the games played by children involve tests, and they are games of will-power. So, far from revealing inner conflicts and torment, they show a part of man's greatness, his thrust forward into the future, high spirits, and also the self-discipline derived from the rules.

One gathers that Chateau is not speaking about egocentric play in this way, but forms of social play which indicate a future towards which the child is straining; the educator is there to help him forward to new paths where he will act as a man, not as an infant. The child is therefore asking tacitly to be shown how to work, and 'aims at what is difficult, not at what is pleasant'. This interpretation seems a very important one, as it shows a departure from the passive nature of problem-governed play, and animal-play. As in other features of the *maternelle* type of child-rearing, there is an emphasis on the dignity of man combined with a belief in the inner urge towards the right way of doing things.[7]

Assessment of Play

The question whether play is effective in treating different kinds of maladjustment in children, wrote one psychologist, has hardly been tackled objectively at all. While there is still controversy about the real effect of play techniques in therapy, criticism of 'free' play comes from Smilansky, who said that for some deprived urban children, this would only duplicate undirected play in the street and home for city children; in poor districts they run about outside, and so 'the kindergarten need hardly offer them opportunities for free play and an outlet for their energies'.

A colleague of Smilansky's, Feitelson, pointed out that play as an integral part of child-rearing activity must be seen in its Western setting. There are Middle Eastern communities where children are brought up with scarcely any opportunity for free play, and immigrant children from the Kurdish mountain area were unaware of play possibilities. Like the Egyptian village children described by

Ammar in 1954, they had not had space, time, or materials for
'undisturbed free play'. Feitelson and his co-workers were able to
teach these play-deprived children to play imaginatively.[8]

Friedrich Froebel, relatively uninformed in the realm of psychology
as we know it, began the day for kindergarten children with 'creative
self-activity'. Children were given the chance to 'work out the ideas
that had been gathering in their minds during their absence from
school'.[9] We have seen the same sort of thing done in an *école
maternelle* by a simple silence-music routine, with the toddlers either
in a circle or Indian file, swaying to rhythms from a record-player
and dissipating their tension and timidity. The authority for play in
early childhood goes as far back as Denis Cochin, who directed teachers
in the old *salles d'asile* that 'as for developing their intelligence, this
should happen gradually, through play'.

Accepting play as a core-activity in childhood (or as Huizinga
claimed, in adult life as well) we have to criticize our leisure-areas and
automobile-dominated holidays. In some countries, restaurants
provide playgrounds and there are a few, very few, English pubs with
swings and slides in the garden. During the hours of motorway
driving which lead to the beaches or hills one can see children cooped-
up like hens in a cage; there are few amenities provided at the food
and petrol stopovers.

Hospitals, in recent times, have come to realize the child patient's
need for play, but surveys of orphan homes and institutions have
revealed a shocking lack even of toys.[10] Legislation will eventually
be needed to remind grown-ups that playgrounds and material are as
necessary as parking-spaces but have a greater claim, as they are for
human-beings. Little work has been done to record the effect on
children of long journeys without exercise, although the effect on
adults of jet-fatigue and time-change is known to be felt for several
days and to require biological re-adjustment.

Child-study records have shown us that the sense of rhythm and
ear-training for pitch and melody develops with the child's growth
itself. Maturation may not come until elementary school level, but
an eighteen-month-old boy will sway to the rhythm of an oboe
concerto on the radio before he can walk safely across the room to
hit the music-box with delight. There is a great deal we do not know
about little children and music; we are only now realizing that music
like language is linked with the home environment. A child from a
music-less home is deprived and needs compensation to overcome the
lag in melody and rhythm training.

The place of music in the history of 'ECE' is at least as old as the
New Lanark school of Robert Owen, when song was a regular feature
of the day. In North America, music in school antedated the arrival
of the kindergarten method by fifty years, but was adopted as part of
that method in the Peabody movement of the 1860s. Jean-Jacques
Rousseau himself was much concerned at the world's failure to
appreciate his system of musical notation.

The nineteenth century was the century of song and brought back
singing to the 'Land Without Music' — Britain. There were huge
singing classes in Paris and Germany early in the century, taught by
the *Mainzer Singschule* method, and the commune schools in France
used a similar method in the 1830s. But it was after the Prussian
victories of 1870 that France, as we saw, associated German success
with German music, and the English 'payment by results' system
placed a premium on melody at about the same time: 'sixpence per
head was paid for each child who could sing a prepared song, and
double that amount if he could sing from notes . . .'

In Hungary, where the English infant schools were imitated
during the last century, little children sang German songs in 1828,
and Hungarian ones after the revolution of 1848; Froebel's didactic
songs were adapted to the national language when kindergarten
methods arrived, and even set to melodies by Verdi. Bartok, Kodaly
and Carl Orff have done a great deal of innovatory work on music
for early education in recent times. An observer who saw and heard
children in the Münich studio of Suse Böhm (pupil of Carl Orff)
reported that children did not have to wait until they had mastered
the instruments. Tiny tots were beating our a rhythm while older
children improvised on xylophones, glockenspiels, and recorders.

Pre-school time-tables do not usually have a set time for music,
which appears incidentally in song and dance. Hungary, again, has been
an innovator, with a curriculum based on Forrai's work, and
intended for use right through the elementary or basic school.
'Repetition of nonsense rhymes helps to develop proper articulation;
folk plays intensify fantasy and awaken collective feeling . . . a sense
of rhythm is developed . . . and seventy to eighty songs or rhymes are
acquired during the pre-school period.' There is no visiting music
teacher in this organization; the usual teacher can lead the pupils, so
that song and music may spring up at any time of the school day.

So much experimentation has occurred with both art and music in
early education that it would be difficult to choose the most significant
ventures, but in view of the references we have made to Itard and

Séguin at least one departure must be cited – the role of music with
handicapped children. Autistic, severely retarded and physically
handicapped children have been reached by music training, and an
absorbing account of such work has been given by Juliette Alvin and
by Philip Bailey, *They Can Make Music* (1973).[11] There are illustrations
in these books which demand our attention, of children classed as
'ESN' or suffering from such an affliction as cerebral palsy making
music in concert together. Patients in institutions and mental asylums
are, in this way, able to find a language in which to express themselves
to the world outside their own personality and suffering.

Directive and Non-Directive Play

Throughout the discussion of modern pre-school methods and
management runs the argument about adult interference, or to put it
more mildly, guidance. Comparisons between what are called
'structured' classes and non-structured classes are commonly made
and the extent to which free play is permitted may be taken as a useful
term of reference between the two. Yet it is not as simple as that,
really. Even when adults interfere rarely, the types of play indulged
in are often guided by the equipment chosen by adults for use in
these 'free' surroundings. The children have to function in part-
response to their surroundings and elders.

At the *Maison des Petits* in Geneva Mlles Audemars and Lafendel
evolved a number of games, toys and contraptions which facilitated
free play and sensory-motor activity. They were of the opinion that
free play was of the utmost importance because it was not for the
child a preliminary operation or an exercise with adult things; it was
the way in which the child absorbed the outside world. Accordingly,
the *Maison des Petits* atmosphere stood a long way apart from the
Montessori room, where play is converted, in a way, to teaching
purposes and cognitive development. It was much more like the
modern English nursery school and its (apparent) free for all. Yet for
Piaget, when he estimated the value of the *Maison des Petits* some
years later, the Audemars-Lafendel setting was not quite free. Even
their games and equipment, their varied array of materials tended
towards work, and as chosen by adults revealed adult *anticipation*
of the result. Bridges, boats, trains, mills and houses appeared from
the small hands of the Swiss children to everyone's satisfaction, as
was intended. Equipment, in a nursery play-room, can become the
obstacle in the way of development, thought Piaget; there is a fundamental difference between children's thinking and ours. The adult

anticipates by theoretical thought about possible results, and then puts his plan into action. The child on the other hand acts without anticipation, and the goal appears along the way. While playing, he is assimilating reality to his particular activity, 'providing the latter with necessary nourishment, and transforming reality according to the many needs of the ego'.

'The whole personality is in the process of expressing itself, and what is happening is a genuine personal act of creation.'[12]

Jean Piaget and Research in Cognition

Jean Piaget is one of the most exciting research scholars in the story of early childhood education. He is still working, as we write, in several capacities as lecturer, writer, and director of practical psychological research. His output of books has been enormous, even when we take into account that many of them have been written in collaboration with experts such as Miss Bärbel Inhelder. Probably no name is so well known to laymen as that of Piaget, even though few of us and indeed few scholars may have read all his works, which now represent over thirty titles and fifty years of research.

Piaget was born in Neuchâtel, Switzerland, in 1896. He studied science and wrote a doctoral thesis on the Alpine molluscs, which is not so improbable when we remember Froebel's one-time passion for mineralogy, and the medical schools which formed the background of Montessori, Décroly and Claparède, whom Piaget joined at the Genevan Institut Jean-Jacques Rousseau in 1921. The institute was strong in personal talent, but hampered by lack of finance, especially in the early years. Mlles Audemars and Lafendel were there, and Mlle Descœudres, who, from observation of five hundred children collected around Geneva, had written her book on *Child Development from Two to Seven*. Claparède himself and Pierre Bovet led this talented team. Apart from their own research, the Genevan Institute was interested in comparative education, and the work of leaders as different as Madame Montessori and Lord Baden-Powell attracted their attention.

On his arrival at the Institut, the twenty-five-year-old Piaget was given a small room (which was all that was available) in which to prepare his work, file his results and sketch out future exploration. In the afternoons, as he was not required to help with other duties, he left for a primary school in the company of one or two student assistants who helped to record the replies of the children. At this level Piaget had the rare gift of gaining the child's confidence very quickly and Bovet tells how Piaget and his subjects often seemed like young pupils chatting together or exchanging confidences. The Institut was already using a number of different tests and Piaget adapted Binet and Burt to suit his own methods, producing altered experiments and remarkable results which more than confirmed the faith of older members in the Institut. Four brief years passed at Geneva during which he accumulated the data for his four early volumes of research into the almost-unknown realm of the thinking processes of children. A shortage of funds made it impossible to retain Piaget in Geneva, and he returned to a chair of psychology at Neuchâtel. Ironically enough, a generous grant from America later in 1925 facilitated the work of the Institut and helped to begin the International Bureau of Education.

Child Morality

Mlle Descœudres had provided a lead for research by her work on morality tests, and from his own questions Piaget collected material for a study on the child's view of justice which later appeared as *The Moral Judgement of the Child*. Children's attitudes, he concluded, were independent of adult views of social morality, and grew out of the social life of children as they evolve among themselves, feeling solidarity or hostility to each other and sensing mutual respect when the 'rules' they create are observed. The social basis of morality is no new concept, and there have been many to criticize this section of Piaget's work, but by the evidence of children talking and thinking about punishment and fair play in their society he illuminated areas which had previously been ignored or regarded as the adult province of knowing and *instilling into* (to use the traditional and significant phrase) the child a knowledge of right and wrong. That the child had a point of view about this had already been accepted by some intelligent educators: Pauline Kergomard was one. But the picture of what that point of view was had been somewhat rough in outline.

In addition to producing a mass of evidence of what little Genevan children thought on punishment, Piaget proposed that different ages of development accept different ideas — that there is a developmental shift between nursery age and elementary school age. 'A sort of law of evolution in the moral development of the child', whereby expiation gives place to reciprocity in child society. They are thinking out the basis of punishment and morality instead of accepting what the adult says it is. Self-determination of moral standards is the opposite end of the world from nineteenth-century practice in 'breaking the will' of the child to restore obedience.[13]

Stages of Development

Extensive observation over a number of years, partly based on the study of his own children, led Piaget to predicate three major stages of development in the young child from birth to eleven years of age (or thereabouts; the time-spans are not rigidly defined).[14] These stages cover changes in the growth of cognition, and have prompted a greal deal of discussion, some of it critical. No one concerned with young children's education can afford to be unaware of the trend in Piaget's theory, which is summarized here.

1. *0 – 18 months*. In Stage 1, sensory-motor operations last approximately from birth to eighteen months. The infant-toddler is forming his ways of behaviour in relation to certain objects which are usually in the nursery-room, and appear to be fixed and permanent. He is exercising mechanisms which begin as reflexes, building a system of movements which, he discovers, may also be made in a reverse direction.

Eye movements to follow an object (mobiles, for instance, attached to the cot), turning, touching, shaking, even sucking are operations during this period of great activity. He or she is assimilating new objects or situations to an existing scheme of things as he is going about the learning process: fresh acquisitions come to enlarge the scheme, to modify it and oblige the individual child to make 'accommodation' and co-ordination possible between previous schemes and novel ones. All this appears before our eyes in the form of actions.

'In the course of six sub-stages, our child recognizes objects, begins to grasp at them, becomes aware that unseen objects are still existing in his world (and have not disappeared from vision to vanish forever); he decides that these objects have some sort of 'permanence', and also he begins to investigate cause and effect.' For eighteen months' work all this really seems quite an achievement, while the brain is forming, the cortex and central nervous system are forming through biological growth processes.

2. *2 – 7 years*. Stage 2 is the period between the second year and seven years of age. It is a period of preparation for formal, conceptual or abstract thought and has also been called the concrete thinking

stage. The infant at stage one was quite egocentric; the growing three-
and four-year-old is becoming aware of outside persons, rules of
conduct and cause and effect. The fact that he has a limited view of
that process, and blames the banana skin for his fall does not change
the fact that he is forming a notion about causes which he did not
have before. He identifies with personal models, person or persons
close to him, whom he regards as omnipotent and awe-inspiring.

3. *7 – 11 years.* Between seven and eleven there ensues a long period
of 'structuralization' when he has to apply his acquired structures to
many different examples. It has been found that the principles are
applied in a certain order: the principle of conservation is not, for
example, applied to volume until after it has been applied to weight
and quantity. The notion of time as a concept independent of spatial
distance — before and after — begins to be formed. Symbolic speech
is adopted although the full meaning is not grasped.

This is not to be understood as a straightforward advance on all
fronts, of course. 'Every new advance acquisition' points out Maier,
'of more advanced objective behaviour initially involves only surface
behaviour. When threatened, the child automatically returns to his
previous intuitive and egocentric mode of thinking and reasoning.[15]

In several works, Piaget and his colleagues have investigated learning
mechanisms and the child's way of thinking logically. *Judgment and
Reasoning in the Child*; *The Growth of Logical Thinking: From
Childhood to Adolescence*; *The Early Growth of Logic in the Child*
are all concerned with problems about learning. Piaget's view on
learning departs from the other theories of learning in several features.
In the work of thinking, or processing data, the brain receives stimuli
which it can incorporate, or absorb while, at the same time, being
altered by this process. The information absorbed is also altered, so
that perception involves a sort of digestive process with the intake
selected, transformed and/or rejected while the organism inside is
changing in response to outside stimuli. So learning is a process in
which there are changes during assimilation of outside stimuli within
the mind itself and the organism is continually active, it changes the
outside surroundings by its activity in cognition. By assimilation,
the child experiences an event in so far as he can integrate it to his
subjective experience: in accommodation, the child tries to incorporate
the environmental experience as it really is, adapting his system to
take in a totally new experience.

Our four-year-old, still limited by the restraints of his first egocentric phase, has to struggle to find a balance between assimilation and accommodation, which is to say that parts of reality encountered again are fraught with a multitude of new shades and elements which can at first be ignored, but which in the long run must be taken into account.

It is within Stage 2, from mid-second to seventh year, that elaboration of mental operations is occurring; this is the time at which the child enters nursery-school or *maternelle* and includes the years which we consider crucial in mental and personality development. The Swiss scholar has not, however, devoted the bulk of his studies to this period, which seems to him a transitional one, between the autistic phase and the beginnings of socialization. Many nursery-school observers would certainly deny that this has to wait until the child is six or seven.

For Piaget the child has begun to make advances over his autistic behaviour phase, between two and seven. In his still-limited view, everyone thinks as he does and understands what he is doing; he is able to move centres of space and its objects from his action to himself, 'and thus locate himself at the middle point of this world which is being born'. He is working hard to assimilate experience and incorporate his findings in an expanded view of the world. But the key point to remember here is that knowledge is inseparable from his internal biological organization: there is a process of interaction between organism and environment which now transforms external reality into an object of knowledge.

Play

Through play, which infiltrates every activity, the child meets his own sort of reality. To the onlooker, this seems very often like fantasy play, but it possesses a rich egocentric character. Piaget (after Claparède and Groos) sees the child playing his way through life; put more strongly, the absence of play becomes a negative factor, retarding progress, leaving the child in his autistic world, out of touch with his environment.

All this has its beginnings in the first stage, where, Piaget stated in a passage which is fundamental to his thought, 'before any language is used, and therefore prior to conceptual and reflective thought of any sort, the baby's practical, sensory-motor intelligence is growing and making its own conquest of phenomena'.

Our two- to seven-year-old, given roughly normal progress, is arranging his concept of space and relationships within it according to his subjective experience. Life has a logic, which is his own logic inside his frame of reference. The same level of behaviour can be seen in adult life sometimes when a point of view can only be explained within the terms of a person's own history.

Child Logic

Two essential phenomena are peculiar to this stage, according to Piaget. Firstly, events are reasoned and judged by their outward appearance, regardless of their objective logic. This process is called 'a reflective level of internalization and of symbolization, permitting reasoning; but originating at the sensory-motor level before the development of language and inner thought'.[16]

An example of this subjective judgement is the famous 'glass of milk' experiment, where a child chooses a small glass filled up to the brim rather than the very large glass filled to three-quarters. His selection is based strictly on his own idea of what fullness is. He may even have witnessed a greater amount of milk being poured into the latter glass, yet he judges as he sees things, i.e. comparisons are purely visual.

Further, the child at this stage does not have the capacity for reversible thought; a good example of what this means is given by John L. Phillips. A four-year-old subject is asked:

'Do you have a brother?' He says, 'Yes.'
'What's his name?' 'Jim.'
'Does Jim have a brother?' 'No.'
Four-year-old ——— JIM
           brother to
but the relationship goes only one way.[17]

In another visual example of the penetrating study Piaget has made of thought processes in childhood, two plasticene balls of equal size are prepared and shown to the child, who is asked whether they are the same size or not? An average four-year-old replies that they are the same size. Then, while he is watching every move, one ball is taken and rolled into a sausage shape and placed again next to the other. (Nothing is hidden from the child's observation.) He now, in answer to the question, says that one has more plasticene content than the other. Usually he chooses the sausage-shape, but sometimes the ball.[18]

Now it is clear that, however we may feel out of our depth when

Piaget or his critics start debating the merits of genetic epistemology, examples like those quoted take us a step further in our recognition of the child as a being very different from ourselves. His different modes of perception have to be absorbed by us if we are to help him to learn and if we are to conduct anything but a *dialogue des sourds*.

Logic before Language

Describing the second period of development in a lecture given many years after his original statement, and after serious criticism had been levelled at his theory by other scholars, Piaget repeated the view that at this stage of childhood sensory-motor intelligence becomes internalized. This 'logic' of intelligence takes shape at the level of representation thereafter, by which he meant not only language but other forms of representation. Among these was the symbolic function (and it may be worth recalling as a footnote here that the Piaget book known in English as *Play, Dreams, and Imitation* was in the original French called *La formation du Symbole chez L'Enfant*). Then there were gestures, which were sometimes idiosyncratic and sometimes systematic (as in deaf and dumb sign language, for example), and imitation as expressed in drawing, painting or modelling. Prior to the formation of language, Piaget insists, the roots of logic may be found at the sensory-motor level, and the fundamental structures of order and inclusion exist there. As a result Piaget views language as 'a necessary condition for the attainment of logico-mathematical structures, but it cannot constitute a sufficient condition'.[19]

Critics of the Piaget Stages

For some students Piaget's stages have seemed open to the criticism that they are valid only in a particular culture. American children appeared to pass a given developmental point earlier than the Genevan children, reported some psychologists. The eminent anthropologist, Margaret Mead, reported that one Pacific island people did not pass through the animistic stage which Piaget said was general among young children. The discussion was complicated by a report that children in American Indian tribes, unlike their Antipodean contemporaries, did follow a pattern postulated by Jean Piaget.[20]

The Soviet expert, Vygotsky, considered Piaget's classification of child language in the first stage far too limited under the heading 'egocentric monologue'. In his *Thought and Language*, Vygotsky put forward the view that the Swiss scientist had ignored some other functions of child language: it may serve to relieve tension, as a director of activity, and also as an instrument of thought, to name but a few of these. Suggestions that Piaget's observations on moral judgement had been unduly limited by his definition of justice came from the American scholar, Kohlberg, who pointed out that norms of justice were not just matters of abstract logic; they were sentiments of sympathy, gratitude and vengeance which had taken on a logical form. Bryant at Oxford expressed disappointment with the book *Memory and Intelligence* when it came out in translation in 1973 and claimed that Piaget and Inhelder had been repetitive in their experiments and unoriginal in their theory. When Dr Bryant read a paper to the British Association at Swansea in summer, 1971, and followed it with an article in *Nature*, a general discussion arose as to whether the celebrated Piagetian 'conservation' experiments had been discredited.

In the Piaget 'number of conservation' experiment, two equal rows of beads are laid out opposite each other and the child is asked if they are an equal number. Then one row is extended to produce one long, one short row. The child's reaction is usually to say that the number is greater in the long row. Now Bryant feels that, while Piaget's inventiveness and experimental ingenuity were not in question, the results may have meant different things. For instance, when the child chooses the longest line of beads, he has been faced with two incompatible judgments which are as good as each other in his view. 'He has to plump for one so he chooses the more recent.'[21] In other words, there is more than one explanation for the child's reaction whereas Piaget stresses only one — that the child does not understand the invariance of number at four years of age.

But Bryant hastened to admit that the questions Piaget asked and the problems which he has introduced into child psychology were brilliantly original; and Professor Lunzer, who sprang to Piaget's defence, pointed out that Piaget's example was the inspiration behind two important teaching projects at present under way in Britain: *Nuffield Junior Mathematics* and *Junior Science*.

Work in progress to furnish statistical correlations on the connection between intelligence, learning ability and the development of logical thought may, under Lunzer's direction, provide some answers and take us further than Piaget, whose life work has centred on these subjects. But even this type of research, went on Lunzer in an illuminating passage of scientific 'confession', would not be enough in the long run. 'What is required is an overall model, supported by experiment, within which what we call learning, intelligence and thinking will be re-defined. More than one breakthrough is needed to achieve this. When it is achieved, Piaget will have been superseded. But not (the observation deserves emphasizing) not in the sense that his findings will have been shown to be spurious. Only that the perspective, broad though it is, is still too narrow and imprecise.'[22]

Piaget in the Classroom

Piaget's reputation stands so high among the educators, in spite of his occasional obscurity, that authorities in some countries recommend him in public but ignore him in practice. The author of an article in the French journal *L'Éducation* suggested that French authorities fail to apply Piaget's lessons because of the difficulties inherent in mastering his theory, and asked whether the honours heaped on Piaget in recent years had not been given partly to silence an unorthodox authority?[23] The question borders on the frivolous, but it is good to see that, particularly in English, attempts are being made to present Piaget in a form useful and intelligible to the teacher or helper in nursery-schools.

Since the 1950s Professor Piaget is usually referred to not as an educationist, nor even as a psychologist, although he certainly has great claims in either profession: he is a 'genetic epistemologist'. This rather intimidating title masks the latest stage in Piaget's personal search for knowledge about the intelligence of man. His scientific background was wider than that of most psychologists and his own inclinations and training drew him towards philosophy as well as science; after 1940, he designed his programme of tests within the Kantian concepts of space, time and causality. His work was directed more and more towards exploring the bases of knowledge; in an explicatory aside he described genetic epistemology as having, as its main problem, 'the explanation of the construction of novelties in the development of knowledge.'

The centre for genetic epistemology in Geneva draws together those who are working in the fields of logic, mathematics, biology, physics and cybernetics as well as in psychology. This inter-disciplinary work Piaget considers quite normal, and indeed essential, and is surprised when psychologists accuse him of transgressing the boundaries of that study.

His research has not only been about developmental psychology; it is itself in continual process of development. At the end of one of the more recent publications, Piaget tells us that we need to under-stand the laws of mental imagery in order to understand 'anticipations'.

The whole subject of anticipation and imagery will therefore form the subject of a new series 'upon which we have been engaged for some time'. Thus the study of logic leads to further experiments about anticipation, and the later tests permit us to criticize some of the conclusions in earlier work. Research for Piaget is a moving stair, and he has this in common with Froebel, that he considers his work as a beginning and not as a complete and rigid system.

PART 2: DEVELOPMENTS UP TO THE PRESENT DAY

7 FRANCE

The vigorous attack on routine and tradition launched by progressives like Ferdinand Buisson and Madame Kergomard seemed to slow down after 1900; finance and politics did not follow very closely behind the flag of innovation, and there was no compulsion exerted on communes to open new *maternelles*. Under the ministry of Combes a determined effort was made to close down religious teaching schools and even crèches run by religious orders, and at the same time reduce enrolments in the *maternelles*. There were seven hundred thousand children attending *classes enfantines* or *maternelles* at the turn of the century; twenty-five years later the total had fallen to four hundred thousand. There had been, it was true, a decline in the birth-rate after World War I, but this had begun to correct itself by 1925, when the figures showed only one out of seven children under six attending some sort of infant school in France.

Enrolments in French pre-school centres showed a decline after 1900, and the tendency continued − as it did in Britain − for many years. Third Republic policy remained hostile to denominational kindergartens and nursery centres, but there was no compensatory increase in the number of *maternelle* buildings, and, of course, communities above two thousand were under no direct compulsion to open new schools of this sort.

Pauline Kergomard had reached retiring age in 1903, and although her energies were undiminished, she made way for younger educators, remaining active as an adviser and friend to the movement she had done so much to shape. She was no longer directing policy, therefore, at the time when the new 'progressive' ideas began to flow into the stream of infant education from Italy and elsewhere. One of Madame Kergomard's closest collaborators believed that she agreed with Maria Montessori's emphasis on freedom, which ran parallel with her own views, frequently expressed. In later editions of the textbook, *L'enfant de 2 à 6 ans* Montessori was quoted approvingly, particularly on all points which related to sensory education.

The period before 1914 was particularly fertile in significant research among French-language scholars and scientists, but it is doubtful whether overworked teachers in crowded urban centres had either time or energy to follow research with experimental method.

Change was in the air, nevertheless, and awaited the chance to slip past the guard of reactionary teachers and politicians. Psychology and development were in the forefront of discussion when Binet's book about ECE, *Les idées modernes sur les enfants*, sold thousands of copies in 1909, and Ellen Key's onslaught on 'soul murder in the schools' had been equally successful a few years previously. Décroly opened his school for normal children in Brussels only in 1907, but he and his group had been publicizing their work in journals before then; Claparède's book on child psychology and educational experiment had appeared in Switzerland where he was organizing the Jean-Jacques Rousseau centre and preparing his introduction to Dewey. All these had begun to affect the higher levels of medical and educational discussion, a generation of younger teachers who had been exposed to the Kergomard crusade had graduated from teachers' colleges, and the best of them were encouraged to enter a *maternelle*. Even if practice lagged behind theory and foreign visitors found fault with much of what they observed (as we shall see), it needs to be repeated that French government instructions were based on study of the child's psychological and biological interests from 1887 onwards.

As early as 1887 the curriculum had placed physical exercises first and beginnings of reading, writing and arithmetic last on the recommendations to schools; intellectual exercise was to be limited, moreover, to two a day, preferably in the morning, and to be divided by 'song, movement, walking or physical exercises'. In 1921 a series of new instructions replaced the old term 'object lessons' with the new 'observation exercises', and the emphasis on observation was striking: the little children were to have free play with toys and common objects and to observe by 'touching, feeling, sniffing, imitating, questioning and answering'.

Prior to these innovations, what had impressed Miss Synge, an English visitor, was the cleanliness of schools and children; if the pupil arrived clean with hair brushed and stockings drawn up, he or she was admitted to the *maternelle*, but otherwise, not. If a child's linen had not been changed on Mondays and Thursdays, it followed that the unfortunate child was dismissed from the school. Similar rules existed in Belgium. Such stern treatment was obviously designed as an educative measure for parents, but they seem draconian when given to three- and four-year-olds.

But when nursery education did begin to come into favour in England after the McMillans and the Synges had fought their battles, it is significant that it was seen to be primarily a health measure.

The general health of school children in Britain (and, indeed, in Western Europe) has improved so markedly that hygiene is no longer the grave matter it was early in the century; with better (but still inadequate) housing for the lower wage-earner bathrooms for everyone have become almost commonplace.[1]

The comportment of the children impressed Miss Synge. She thought there was less discipline, less sitting in desks, less marching than in England. The children sang as they entered or left the class-room in those faraway years and there was playing of ball in classroom (*sic*) and courtyard, more toys — horses, carts, buckets and spades. What was lacking in France and Belgium was more time for rest, and the daily timetables were 'breathlessly full', she thought. The banishment of reading, writing and arithmetic from the daily occupations of little children in Belgium and France was a reform which made a great impression upon the visitor, and which she duly reported as a move in the right direction for England to copy when reorganization of the infant schools began. On the debit side, however, was the failure, in both France and Belgium, to capitalize on Froebel's revelation of the value of nature work, the observation of plants, flower and fruit, and follow Froebel's indication of the path from this natural growth to the realization of a higher power than that of man.[2] Few fresh flowers were to be seen, or growing plants in pots: the gloom was heightened by the black dresses of the *directrices* and their assistants.

Another visitor, this time male, was more critical. The American educator, Farringdon, in 1906, felt that the timetables were not only full, but unbalanced. 'It is chiefly work and little play,' he said, 'in spite of the social and economic, rather than educational, principle underlying their organization.' Thus, in spite of all Pauline Kergomard's enlightened activity, and the entirely opposite intentions of the Ferry-Buisson planners, we are thrown back on the shelter-principle of the *salles d'asile*, and Farringdon seems to have felt that it was unwise to forget it. Moreover, he went on, the spirit of enjoyment which underlay the play of American kindergarten children in the schoolroom was quite unknown in France. The ideas of Froebel had as yet had little influence on the *écoles maternelles*, and they had been rightly criticized for hurrying the children along too rapidly and making the work too serious. It is not clear how many schools Farringdon visited, and his criticisms seem to be based on what he saw of the school — or the older class in the school — which was attached to the teacher-training school at Batignolles, in Paris.

More informative than Farringdon's impressions of rather restricted inspection are the extracts he quoted from the day of a teacher in an *école maternelle*. It does not seem radically different in organization from the typical day of the 1870s, although methods used inside the classes classes have changed enormously. Significantly, it concludes with the observation that,

> when the children leave the *école maternelle* at six years of age, almost all of them can read readily, write legibly, and perform some simple operations in addition, subtraction, and multiplication.
>
> From the time when the *école maternelle* opens, at eight o'clock in winter and seven o'clock in summer, the children from two to six years of age come in the company of some member of their family — an older brother or sister who is on his way to the adjoining school, or perhaps the mother.
>
> The teacher on duty receives them and has the children that eat luncheon at the school arrange their baskets in a place by themselves. Then all the little folks take their seats on the benches of the court. Until nine o'clock, the regular hour for opening school, the teacher has the children spend the time in singing or in some light gymnastic work.
>
> We might add that the *école maternelle* is a mixed school and there is no separation of the sexes in the classroom, in the court or on the playground.
>
> At nine o'clock all the teachers appear. Each one takes charge of her own class, conducts the children to the toilets, inspects their hands, their handkerchiefs and their clothes, calls the attention of some to their faults, rewards others for their general neatness, and promises to be lenient with those who are very clean the next day.
>
> They sing as they go to their classes. When everybody is seated the class work begins.
>
> In accordance with the program, twenty minutes are spent in reading, five in singing, twenty in writing and ten in language work.
>
> For the reading, movable letters are used or else the teacher writes letters or syllables on the blackboard, always giving the sound with the character.
>
> At quarter past ten there is a half-hour recess. The children play freely but they are under surveillance.
>
> On returning to the class, the roll is called, and then follow simple lessons in history, geography, or object lessons, according to the program.

At quarter past eleven, the teacher appointed to look after the luncheon hour conducts to the court all the children that eat luncheon at the school.

Behind these come the children that go home for the midday meal. A teacher sees them to the door of the school where the parents are waiting for them.

The maid helps the teacher in seating the children at the tables and in passing the food. The poor receive their soup and vegetables, sometimes soup, vegetables and meat, free; the others pay ten centimes (about two cents). During the luncheon, the teacher and the maid continually call attention to the need of cleanliness and even interrupt the meal to make important suggestions. Luncheon is over at quarter past twelve.

The play of the children is free. The teacher in charge is now relieved by another. The surveillance is usually restricted to preventing dangerous games; but a teacher who really appreciates her responsibility directs the play, participates in it and takes personal interest in all the little children who have so much need of good advice or kind words.

At one o'clock, the children are taken to the wash room and the toilets. They sing on their way to their class rooms, and then follow the ordinary class exercises: reading, arithmetic, interspersed with memory work or singing. Then various exercises continue until half past two, when there is a recreation period of half an hour. Twice a week, after this period, each class has gymnastics: simple movements of the arms and legs, marches, games.

After the recreation, there is either manual work or designing. These exercises consist of folding, weaving, cutting or pricking. The design is either drawn in a blank book or fashioned with little strips of material.

At four o'clock, the children that go home alone are led to the door, the others await their parents.

The school closes at six o'clock in winter and seven o'clock in summer.

When the children leave the *école maternelle* at six years of age, almost all of them can read readily, write legibly, and perform some simple operations in addition, subtraction and multiplication.

In some quarters of the great cities, the children are poorly clothed, but generally speaking they are reasonably clean. It is very rare to see a child with a soiled frock on Monday.

The education often leaves much to be desired; the child

confided to our care expresses himself in a very rough fashion; he strikes his comrades and they retaliate, but he soon loses these bad manners, and all the poor little children who have so much need of affection, like all children of their age, become attached to their teacher. They are very happy when they receive her caress, and take it as a severe punishment when they are deprived of this. So the discipline is reasonably easy.

Innovation and Reform: 1922 to 1940

The years after the First World War were years of numerical stagnation but classroom reform for the *écoles maternelles*. One in seven of the under-sixes was accommodated in the mid-twenties as compared with one in four when the century began. There was little new construction of *maternelle* buildings, which numbered about four thousand after the war, and the smaller population of pupils enabled the government to limit each age-group within the *maternelle* — small, middles and older children — to fifty. Many schools had only one hundred pupils in all, and although there were still more children than a teacher could really handle effectively, conditions were better than they had been.

Before 1914 (to take a convenient date) the outside appearance of the *maternelles* had been forbidding. Inside the atmosphere had also been gloomy, in spite of the efforts of enlightened *inspectrices* and school principals. To parents and the older generation a school was a school where you learned your sums and your spelling-book; it mattered little whether it was qualified with the adjective '*maternelle*'. Madame Kergomard's insistence on the need for life and Dr Décroly's demand for a school *de la vie et pour la vie* (which by *life itself* prepares the young for life) fell on stony ground in that faraway world of pre-1914, when France was determined not to fall behind Prussia in school efficiency.

Like the grapevine itself, educational reform is slow to yield fruit, and the ideas of the 1920s were not so much novel as newly acceptable. Free to travel at last, Madame Montessori lectured in London and the United States, arousing interest everywhere. The work of Décroly was widely discussed among francophone educators and made the basis for classroom experiment. Claparède's introduction to Dewey had appeared at the Institut Jean-Jacques Rousseau, where Jean Piaget arrived in 1921; the *New Era* magazine, which prominently featured all 'progressive' education techniques, was published in French as well

as English, and held conferences in Continental resorts. News of
Gesell, Watson and Thorndike in the United States or Charlotte Bühler
in Vienna filtered through to the inspectorate of Paris and the
academies in France.

Colour was one of the novelties in the *maternelle*. Teachers began
to rebel against blank grey walls and enlivened them with 'an amusing
frieze of white geese', and pink borders, while each child's locker held
a rose-pink pail for plasticine. Blue and white flower pots had begun
to appear, and there were brown beech leaves and a bunch of mistletoe
hanging from one wall. Black pinafores and the *directrice*'s black
dress were replaced by brighter garments. The process was not general,
or sudden, but it had begun, like fox-trots and the movies, and the
gay twenties reached the *maternelles* after some delays.

At first the plethora of new methods and suggestions posed a
problem for the inspectorate and those who were supposed to guide
the *maternelle* policy. There was a great deal of support for Montessori,
and in several countries Montessori schools were founded: should the
Montessori method be recommended for general use? Décroly's
'global' method for the approach to reading was widely discussed,
and in common use in schools in Belgium: should it become the rule
in the *écoles maternelles*? Adolph Ferrière, and Dalcroze were other
innovators whose suggestions were welcomed by progressive circles;
should the activity school and eurhythmic exercises be adapted into
the *maternelle* syllabus?

The instructions for 1923 replied with caution to these grave
questions, counselling an eclectic approach and a wait-and-see attitude
towards the latest fashions. The best method would be the one which
produced the quickest and most lasting results. 'Between the single
letter method, the syllable method or the global method we decline
to make any choice; there are experiments at present in progress which
will decide the issue. The best way of going about things must be the
one which interests a child in that thankless task which consists in
linking sounds and shapes which have no apparent relationship.' No
single method was chosen as sufficient for general use in the *maternelles*, although parts of all the new contributions were freely to be
adapted, should the teachers so wish, to French conditions.

The French reception to the new way of things was traditional,
therefore; the *salles d'asile* and *maternelles* under Mme Pape-
Carpantier and Pauline Kergomard had slowly, and, as it were,
reluctantly, admitted Froebel to the schools. Their successors were
equally unprepared to admit Montessori as *a philosophy* or Décroly

as a single, exclusive, method. In consequence, the *maternelle*, except in a few isolated cases, accepted new ideas far less than is usually said to be the case.[3]

Writing in the 1930s, another visitor, who found much to admire in the French system, described the eclectic approach and wide differences in method. In music teaching she saw a wide range in methods, varying from a tuning-fork, struck to set the note for singing national songs, to sophisticated use of the Dalcroze method. The more 'modern' schools, as Miss Hawtrey termed them, came to reading by the Décroly path, beginning with a general impression of the whole, and later analyzing the sentence into its components. But inside one school, there was one class learning by use of separate letters of the alphabet while three others were following the *méthode globale*. When the visitor pointed this out to the *directrice*, she was not at all concerned, and pointed out that the teacher using the single letter method succeeded perfectly well in teaching her children to read!

The work of spreading the right sort of news to outlying *maternelles* was held up by government unwillingness to pay for more inspectors (and it had been a long fight to conquer prejudice against women inspectors, strange though this may seem today). By the 1930s there were twenty *inspectrices* and four *inspectrices générales*, who were exclusively concerned with the *maternelles* and who, of course, had passed the examination known as the *certificat d'aptitude à l'inspection*. They were overworked like the teachers in their departments, of which large areas they often had several in their charge. The lady in charge at Dijon had to apologise to an English visitor for being unable to meet her; she was leaving at 5 a.m. on a journey to the furthest communes of her *second* department. Five *inspectrices* were appointed to the Department of the Seine, and were fully occupied by their duties; one of these was responsible for three hundred *écoles maternelles*. The independence of the inspectorate was, however, one of the factors in retaining its hard-won autonomy of organization and method.

Innovation and Expansion: Building Design

French architects were given the opportunity in the late 1930s to blend functional utility with imaginative experiment, enabling the *maternelle* to move irrevocably away from the barracks building of the *salle d'asile* tradition. They also made the most of their opportunity during the period of expansion which occurred in the post-war period. A country like France with such a diversity of climate and scenery, offers particular attractions to the painter, designer, and architect; there are *maternelles* which have been designed to blend with the sun, sky and sea of the tourist-poster South and others which look out from the top floor of modern tall buildings towards rural scenes which are invisible from city-streets or low buildings like the neighbouring *lycée*. No stark brick fortress awaits the toddlers on their first day at school, as in some of the older centres in Paris and other northern towns – the new-style *maternelle* is 'hewn from the sky and sunshine' as admirers put it, rather than from dreary city blocks, and one immediately receives the impression that this is, indeed, not a school in the ordinary sense of the word.

The entrance to one recently-built *maternelle* lies through a park planted with shady trees, which in turn leads to a small orchard, then to a lawn of green grass and only then to the long low attractive building. The visitor feels that the centre has grown, as it were, amid a small farm property. Outdoor space exceeds the covered ground by more than ten to one, and the play-grounds lie beyond the conventional *cour* (play-yard) on the far side of the building. (It is a convention with the *maternelle* that little children are released directly from the classroom into the *cour* at playtimes by the simple process of opening a door; no organizational fuss is needed because the yard is always clearly visible, is always enclosed, and is guarded by a *femme de service*.

Another new model *maternelle* employs a centrifugal concept with a very large play-room, open on five sides as its centre. The octagonal classrooms which lie beyond the playroom are separated from it by patios planted with flowers and herbs, so that the many-sided class-rooms look out through windows on four of their sides. Inside the building the way to the classrooms is lined with plants with the result that there is no longer any clearcut division between life inside and life outside; they are fluent and reassuringly the same. The smallest children (*les petits*) occupy the section near the entrance, although separated from it by an entrance hall. Their room is adjoined by another octagonal room designated as a rest room; the *directrice* has her offices nearby and can be reached through a door from the rest-room. The lavatories are close at hand, as are the storage spaces for equipment, toys, and playthings. Within the infant room itself there are of course a sink, taps and ample cupboard and shelf space. At the other age levels, the room which the older pupils (*les grands*) occupy is farthest from *les petits*, and only the second and third classes are contiguous.

One standard pattern is to base the *maternelle* on four classrooms. There are three age groups, the *petits*, the middle group (three and four years old) and the *grands* (between five and six). A child may be admitted at two. The middle group may share two rooms: the other two groups are kept apart, and a wash-room with WCs is usually adjacent to the *petits*.

The new schools were functionally adapted in some cases to the ages in the *maternelle*, with separate corridor and playground for the 'babies'. They were built at a time when living standards were rising and technology had brought cheaper toys into French families. New buildings favoured the growth of the distinctive French style of nursery school care, which is national without being nationalistic, inventive and literary. Language in all its forms is considered important in the *maternelles*: clear speech and polite, grammatical French is expected from the older class, who have been prepared for this at the lower level. The medium for good language development is the teacher's example, shown particularly in the telling of a story with great skill. Miss Hawtrey, visiting from Britain in the 1930s, spoke of the remarkable artistry of young French teachers displayed in the tale well told. The foundations of this were laid during the gloomy years of declining enrolments and public apathy before 1914, and this was one occasion when North American example proved helpful to France. The Froebel revival in the former country inspired widespread discussion at educational conferences about the importance of storytelling and the oral tradition reached a level of high skill in France.

Literacy and Language

A paramount principle of education is the correct use of language in the classroom, according to one *inspectrice-générale*, who brings the subject of language development into her description of toys in the baby class: 'they may keep them for a long time; but they have to bring them back where they found them, and replace them in good condition. As they learn to be orderly, so they learn, too, about speaking properly because they have to ask for their toys, not just grab them whenever they wish; in order to ask, they have to speak; they have to use the right word, and the appropriate form of polite speech. In this way the little fellow begins to learn.'

She returns to this theme again, to emphasize the interplay between teacher and child with language-learning: more complex materials are available when the child is a little older and asks his teacher for them. At every point the right word (*le mot exact*) is given first by the teacher, and repeated, understood, wisely employed by the child. Language exercises like these are the best possible method, 'because they teach the pupil to employ the right word to indicate a particular object or to attribute a particular quality to it'.[4] One is reminded of the emphasis placed on language development in some compensatory programmes, and two features recall points made by Russian research workers: one is the need for adult help and direction at a time when curiosity without guidance is not enough; the other is recognition of the unusual sensitivity to language possessed by the child between about two and five years of age. 'All the efforts of adults would be entirely useless if the children of younger age were not to show this high sensitivity to composition and pronunciation of words.'[5] Between two and seven the Russian child virtually masters Russian grammar, and the French child is expected to be on the right road to the same sort of achievement.

Several masterpieces of foreign children's literature from foreign countries appeared in French translation during this period. (*Eric or Little by Little*, 1918; Kipling's *Just So Stories*, 1912; Lewis Carroll's *Hunting of the Snark*, 1949.) But the nineteenth-century bestsellers such as Hans Christian Andersen's *Tales*, Madame Bruno's *Tour de France de Deux Enfants*, Hector Malet's sentimental *Sans Famille* and Louisa May Alcott's *Little Women* kept their place on the nursery shelf and were joined after 1927 by a remarkable indigenous series called the *Albums du Père Castor*.

Pierre Faucher, the originator of 'Father Beaver' was a teacher who gathered around him a group of story-tellers, psychologists and expert artist-illustrators who helped him to produce a series of three hundred and fifty albums which had a powerful influence on young French children. In order to create books which were for children and taken from children's real interests, not imposed on them by adult taste, Faucher experimented with an observational school for children between four and twelve. His series has been widely distributed in the *maternelles* where they were the agents of Faucher's serious purpose: to touch some of the deep chords in the child's emotional life, support his creative urge and foster his need for contact with every possible type of natural life around him. 'Father Beaver' and his books have been among the strongest influences on the cultural background of children in the French *maternelle*, and are probably unique in their combination of intelligent purpose and material success among children's books today.

Literary and Social Class

The standard French demanded of our *grands* in the *maternelle* is a middle-to-upper class literary language; tenses, moods and vocabulary test the child's attention and prepare some of them for their future career in *lycée* and university. These are likely to be children from highly literate (educogenic is the word we are trying to avoid) middle-class homes. Like their colleagues in Britain and the United States, French teachers are much concerned with the problem of social class and educational opportunity; Gilly's inquiries (1967) into the background of retarded primary pupils in the Paris region revealed that nearly six times the number of children from 'literate' homes (teachers, liberal professions, management) belonged to the labouring classes. 'From the end of their first year in compulsory education, children from poorer homes tend to be numerous among those who are 'kept down'. If the first year is too great a challenge for these children, the *maternelle* is likely to be asked to do more (despite staff shortages and unsatisfactory conditions) to prepare them for the intellectual work of primary school.

To expect the *maternelle* to remedy the defects of society is to ask too much, of course. Recent surveys have indicated that in spite of the presence of a highly literate, 'cultured' stratum in French society, the habit of book buying is comparatively restricted. French lending libraries, which are improving, it must be admitted, are nowhere as numerous, well-equipped, or accessible as libraries in Anglo-Saxon countries. (When we were visiting *maternelles* in the South of France, the local town, whose name is an international byword for art and artistry, was just opening its first municipal library. In Nice, conditions were overcrowded and chaotic.)

In one of the rare university studies of the question, a member of the University of Tours, André Mareuil, has emphasized the importance placed upon legends and fairytales in the *maternelle*. Quoting the opinion of Alain (a highly influential educational thinker of the 1930s, whose sister, interestingly enough, was principal of an *école maternelle*) and Van Gennep,[6] he attacks Madame Montessori for deploring the use of the fairytale at pre-school level. Montessori, with her insistence that the child's imagination should not be allowed too free a rein, stands at the opposite pole to the *maternelle*, which sees in these folk-sources of literary culture *'fortes et toniques vérités'* — truths both stimulating and substantial.

Educational research, much occupied, even in France, with relatively trivial investigations, has practically ignored the question of 'which culture in the nursery school?'. One or two professionals in other countries are beginning to show real concern at the weakness of our answers. For example, Lesley Webb in England asks almost the identical question posed by Monsieur Mareuil in the Tours article: 'We cannot, therefore, evade the question: What kind of society are we preparing them for?' If we are preparing them, through our literary culture of folktale and songs, for the society of the future (and showing considerable bias against working-class children, it seems) we need to ask whether the goal has been defined, and also whether this society will retain what we call human values. The vigorous and at times virulent debate in the United States about the 'structured' language programmes for disadvantaged children versus 'traditional' kindergartens appears to step into the soft grass verge of this problem, but slips away from it by bringing up the old bugaboo of intellectual gain. There is no culture, except IQ culture, Mr Bereiter seems to think, and pre-schools without IQ gain would be better called child-minding centres than educational places. He consequently dismisses the tens of thousands of kindergartens in the US from discussion of education. Yet it was to psychologists that Professor Wallon appealed at the College de France to indicate the form of society needed to assure man's development and dignity. One wonders where they will find replacements for the paradigms of nobility or generosity which both Froebel-inspired and French *maternelle* centres have found in this wealth of folk-story.

Expansion: The Maternelle Boom

After the end of World War II, France embarked on a voyage of reconstruction under the guidance of Jean Monnet; political changes in Paris intermittently slowed down the progress of the plan to re-build the economy afresh. At the time it seemed as if the northern part of the country needed to be rebuilt *in toto*: roads, ports, bridges, town-centres were all devastated by the armoured savagery of warfare. There was a shortage of teachers, and funds for education had to be allocated in the order of priority set down by economic experts. The primary schools, which had been boosted by the Third Republic in the 1880s, had to wait their turn while the *lycées* and higher education establishments were prepared to receive the cadres of a new society. But with the post-war years a new spirit of criticism pervaded the intellectual world which emerged in education as a movement for reform. Even now, thirty years afterwards, the process is by no means complete, and critics direct their campaigns against a rigorous system which was designed to provide 'a bourgeois minority with the loftiest academic disciplining in the world'.[7] Not only the selectivity, but the severity of a system which appeared to demand too much from children even in elementary school came under attack; health experts and teachers united to alleviate the work-load and time-table in elementary schools under the *tiers-temps*. The rigid series of examinations which harried young French boys and girls as early in their lives at ten and eleven years of age were attacked by an enlightened *inspectrice-générale*, even though examinations remain to this day, the valve by which the regime controls entrance into the powerful public service. The competitive nature of the outlets at school-leaving levels imposes considerable strain on the French youth-population at senior high schools when only a small percentage at the top end of the examination results is accepted for higher training and university entrance. Even the big increases in provision of universities which occurred after the events and protests of 1968 have not settled the problems involved in demands for change and reform.

In this turmoil of reform and reconstruction the *écoles maternelles* were not forgotten, and the arguments about their place in the Fourth Republic inevitably reverted to discussion of their dual function, both social and educational; the problem of the goal of 'ECE' was raised again when a national elementary education system had to be virtually rebuilt and a work-force accommodated to newly planned industry and housing. The 1950s and 1960s witnessed an astonishing expansion of pre-primary education in France, of which these figures give a clear indication: in 1948-9 there were just over 400,000 children in the *maternelles*, which was about the same number as in 1921. Ten years later, no less than 786,528 children attended the *maternelles* and the few *jardins d'enfants*. The enrolments and new buildings thereafter multiplied in startling fashion:

1958		786,528
1962		982,193
1966		1,214,688
1970	(estimated)	1,832,000

These figures do not include children in the *classes enfantines* section of elementary schools, whose numbers represented, in 1961-2 an additional 190,000 and in 1967-8 another 235,400. The total in the year 1971-2 would therefore rise to two millions in the public sector alone, representing children of both sexes between the ages of two and six; thus enrolments had almost doubled in the ten years after 1960 (when there were 878,450 in the *maternelles*).[8] By the mid-1980s, it was estimated in government circles, *all* children between two and six would be in attendance at some sort of school establishment.[9]

Other Countries

Making a brief comparison with some other European countries we may note that the Netherlands accommodated eighty per cent of her four-year-olds, Belgium ninety per cent, and Italy fifty per cent in 1970. The United Kingdom, according to an official circular issued late in 1972, offered nursery-school care to fewer than thirty-five per cent of the four-year-olds, and five per cent of her three-year-olds. The disparities are indeed wide, even in such a small area as Western Europe.

The social background of these three- and four-year-old *maternelle* pupils varies widely, and parents in comfortable circumstances use them as much as their fellow citizens in working-class suburbs. The role of the schools is not only dual, therefore (social and educational) but multiple, as its facilities become more widely known, and parents in easy circumstances are attracted by what the *maternelle* can offer as a first step in the important matter of education. The number of working mothers is difficult to estimate,[10] but changing conditions in big towns and cities, where mothers are frequently isolated from relations and grandparents by residence in apartment buildings, certainly favour the *maternelle*. Travelling about in a large town is now becoming increasingly difficult and shopping with one or two toddlers can be a mother's nightmare. A study carried out on four large housing projects in the Seine-et-Oise area adjacent to Paris is worth mentioning; it found that eight-five per cent of the population of small children attended nearby *maternelles*, but only two per cent of their mothers went to work. There has been a shift in attitude towards the *maternelle*, therefore, during the last fifty years; there is little or no stigma attached to the custom of depositing the three- and four-year-olds at school for the morning and afternoon session, and likely educational advantages have received more publicity in the last decade.

BRITAIN

> Nursery schools have as their primary object the physical
> and medical nurture of the debilitated child.
>
> Board of Education, 1936

> The Nursery school is first and foremost an educational
> institution, which takes *the whole child* for its province.
>
> Phoebe Cusden, 1938

The McMillans

Health and Nutrition in Bradford and the East End

After Robert Owen departed for Indiana and the Lancaster gallery
method took over in Britain, infant education, as we have seen, went
through the slough of despond. Except for the fortunate few, children
were neglected, crowded into infant schools for want of anywhere
better, prone to disease and malnutrition. The kindergarten, limited to
the fee-paying middle classes in general, was a privileged reserve; child
welfare in the broad sense had to await the battles fought almost
alone by the McMillan sisters, Rachel and Margaret, in Bradford and
London.

Curiously enough, the McMillans had an international background
which linked them with movements for improved services in hygiene
and nutrition in Europe. They had been taken to North America
when they were still young, but brought back to Scotland after their
father died. They both had a gift for languages and were well acquainted
acquainted with Séguin: Margaret studied music and languages in
Germany, Switzerland and France before working in London's West
End as a lady's companion. Like Pauline Kergomard, Ellen Key and
Maria Montessori, she believed in fighting for the rights of women,
but also joined the socialist movement and entered the lists on the
side of the working class. It is said that her fashionable lady employer
decided Margaret had to leave her service after being seen in Hyde
Park haranguing the Sunday crowd on behalf of striking dockworkers.

Margaret McMillan is a difficult figure to incorporate into the
story in a way; her personality had many facets, but it had not been
formed in classroom, college or hospital. She had insight and Celtic
charm, coupled with personal experience of poverty and suffering and
a burning devotion to the underdog in British society. Her reading

background was unusually wide for a young woman who was acceptable in polite drawing rooms of Mayfair and Belgravia.

She had mastered Rousseau, Pestalozzi, and Froebel. Karl Marx's *Das Kapital* she had read from cover to cover. She had ploughed through the works of neurologists like Donaldson and Lombroso, and of psychologists like Mosso and Claparède, and was familiar with almost every scientific textbook on mental deficiency from Séguin onwards.[1]

After her experience as a lady's companion, Margaret moved north to Bradford, joined the Fabians, worked as a Labour Party organizer and was elected to the city Schools Board, to fight the battle of the slum child. She considered that the condition of the poorer school children was worse than had ever been described, and wasted no time in campaigning for school medical inspection, then unheard-of, and school baths. Baths she succeeded in introducing at a school in Bradford, years if not decades before the rest of England followed the example, and although the achievement was a solitary one, it attracted a lot of publicity. Then she turned her attention to dietary deficiency, criticizing compulsory schooling for little children who had not been fed. The government, she pointed out 'does not compel parents to feed their children: hence it is certain that, to some of these hungry little ones, free education is less of a boon than an outrage'. The McMillans were true forerunners, who thought like the Continental reformers that cleanliness, health inspection and proper nourishment were the real bases of an intelligent education system. (Not until 1907 were local authorities obliged to provide for medical inspection of 5 year-olds.)

Overwork and ill-health compelled Margaret to give up the crusade in Bradford, and she returned to London where she was reunited with Rachel, who in the meantime had done the necessary training and become a health inspector in the nearby county of Kent. Facing the problem of sickness and unhygienic living conditions among poor children in the dockland East End, the two sisters determined to see what results sanitary surroundings and fresh air might have on slum dwellers suffering from rickets and other ailments. Their first open-air shelter camp was not the outcome of a spinsterish urge to do good among the street urchins; nor was it just well-meant philanthropy. The project grew out of Margaret's early work in Bradford, and was meant as a scientific experiment towards definite ends.

Deptford

After clinics had inspected numbers of sickly children in the East End
many were found to be in need of treatment, but no treatment was
forthcoming because of lack of interest or facilities. In 1910, with
boundless zeal and determination, the McMillans set up a clinic in
Deptford, helped by funds provided by an idealistic American soap
manufacturer. (The first government-authorized school clinic in
England owed its existence to their agitation.) It is with Deptford
that their name will always be linked, for the clinic became a nursery
school, and nearby now stands the training college named after Rachel
McMillan.

While a doctor and a nurse in attendance at the clinic operated
on twenty children each week for tonsillitis and adenoids, in other
rooms children were shown how to breathe properly, and exercises
were given to remedy deformed little spines. When they saw that some
of the good was undone when children returned home to wretched
overcrowding and infection, they persuaded some parents to leave
their daughters, aged between six and fourteen to stay a few nights,
sleeping in shelters put up for them in the garden. The garden soon
proved too small, and they moved into the churchyard of Saint
Nicholas next door, setting out the stretchers between the grave-
stones, an act of practical ingenuity which aroused some criticism
among the living residents of Deptford. But the sisters were used to
criticism, and found that the girls improved in health, for even this
environment was better than what their homes provided.

Partly by the force of practical observation and partly through the
theory of kindergarten education, with which they were well
acquainted, the McMillan sisters began to wonder if they could provide
any permanent benefit for these East End children without beginning
much earlier, in the toddling stage. Circumstances contrived, as before
in their crusades, to see their work begun within a comparatively
short period. The connecting link between the Night Camp and the
Nursery School to come was one of their girls, Maureen, with a baby
sister, Rosie.

One day when Maureen had finished making her bed and was
helping to lay the table for breakfast, a sudden thought struck her.
She slipped her hand into Margaret's and said wistfully, 'I don't
half wish our Rosie could come here and play. Wouldn't she love
the water and them marigolds and the pussy on the wall!'

Margaret looked down at the eager little face. 'How old is your

Rosie?' she asked. 'She's only a nipper, miss, just two – and she doesn't go to school yet. My mum says she's always under her feet.'

'When you have finished your breakfast, Maureen,' said Margaret, 'run home and ask your mother if you may bring Rosie here to spend the day. You can take her back this evening before you have your supper.'

When Rosie, stout, pale, curly-haired and running-nosed, arrived, it was, in a sense, the start of the open-air nursery school. Soon there were six children, housed in premises rented from the council at one shilling a year: within a month, there were thirty. The Open-Air Nursery School Movement had come into existence.

On warm evenings, after the bath, they would run in couples, these little three and four year-olds, down the length of the oblong shelter and back, rejoicing that there were no tables, no chairs, no rules to keep them any more from this new, strange, life and movement. They ran and ran, and would hardly stop running.

'What is this?' they seemed to say. 'The world is not a little room, it is not a pavement, it is not a classroom.' And they went on running.[2]

It is a moving experience to visit Deptford today, to see the imposing training school which became Rachel McMillan's memorial and the unpretentious, still-functioning nursery school between the roaring trunk highway to Woolwich and the churchyard where Christopher Marlowe was buried. There is a photograph of Margaret looking down from the wall, and one of Queen Mary visiting the children she befriended in the 1920s at Deptford. It is a reminder that the sisters had no private financial resources, and brought their dream to reality by their ability to convince others that something must be done.

The little school, like their earlier effort with the child clinic, was not an isolated individual attempt to act the philanthropic role among the poorer classes. The school was from the first for research and experiment – 'action is research' wrote Margaret McMillan – on the effects of poverty on child development.[3]

The open-air nursery school was not only a health centre, a sort of children's *Kurort*, in Margaret's opinion. Despite her Marxist reading and her shrewd Scottish commonsense, there was a strain approaching mysticism in the way she viewed the possibilities of these centres. In common with Oberlin, Froebel, and Montessori, she found scientific experiment was insufficient, and wrote of her hopes that the masses would find a force of intelligence awakening within, a force which was dormant in societies founded on slavery and privilege.

The McMillan theory of the value of the open air and sleep proved itself a success. Their children became resistant to illness in a neighbourhood prone to epidemics and deficiency diseases: when over seven hundred children between one and five died of measles, there was not one fatal case at the Deptford school. Rickets responded to treatment there more quickly than elsewhere, and when the children were examined on arrival at infant school, aged five, local medical officers reported that their health was better than that of children who had not attended. Thus the doctrine of fresh air, even though it was then the smog-filled air of the East End, became part of the English tradition in nursery and infant schools. Late in life Margaret wrote her philosophy of the nursery school, and criticized the idea of a large, strongly-built school for little children. The school of tomorrow, she said, 'will be a garden city of children . . . a place of many shelters — a township, if you will, of small schools built as one community, but with every shelter organized as a separate unit, designed to meet the needs of children of specific age or stage of life.' She rejected the infant schools of the twenties as efficient, comfortable, but unadventurous.

When World War I came, the sisters faced tremendous difficulties which were almost too much for them. They found that rich friends and sympathizers came down to help but seemed to melt away, or 'strange to say, they did not help us at all. It was as if they touched the work only to make ruinous explosions. A kind of moral chemistry, of which we were mere helpless witnesses, seemed to reveal itself,' remarked Margaret of this time.[4] Overworked and harassed by night bombing raids, they themselves suffered from illness. Their American benefactor, Mr Fels, died suddenly and all their resources seemed to dry up. Two sick and motherless boys, whose father was at the Front, had been left as boarders in their care. But in wartime money has been found more than once for children's care ventures, and a grant of sevenpence a day per child under five proved the Ministry of Labour's silver lining.

The Fisher Act, named after their friend and supporter, H.A.L. Fisher, was passed through Parliament in 1918, but Rachel had not lived to see the changes which followed this 'education' act. Half-time and employment under twelve was at last forbidden after a hundred years of misery and prosperity; the struggles for children's rights

appeared to be won at last. Local education authorities, under
Section 19 (a) were empowered to supply or aid supply of nursery
schools and nursery classes 'for children over two and under five . . .
and whose attendance at such a school is necessary or desirable for
their healthy physical and mental development.' The way lay open
for increasing the number of open-air nurseries, to improve the well-
being of the war babies, or so it seemed for a time. Yet economic crisis,
so frequently the excuse for an attack on education expenditure,
was invoked by the Geddes Committee to bar the way again to
nursery education in 1922.

Instead of sharing in the benefits of victory, nursery school
supporters in England found themselves forced to struggle once again
for public assistance. During this period they banded together to form
the Nursery School Association (1923) which produced thousands
of copies of pamphlets (200,000 in 1929 alone) with which it
attempted to convert flinty-hearted local councillors and the public at
large to the cause. The Froebel Society, after fifty years of worthy
activity, was finally recognized by the Board of Education in the 1920s,
which rounds off the strange history of Froebel-inspired organizations
and their treatment by governments after 1851, when Prussia banned
the kindergarten.

Child and Society

Outside the Schools

The social history of childhood was entering a new chapter in the
1920s, and many changes had begun to affect life before August
1914. The post-war world offered a confusion of old and new customs,
inventions and attitudes, all of which affected children in some
degree. The nineteenth century was a long time a-dying, but the
twentieth century did not arrive at a chronologically neat moment,
either. In one decade appeared inflation and depression, before a
child born before the Armistice had time to reach secondary school.
Household help and nursery maids disappeared from middle-class
homes and there were for a time jobs available for young women in
the post-war world. There were cheaper clothes, cheaper prams, and
the appearance of a cheap motorcar; mass-produced toys arrived from
Japan and sold in cheap stores. Parents went to the movies, did the
fox-trot, smoked more and more, and used the telephone as if it were
not a new-fangled disturber of the peace. Home movies, of course,
were the privilege of the well-to-do, so the under-fives were not

bombarded with entertainment until mass-produced television sets appeared many years later. But the influence of the cinema began to permeate the world of childhood in all sorts of ways, changing it as the motorcar changed the village streets and made them unsafe for children's play on the way to school.

The affluent had always been able to afford trainsets which were improved each birthday by adding signal-boxes, Pullman coaches, and fast locomotives. Now poor children came into their own when mass-produced toy cars, trucks, buses and tanks appeared on the market. Military equipment has succeeded to the sailor suits and cowboy outfits, of the twenties, which seem harmless enough in retrospect. Sub-machine guns, rocket-launchers and other basic items of terrorism are manufactured in quantities probably comparable with the exports of the 'real thing', so true it is that the obsessions of adults are transformed downwards to become the toys of children. We are following a long and unpraiseworthy tradition which goes back at least to the 'model guillotines' which were given, according to Goethe, to little patriots during the Revolution for the execution of toy aristocrats.[5] Parents who do have access to playgroups and nursery schools may learn the value of educational playthings, and not necessarily those complicated and expensive contraptions which require no greater effort from the child than pressing a button or winding up the clockwork.

In one respect British children were fortunate, if they lived in a family, that is, which was accustomed to read aloud. From the early nineteenth century books which were acceptable to little children began to appear, and reached a high standard even before *Alice in Wonderland* was written (admittedly, for children of reading age) in the 1860s. Our daughter, who is under five and cannot read by herself yet, keeps a special place on the table for *Little Black Sambo* which, the reference books tell me, was published first in 1899! The Beatrix Potter classics began to appear in the early twentieth century and a masterpiece arrived with Kenneth Graham's book about the adventures of little animals in the English countryside, *The Wind in the Willows* (1908). Story books for children became an industry in the 1930s and now thousands of new titles appear each year, although few writers can compete with Grahame, Kipling in his *Jungle Book* period, or A.A. Milne's adventures of Pooh Bear. There was, too, a one-way traffic in these classics across the Channel; the *maternelle* may have learnt little from the nursery-school, but French children revelled in the translations of English and American children's books which followed in the wake of Kipling (*Le Livre de la Jungle* was printed for a French audience before 1900), and Uncle Remus.

Artificial barriers and the propaganda prejudices of wartime blocked the interchange of ideas in 1914–1918. But 'the Armistice was soon followed by an outburst of creative energy' and the 'idealists, free at last to raise their voices, shouted their ideals from the housetops', as Goldring put it in his provocative study, *The Nineteen-Twenties*. Intellectuals, whether officers or other ranks, returned from the trenches with the determination to improve on what had been. The French officer-intellectuals who called themselves the *Compagnons de l'Université nouvelle* issued their manifesto in 1918 and this was paralleled by several experimental departures from tradition in England. Although 'the younger generation, as events proved, fatally misjudged the power, the astuteness and the solidarity of the old', in many, the ferment in educational thinking, which brewed about the yeast of 'progressive' ideas has not even now entirely settled. 'Educational ideas that seemed startling in 1914 are hardly likely to perturb the world of 1920' wrote one of the stalwarts optimistically, and although they did perturb and were rejected by the well-established British élite system of grammar and 'public' (meaning private) schools, the dust was not quick to settle.

1921 is a year one can take as a linkpost: the year when, in France, new regulations were issued for the *maternelle*; France, too, was host to an international conference called by a journal known as *The New Era* in Calais that year. The theme was 'the creative self-expression of the child', and a youthful A.S. Neill, later founder of Summerhill, spoke on one of his pet subjects: the abolition of authority. In London that year, Queen Mary opened the London County Council extension to the Deptford Nursery School and in characteristically negative mood the government warned of the need for economy and forbade new nursery schools 'except in special circumstances and on an experimental basis, where existing buildings are available'.

In the previous year, Percy Nunn's influential book *Education, its Data and First Principles* had been published, Susan Isaac's *Introduction to Psychology* came out in 1921, and from the conference at Calais was formed the international *New Education Fellowship*. This loosely-knit organization was open to anyone who subscribed to the journal which became known as *New Era* and was published in fine style, expensive print and paper with good illustrations and editions in French and German. Turning over the issues of *New Era* from 1920 onwards, one can feel the ferment in educational ideas and see how it was stimulated by interchange of ideas with other countries. Also one is struck by the way in which the new ideas came from sources close to early childhood education, and from there penetrated upwards into the stodgy classrooms of the adolescent, but slowly.

The first volume of the magazine, published in 1920 by Mrs Beatrice Ensor, had no less than four articles on Madame Montessori. It was co-edited by A.S. Neill, who stayed on the Continent after 1921 and sent back an enthusiastic article on the Dalcroze training in eurythmics in Dresden. The news of Décroly's discoveries in Brussels appeared in three articles in 1922: sex education for children was discussed, and the work of advanced schools on the Continent and the Institut Jean-Jacques Rousseau. Volume 4 discussed the Dalton Plan, based on the assignment system, and so successful in England — and elsewhere — that one writer later said that after its originator, Miss Helen Parkhurst, visited England in 1921 'Daltonism in some form or other broke out in school after school'.[6] It also 'broke out' in France and was applied experimentally in the *écoles maternelles*. Self government in the classroom was discussed, eurhythmics — which was beginning to penetrate the gymnastic classes in many schools, and Ferriere's *École Active*, based on hygiene and the 'culture of energy'. Dewey and also the Winnetka method were the subject of articles in 1926, Décroly returned to the journal in 1927 and throughout the twenties there was further treatment of Montessori and the Montessori movement.

The impact of Madame Montessori on England grew forcefully after her visit in 1919, when she was fêted at the Savoy Hotel, with H.A.L. Fisher in the chair. When she offered a training course in that year, there were one thousand applicants for three hundred places in London. She returned every second year and received considerable publicity, so that her influence penetrated far beyond early childhood education and affected even secondary education for a time. Clad in long robes which accorded with her dignity and magnetism, she seemed like the high priestess of some new cult. Her influence brought the child-centred revolution in education to the eyes of the public at large; she was cited with the kindergarten, Dewey, and the nursery school movement, in the Hadow Report (1933) as one of the main influences on teaching in infant classes.

Hadow

Prior to publication of the Hadow Report by the Board of Education in 1933, Susan Isaacs, Grace Owen, Dr Montessori, Arnold Gesell and

countless educators and medical advisers were consulted on the
history, practice and possible improvement of Infant and Nursery
Schools in Britain. An appendix contributed by Professor Harris, MD,
described anatomical and physiological characteristics and development
of children between the ages of two and seven; another, by Cyril Burt
and Susan Isaacs, offered an account of the emotional development
of children up to the age of seven plus.[7]

Carefully written, efficiently edited, and very well printed by
His Majesty's Stationery Office, the report is a standard work of
reference on both attitudes and achievements in early childhood
education. The Hadow Committee was only empowered to make
recommendation, of course, under the English system of administration, and it did advise school groups for the under-fives in rural areas
whenever practically possible, and gave its opinion 'that the nursery
school is a desirable adjunct to the national system of education'.
Moreover, it defined the purpose of schools for the under-fives in
these terms: 'The fundamental purpose of the nursery school or
class is to reproduce the healthy conditions of a good nursery in a
well-managed home, and thus to provide an environment in which the
health of the young child — physical, mental and moral — can be
safeguarded.' (Conclusion: para. 40.)

In the early twenties, officialdom had restricted admission to those
children for whom attendance was 'necessary or desirable for their
healthy physical and mental development'. The emphasis had been
on health, for so much of the McMillan gospel had penetrated to the
official mind, but no more. The question of the fate of children under
five, it was said in 1919, was primarily one of health, and only
'incidentally' one of education.[8] At the time there were plenty of
day nurseries where the children were kept sitting in their places,
correctly clothed and still. Their health was being preserved from
contact with disease in the street, but as a means of generating rickets,
one reporter commented that this treatment could hardly be bettered,
and if the children could be kept from being run over, they would be
better in the gutter.[9] Because of their role, which was considered to
be a socio-sanitary one, Hadow admitted that nursery schools
recognized for grant 'have only been provided in crowded urban areas
where housing conditions are unsatisfactory' (para. 22, p. 42). For
many years to come, the survival of slum conditions in Britain
reinforced this attitude, which drew empirical support from the
evidence of medical inspections in elementary schools. Paradoxically,
the high standards laid down by regulation to govern the design and

staffing of nursery schools helped to defeat the main object, as the cost — even after the Geddes axe had been lifted — deterrred authorities from constructing them.

Under simplified regulations issued in 1925 and 1929 (when the Ministry of Health co-operated in the production), the authorities recognized the feasibility of much larger schools, containing provision for 150 to 200 children. They must give children the opportunity for rest, meals and recreation; part of their responsibility was to attend to the health, nourishment and physical well-being of the child. The joint circular of 1929 revealed the influence of the new ideas which had spread through progressive circles in education during the post World War I period. It was at last admitted that the purpose of the nursery school was twofold: *nurture* and *education*. The whole and undivided personality of the child was at last to be considered worthy of attention below the age of five, and, as Miss Grace Owen had pointed out in the previous year, British schools would realize that the relations between the mental and emotional life of the child were so close and subtle that 'one of the pitfalls most to be avoided is that of allowing a little child's education to fall into compartments each dealt with separately'.[10]

Self-portraits of some typical centres which shared in what has been called 'the warm simplicity of the early nursery schools' were printed in the *New Era* late in the twenties. They provide a valuable reminder of the heroic work being done by a few in scattered places up and down the country, and also convey an impression of contemporary attitudes inside the movement.

There was the Princeville Nursery School in Bradford which had four rooms opening on to a verandah and a garden, where the day began with a bath and then activity in the garden. Flowers were plucked and placed in jars, windows cleaned, a doll's house swept and dusted. The baby's nervous system was induced to respond to colour, sound, rhythm, form, and touch, developing his motor and sensory power through auto-activity. This activity was neither 'kindergarten nor play school, nor games and pretty employments devised by the teacher', said the manifesto. It followed the line of physical and physio-logical development by the child, and was, in that sense, systematic.

There was a nursery school in Sutton, a poor suburb of London, which had grown from a free kindergarten begun by a local resident, with five children. It now looked after 125 children in airy premises with a big garden. Youngsters who arrived delicate and listless soon developed into healthy vigorous children.

In Derby, there were 80 children under a trained Superintendent
with a special qualification for nursery school work.

It is not all play. This little girl so carefully carrying a plate of
soup to another child at the dinner table is learning control of
limbs and body, and also to supply another's need before her
own. This group of bairns so joyously doing rhythmical exercises
to music is learning to *listen*. In the yard are sand-pit, see-saw,
rib-stalls, rabbit hutches, toy house.

Birmingham had a nursery class attached to a Council Infants'
School, taking thirty-four children from one of the worst city slum
areas. 'The selection of the children is one of the greatest problems.
There is a long waiting list and the claims of the child whose sole
home consists of a top attic have to be weighed with those of another
whose mother is dying of cancer in a back-street house.'

Children from poor streets were taken to Fairfield, Darlington,
by bus. About seventy children between two and five attended daily,
were given brown bread and butter and milk for lunch and a hot
dinner followed by sleep. Montessori principles were followed
(as they were in other nursery schools at this time) in training the
senses, but, in spite of the good surroundings and equipment, it
seems as if Fairfield's main task was to restore the children's health.
'On admission, many are found to be suffering from rickets, enlarge-
ment of tonsils and adenoids, defective vision and general pre-tubercular
conditions of the chest and glands.' Weekly visits were paid to this
school by the doctor (who was presumably paid by the British and
Foreign School Society, the owners of the school and a nearby training
college). Each child was given cod liver oil daily and a large number
had Parrish's chemical food in addition. Special cases were given sun
treatment and massage. When they reached school age, most of the
children were completely cured. Records of health, monthly weights
and home conditions were kept: not surprisingly, there was a long
waiting list for admission to schools such as these.

Finally, there is the enthusiastic contribution of a staff-member
(one suspects) at the Sun Babies Home, Hoxton, London:

Hoxton! Half-open shelters, painted orange, round a very green
lawn! At one end, before the main building, a flower bed with
plants for study; at the other a gaily paved play-place with ladders
that may be climbed. The day nursery babies are in their cots or

round their kidney-shaped little tables; the school children (four
and five years) in orange and blue overalls, are busy with Montessori
apparatus or with toys.

Over (but never above) the day nursery is matron, helped in
complete liaison by the nursery school teacher (trained in Australia),
who is assistant matron and lives in with the nurses. She is
responsible for the health and training of fifty-odd people from
nought to five years old and of a staff of seventeen, some of whom
are probationers whom she trains. She is also storekeeper, account-
ant, secretary, administrator of violet rays, friend and adviser to
mothers, hostess to many visitors, idealist and practical business
woman!

The nursery is a training centre for nurses, the course being two
years, and there is now a psychotherapist on its committee.
Systematic psychological and physiological records of the children
are kept.

The Development of Theory: Susan Isaacs and Geoffrey Pyke

Encouraged by the 'winds of change' which were blowing across
England, some intelligent and independent-thinking educators began
new schools, along progressive lines, where experiment with freedom
of decision, self-government, unconventional time-tables and fluid
rather than rigid authority-patterns was encouraged. One of these
was the Malting House School, a small venture at Cambridge begun
by a brilliantly gifted young financier who was interested in education
and the new psychology on childhood, Geoffrey Pyke.

A small number of children between two and a half and ten and a
half, intellectually gifted above the average, some of them 'disturbed',
were enrolled by their parents at Pyke's school. Science equipment
included a laboratory with bunsen burners, tripods, flasks, and the
rest, dissecting instruments and anatomical diagrams. The Montessori
aids were used, Linay number apparatus, and material from the *Maison
des Petits* in Geneva. Pyke paid a large salary to the science master, who
came from the United States with high qualifications. There was a
garden with a sandpit and 'Jungle-gym' climbing cage, a variety of
animals, an aquarium, and a wormery. Within the building the rooms
(apart from the 'lab') were filled with tools and materials which the
staff thought might interest the children, and when they arrived,
they found that they were free to wander about and take up whatever
pursuit attracted them. An exception were the 'quiet' rooms, and those

fixed times set aside for the teacher of eurhythmics.

At Malting House, Pyke engaged teachers who were prepared to follow the children's choice of occupation, develop any spontaneous interest shown by them and observe their reactions and progress. There was little formal discipline (in which of course this school was not unique) and they could smoke, or play with water and fire. When Pyke had a film team down to record the activity of the pupils, a bonfire was being used as centre of interest in a free-play exercise. It was such a success that it spread across the garden and into the trees on the boundary, destroying a moored boat before it was curbed.

Obviously, the principal of such a school as this had to have special qualities, and Pyke also wanted — and advertised for — someone with high qualifications and readiness to study the development of the individual child as it progressed through the school. Susan Isaacs (born Susan Fairhurst of a large family in the Midlands) was then thirty-nine. She accepted the post and, remaining for several years at Cambridge, filled notebooks with the observations later included in her two important books, which were completed after she had left the school and it had closed down for lack of finance. They were: *Intellectual Growth in Young Children*[11] and its successor, *Social Development in Young Children.*[12]

Susan Isaacs combined the zeal and humanity of the McMillans with a considerable, and unusual, background of study. Her mother had died when she was six and so, like Margaret McMillan, Pauline Kergomard and Froebel himself, she had been brought up by older siblings and a single parent, her father. The family was not very well off, and so she had to make her way into some occupation or other which would keep her in life. But her father barred her way to the university in Manchester on some vaguely religious prejudice which diverted her studies from the paths to which she was drawn. This is not without significance for our story, because it meant that she was introduced to the idea of teaching as an alternative career, met someone of central importance in the infant school movement, Miss Grace Owen, and went through the preparation of teacher training before she managed to enter Manchester University with Miss Owen's help.

At the university her intelligence was recognized as exceptional; she read philosophy under Professor Alexander, and went on to do psychological research at Cambridge after winning a scholarship for one year. Before going to join Geoffrey Pyke's school she had, in fact, lectured in infant-school education, taken university extension groups for discussion of psychology in London, and published her

Introduction to Psychology. She thus had a wide personal background of experience, knowledge of Froebel and other basic theorists, and a growing mastery of the fashionable subject of the epoch: psychology and psycho-analysis. At the training college in Darlington she had, however, insisted that her students begin their study of child psychology by a thorough grounding in biology; her writings bear witness that she was no impractical theorist, but open to suggestion and ready to admit herself at fault in her conclusions.

The brief life of the Malting House School gave Susan Isaacs a chance to set down her observations of individual development, discuss what was happening with her colleagues and fellow psychologists, and follow up the individual record through from year to year. With the McMillans and the other pioneers, nursery education had been put on firm ground through their well-balanced proportions of physical and personal education. It had been done through inspiration based on the nineteenth-century message of Froebel, Séguin and others. But it lacked a national basis of research, experiment and scientific authority. Pyke was well aware of the work being done by Jean Piaget, and helped to bring the Swiss expert to England, where he visited Malting House. Susan Isaacs, although critical of some aspects of her work, was equally aware of the valuable lessons being imparted to the educational world by Montessori, and used her material at the school. With her second husband, Nathan Isaacs, a lifelong student of psychology who wrote commentaries on Piaget's findings, they made a formidable team at Malting House, a sort of Brains Trust in early childhood education!

When the school collapsed, Susan Isaacs was drawn towards professional work in psycho-analysis, for which she had qualified herself in the twenties. But some people discerned the immense potential value of her work on child development, and persuaded her — and the University of London — to arrange a course in the study of young children which she directed from 1933 to 1943. Thus her knowledge and scientific approach were not lost, but helped to train a generation of graduates in education whose influence was then felt in primary schools and training colleges. So, for a time, child development studies and research bade fair to become accepted in the world of learning.

Reflecting on her experience in school and laboratory, Susan Isaacs wrote in 1937, summing up:

If we were asked to mention one supreme psychological need of the young child, the answer would have to be 'play' — the opportunity for free play in its various forms. The child needs the opportunity for imaginative play, which should be free and un-hampered by adult rules and regulations; he will use it to solve problems by magic, to create playmates or brothers and sisters for companionship, to become a person he has invented, or an animal, to dress up and people his world with different characters of fantasy.[13]

On the question of hygiene, so important to Ferrière and to the founders of the *maternelles* in France, it is interesting to compare Susan Isaacs on Malting House, where there was a lot of outdoor work, messy activities, like modelling and painting, and gardening, all of it incompatible 'with much attention to cleanliness for the mere sake of appearance. But they were asked to wash their hands before each meal, as a matter of course'. There was no emphasis on formal discipline, so it comes as rather a surprise to learn that on this subject Susan Isaacs was something of a traditionalist: when resistance was encountered, command was used in the last resort.

Like any other intelligent teacher, she was able to learn from her pupils, and what she saw at Malting House led her away from permissive positions towards a compromise between traditional rigid rules and liberty. (She was herself changing under the process of psycho-analysis, and, when she came to write about the school experience, had begun to practise clinical therapy.) The Super-Ego was inevitably part of the child's make-up, she had come to believe, and conflict stemmed from uncertainty about the child's own destructive potential. She wanted him to be reassured with firm but kindly control which would 'represent to him a stable and ordered world of values'.

One of her fellow workers at the school, Evelyn Lawrence, said that she there recognized 'the young child's need for order and stability, for adult support of his loving and constructive impulses against his own hate and aggression'.[14] This did not mean that, thereafter, she joined the old school of conservative 'spare the rod and spoil the child' experts whose influence in England has always been strong, for she felt that most schools begrudged sufficient freedom to the child.

By her published writings in the 1930s and her increasing reputation as a lecturer and authority on child development, Susan Isaacs helped to give the nursery school movement — which she supported energetically — intellectual prestige and a theoretical background which was lacking since the decline in Froebel-based studies. Of course many nursery schools were health-oriented, and indeed had little time to spare on psychology when managing a hundred infants in cramped urban conditions. But her ideas were disseminated by her students who became, many of them, college lecturers, and in their turn trained the leaders of the following generation. (One of them told me how much she owed to her lecturer, Miss D.E. M. Gardner, who had herself been a student at London with Susan Isaacs.) In this way the English nursery schools acquired native characteristics which drew on sources such as Froebel, the open-air schools and Montessori, without confining their style to any one of these.

Susan Isaacs, herself childless, believed, with Pauline Kergomard, that a nursery school was not in its essence a substitute for a good home. Yet she considered that it possessed the following advantages:

1. It is a bridge between home and the larger world.

2. It helps the older child of two or three who suddenly finds a new baby in the home, because he can make his own friends and have his own life.

3. Even in an ideal home at the end of third year a child needs more companionship from other children.

4. Space is offered which is only available in wealthy families.

5. Instead of random toys picked from a commercial toyshop, appropriate play material for each phase of growth can be provided by a nursery school teacher.

6. Skilled help with child's efforts to learn and understand, with anti-social impulses, with defiance or quarrelsome behaviour and the home problems which are its source can be provided, and even mothers sometimes assisted to gain further insight.

7. Companionship and wider contacts help to 'lessen the pressure of feeling in the child's relation to his own parents and to his brothers and sisters', so making for a balance and harmony in the whole development.[15]

The emphasis is on adjustment to society and achievement of balance and control over anti-social outbursts through play, expert assistance, and care. In only one item is there a hint of intellectual development and there is no suggestion of any responsibility towards the first stage in book-learning or the 'three Rs'.

Provision in Britain: The Reasons for Inaction

The sympathy, infrequently expressed, of the political parties, the pressure exerted by the Nursery Schools Association, and the needs of mothers and children failed to overcome the difficulty of financial shortages during the depression years. This was curiously in contrast to policy in the United States of America and other countries where provision increased and relieved part of the problems of parents during the recession years. At the end of the 1930s (despite a token of further official support in Circular 1444) schools were still few and (geographically) far between in Britain. There were forty schools maintained by local education authorities and forty-five voluntary schools which received grants from the Board of Education. Only twenty-six local authorities (out of three hundred and sixteen) had assumed responsibility for nursery schools, and even with a falling birth-rate, less than one-tenth of the total two to five age-group were on the registers of public elementary schools. Most of those were over four years of age. including what are called in England the 'rising-fives' — children whose fifth birthday overlaps the school calendar — and therefore were contained in classes, not in proper independent nursery schools.

The bare figures indicated a drop in the percentage of school attenders even in comparison with 1919-1920, and more than one million and a quarter children were not in pre-school care of any description. Public interest had been aroused in some quarters which were intellectually influential rather than numerous, and the Board of Education had sympathetically approved proposals to build thirty-four more nursery schools. Clearly, the infiltration of progressive ideas, the improvement in medical services and attention to dietary deficiencies had done much to improve the lot of school children in the areas where local authorities had taken up their responsibilities: but these were lamentably few. The presence of nursery schools was too rare to be remarked by the population as a whole, and this after thirty years of effort.

England has always baffled analysis, and social historians do not find clear-cut solutions any more than political experts or election predictors. Or not those which are expected. Having reached a high point of nursery schools at the time of Munich, one would expect numbers to remain static or even decline as a result of war expenditure, lack of staff, priorities in other directions. The opposite was the case, and where we have seen our total creep hesitantly up by an increase annually of two or three new nursery schools during the thirties, wartime conditions resulted in a leap forward of hundreds. No statistics were kept during the war, so we are confronted with the remarkable figure of 370 maintained schools which, with 41 voluntary schools, looked after more than 90,000 under-fives. Had this rate of increase been maintained, or nearly so, there might be between 1200 and 1500 nursery schools in Britain now. There are, in fact, 500 and a total of about 270,000 pre-school age children attend both infant departments and nursery schools. Yet the population of this age-group in 1970 was around two and a half *million*.

The admirable sociological study by Tessa Blackstone still leaves us in the dark about the underlying causes of inaction in England. It did appear that the rural agricultural areas of south-western and eastern England were among the most barren of pre-school provision; the presence of patches of heavy industry within these regions accentuated the problem without explaining it. High provision, such as there was, occurred in industrial towns, particularly in the Midlands and the North. (London by virtue of its long history of liberal concern for welfare, and its connection with Buchanan and Wilderspin is a rather special case.) While warning of the possible inaccuracy of drawing conclusions at this stage of research, Dr Blackstone remarked that in one county 'those who hold negative attitudes tend to be men, elderly or in late middle age, Conservative and opposed to expanding the social services'.[16]

Others were able to point to the general improvement in living conditions and, falling back on the laissez-faire arguments which have proved their worth in halting change, say that mothers now could mind their offspring in decent homes. 'Today, thanks to better housing, the suburban garden, much more liberal provision of open spaces, the spread of labour-saving devices in the homes of the people and the ubiquitous pram, a much more sensibly educated generation of young mothers can much more readily keep their children at home until they are five'.[17]

Population change and other factors were to disprove these complacent observations after the war. The nursery-school movement, which had evolved a model institution for development of *the whole child*, seems to have been the product of an advanced social conscience still all-too-rare in Britain.

Britain had by the 1940s established her principles for the nursery-school, based mainly on the Continental tradition of the whole child as interpreted and adapted to local needs by the McMillans. Some important additions and alterations were indicated by the Hadow Report and the influence of Susan Isaacs. After World War II a medical consultant to the World Health Organization, John Bowlby, compiled an important report for WHO on visits to France, the Netherlands, Sweden, Switzerland and the United States as well as his native Britain, so producing one of the few comparative studies of childhood available in the 1950s.[18] *Child Care and the Growth of Love*, which has been through a number of editions, graphically brought before the public the plight of children deprived of a dependable relationship with their mother.

Bowlby collected in this report a mass of evidence to show that much much delinquency and severe disturbance came from a lack of maternal affection and attention during the first three years of life. Research in the USA and in Britain led to the same conclusions, and there was no longer doubt that 'the prolonged deprivation of a young child of maternal care may have grave and far-reaching effects on his character and so on the whole of his future life'. Moreover, impaired intellectual development, motor skills and language accompany deprivation in early childhood. One study quoted by Bowlby was of seventy-five babies reared in families during their first year of life. The institutionalized babies were slow in acquiring head control, in sitting erect, standing and walking. There was backwardness in vocal behaviour early and this became more noticeable, with the babies in institutions slow to talk. They did not show signs of developing an attachment to any nurse, did not develop a sense of trust or seek help from adults when they needed it. Toys did not interest them very much, they did not seem to mind when toys were lost, and they seldom played spontaneously with them. 'Affectionless characters,' as Bowlby called them, were in the making. Children in hospitals for treatment also have shown signs of disturbance at separation from their parents, and this is most marked in children between two and four.

It was not Bowlby's intention to formulate empirical laws; he hoped that research would alter his findings rapidly and drastically, and in accordance with that belief the conclusions of recent research were added to the book to show where, if anywhere, the observations he had recorded had been criticised or their implications queried. Even in the first edition it was pointed out that, although the evil consequences of deprivation were now obvious, the question of *how much* deprivation children of different ages can withstand had not yet been determined.

There was a further question about the age at which infants were worst affected by mother loss. Bowlby inclined to the view that the worst effects accompanied loss after the age of six months and Anna Freud agreed with him. But work done by Goldfarb on adolescents who showed social maladjustments led clearly back to indicate special danger in a child's first year rather than in later ones. Variations in the extent of damage done were shown in later research and led to re-examination of the mother's role: was it necessary to limit foster-mothering to one individual, or could a succession of substitute figures care for the child without more serious harm being done? In

some American universities where students are trained in home management, babies are cared for by a succession of students, each one for a
few days only, and eventually go to foster-homes of adoptive parents.
One follow-up study of children such as these who had entered foster
homes and then been adopted at twelve months was made when the
children were up to fifteen years older. On tests of ability and personality, there did not seem to be any significant difference between the
motherless group and the control group which had been brought up in
a family. But the test did not indicate, and was unable to estimate, the
capacity of the children for affection and relationships with others.
Much more work will have to be done on this, and until it is done most
of the evidence will obviously come from negative symptoms and
exhibitions of violent, anti-social or delinquent behaviour after early
childhood.

The position of the mother was investigated and the child-mother
relationship queried by the anthropologist, Margaret Mead, who
suggested that, in some cultures other than Western European, care is
diffused among several figures and so the severe trauma consequent on
loss of the single mother figure is mitigated. It was not, however,
Bowlby's position that only the natural mother could prove adequate,
but only that a major mother figure was desirable, assisted wherever
possible by other figures including a father figure.[19]

The fact was, that the only scientific observation of experimental
child rearing was reported from Israel, where the care of the natural
mother is replaced by that of the *metapelet* in the *kibbutz*. After the
child has been weaned, he is removed from the parents, but not
completely. There is a daily visit to the parents' room which may last
for a few hours, and more on Sundays. The children spend most of
their time in the 'Children's House', and this can, in some cases, begin
on the fourth day when he joins about twenty others in the care of a
metapelet and her helper. During the first six months of life the infant
remains in the 'Children's House', where he may receive the mother's
visits; the toddlers' house is the next step some time during his second
year, and between three and a half and four there is a further shift to
the kindergarten house.[20]

Israeli children raised in this way were reported to be free of the
disturbing features of, for instance, adolescent life in America. There
were no drop-outs, no youths who found life pointless and they became
(according to Albert I. Rabin in 1958) hard-working, responsible
citizens. Thus the Israeli experience seems to deny Bowlby's findings
unless we examine carefully what in fact he said about the *kibbutz*

method. Quoting the Lasker Child Guidance Centre in Jerusalem, he pointed out that there is no certainty that children do not suffer from the separation, that the separation is not complete and the child sees enough of its parents to establish a close relationship, and that there have been signs that the separation is being modified as mothers bring pressure to bear so that they can see more of their children. It may be too early to judge the long-term effects of the *kibbutz* system on the security, affections, and social outlook of the adolescent and grown man or woman. One of the complicating factors is that group life in the *kibbutz*, the communal outlook and strong morale probably served to modify the effects of separation at infancy for the adolescents. The importance of the experiment hardly needs to be emphasized and one Jewish psychologist described it as the 'most unique contribution' of the *kibbutz* to present-day society.

Dr Bowlby's first book may not have developed his themes of the importance of attachment and separation to the human animal as thoroughly as the author wished; but such a long period elapsed before publication of *Attachment and Loss* in 1969, that the evidence and arguments he produced in *Child Care* influenced a generation of practitioners in nursery school education, and also, incidentally, caused a review of the whole basis of Western institutionalized care for children, the sick and the elderly. In Britain, it served to underline the importance of the mother's participation in early childhood education, and to lead students to query whether children at five should be kept away from home for a whole day. What was the optimum time a child could spend in a nursery school? How closely could a mother co-operate with the teachers? These questions acquired a more intense significance after Bowlby's *Child Care* appeared.[*]

In the school, experiments were made to repalce the full day with either morning or afternoon sessions in order to overcome the child's first school-phobia and separation worries. A colleague of Bowlby made a film on infants admitted to hospital (*A Two-Year-Old goes to Hospital*, J. Robertson, 1952) which had a considerable impact on the medical world and laymen alike. Largely as a result of this work, hospital authorities were brought to admit the need for parents to

---

[*] After time had passed there was some criticism of 'methodological flaws' in some studies collected by Bowlby in his monograph for WHO. This seems to be endemic in research on psychology; at least since 1878, when G.S. Hall described the great Wundt's experiments at Leipzig as 'utterly unreliable and defective in method'. Progress in this area seems to be made in spite of methodology. There are both critics and admirers of Bowlby as there have been of other pathfinders in child studies.

visit their infants daily after admission, and in some cases, to stay with them overnight. During the 1950s and 60s, therefore, child-parent relations assumed a new importance at about the same time as researchers in North America were investigating the effect on orphans of a relationship with older girls in an institution. Another significant step forward had been made to break the research fashion of examining children in isolation from their loved ones and the environment around them.

After the Second World War, provision of nursery schools slackened to a halt in Britain. Nineteenth-century social injustice and the 'assumption of grinding poverty' itself were out of date in an affluent society, which could afford to create the welfare state. Even during wartime, day nurseries had been neglected by the authorities, and the Health Ministry recommended in a circular that little children should stay at home with their parents. The circular did not explain how, in material terms, working mothers and single-parent families could provide for this. Despite what Lord Butler said in 1944 (and Hadow had said in 1933) there was comparative stagnation after 1952.[21] Circular 8/60, of 1960, put an end to the construction of new nursery schools for the time.

Better homes, and more of them, there may have been, but social critics were dissatisfied with the space available for children at play. Alleyways and slum courtyards had not disappeared from London and other cities; for those fortunate enough to have been re-housed in flats, there were other problems. Children confined in new blocks of high-rise flats had not been given enough play space, let alone green grassland.[22] Enviously, social workers looked at the example of Copenhagen, where building regulations laid it down that play space must have priority over car space.

In an overcrowded island, there had been a shortage of play space, unfortunately, before motorcars became part of the general public's way of life. There were, however, open spaces which appeared in the wake of industrial development and Holme and Massie point out that demolition sites and old bomb sites could be used for off-the-street playgrounds.[23] Once again, Denmark showed the way with mobile playgrounds which could be erected on building sites as they became available. School playgrounds are left open and idle during much of the day and holiday time; dismal surroundings in their way, but better than nothing for city children hounded by lorries and cars. Investigating nineteen separate boroughs, it was found that just under half of a given sample did in fact possess

WCs. Only forty-three had washbasins, and many playgrounds had a WC, but could not claim it was clean. 'By any standards,' commented the authors in a very commendable spirit of moderation, 'this is shocking.'

Provision for the under-fives was found to be minimal in many boroughs. Six had no local authority day nursery at all: fifteen out of thirty-six areas reviewed had none, while eleven had one local authority nursery, seven had two, two had three and one had four. The general picture displayed one day nursery for 7,957 children at worst, and one day nursery for 1,460 children at best.

Not everyone accepted this situation without protest: two interested groups formed of teachers and parents decided independently to do something to disturb the general complacency. The National Union of Teachers reported from the answers of teachers in two hundred and sixty nursery schools and four hundred primary schools containing infant classes. This piece of research gained wide publicity and some brittle questions were raised in debate in the House of Commons as a result.[24]

Four-fifths of the respondents were satisfied with plumbing and hot-water facilities (which meant that fifty or more schools were sub-standard in this respect). Many complained that buildings in use were wartime structures put up as a 'temporary' expedient in a national emergency. These shabby structures had outlived their planners' intentions some years before, and despite heroic efforts to repaint the fabric and brighten the interiors they offered the the public a third-rate image of early childhood education. Long waiting lists still existed, just as they had in the thirties, and principals were forced to discriminate between deserving cases. Eighty per cent of the nursery schools were in areas described as mainly or entirely working-class and less than five per cent were in mainly or wholly middle-class districts. Thus the local government-supported school was still to a large extent regarded as meeting a social and sanitary emergency rather than as an essential educational unit for the child's development. In the middle-class areas, independent, fee-paying nursery schools increased in number during the 1950s and 60s, revealing the growing interest in early childhood education among those who could afford to buy it.

Tired of official inaction, one mother decided to form a 'play-group' for the sake of her own child, and wrote to the *Guardian* newspaper about it, First in their hundreds, and then in their thousands, mothers and sympathizers all over the country took up the idea which has grown from this grassroots beginning to become the pre-school playgroup movement in Britain. This voluntary enterprise defined its unit as a group of six to thirty children aged between two and a half and five who 'play together regularly'. The sessions are usually half-days, which may be arranged (when there are volunteer mothers to help) thrice weekly. A private house or an empty village hall served as the 'school': while one or two parents served full-time in supervision, they co-opted mothers of their 'pupils' on a roster basis. Toys and play-materials were lacking but eventually appeared; grudging approval of parish and local authority was given. Central government, seeing the speed with which the movement grew and the self-help principle which excused authorities from heavy expenditure, became interested and finally benevolent.

By 1967, there were about 3,200 playgroups established in England and Wales with 80,000 children in attendance. The Pre-School Playgroups Association estimated in 1969 that this figure had grown to 116,000 and was still increasing; in 1974, an estimated 250,000 children who would otherwise have been confined to their houses or flats in wintertime were given hours of social mixing and joyful and noisy *play*.

The Department of Education and Science made a grant of £3,000 a year from 1967 to the new association, valid for three years. A national adviser was appointed who managed to organize an office, conduct a survey of needs and achievements and issue a report which broke new ground by offering information and advice to mothers and tutor-helpers in the movement. A national organization was planned, with regional advisers to help with the practical problems of running a new adventure in early childhood.

Other government departments were attracted to the idea, and the Secretary of State for Social Services gave evidence of practical faith in the PPA by announcing a grant for a national headquarters and an annual subsidy of £45,000. Then the Urban Programme was set up to assist dwellers in deprived, or 'twilight' areas, and it had contributed £250,000 by 1971 for playgroups and playgroup-advisers. Local authorities, always slow to move, especially in rural zones of Britain, made widely varying grants of money from as little as £25 to as much as £9,000.

When the movement began, it earned the reproaches of older-established organizations for its middle-class background and it was rightly pointed out that it could not compare for efficiency with properly-run nursery schools headed and staffed by trained personnel.

Yet it was precisely in middle-class areas that, according to the National Union of Teachers, there was little nursery school activity: it was a new, exciting trend — why should its class background be held against it when so many children were being helped?

In many playgroups the staff is untrained, but as early as 1965 a survey revealed that fifty-three per cent were run by a qualified supervisor, and eighty-one per cent had a qualified supervisor, or assistant, or contact with a qualified person as adviser. Mothers who help the groups have had experience and training of a sort in their own households; what are needed are more part-time courses and visits from area organizers.

An advantage of the playgroup movement is that mothers and the neighbourhood become involved, talk about early childhood and are asked to act on its behalf. Whether middle-class or not in its origins, there is hope that it may extend throughout the country. In one poorer part of Glasgow there were, in 1972, fourteen playgroups, and in one Scottish county thirty-five per cent of the relevant age-group attended.[25] This is little less than remarkable when we consider how short a time the movement has had in which to grow, and how diminutive is the national over-all average of only *five per cent* of three-year-olds in nursery schools.[26]

When the Urban Programme received an application from the medical officer of health in the London Borough of Southwark, it made a grant sufficient to start no less than twenty playgroups in the borough. The education authority meanwhile allocated a large sum to set up nine new nursery classes in primary schools. This effort was observed and reported on by the National Children's Bureau at government request, after its inception in 1970, in order to see whether funds were being spent effectively in an 'area of social deprivation'.

After twenty months' study, the conclusions were favourable to the cause; mothers and children were benefiting from this new approach to family problems in a deprived area. But perhaps the most interesting feature of the report was not in its broad conclusion, but in the ancillary questions which were asked by the researchers. Mother participation, it was suggested, might become a fundamental condition of grant aid. Further, the contrast between the way playgroup leaders had learned (at courses provided by the PPA) to handle children, and the way some mothers did so emphasized an urgent need for more discussion, seminars or meetings and information for mothers.

The closing of playgroups for twelve weeks of the year at holiday times was also queried, for it seemed to leave mothers in deprived

areas without a refuge just at the time when they were burdened
with duties.

One interesting question was put to supervisors. How did they
select a child when a vacancy occurred? Did they choose the top name
on the waiting list, the oldest, or one in special need? Groups expressed
reservations about accepting children with special needs, because their
attendance was likely to be short, erratic, and mother participation
was often minimal. Under half said they would accept a child who was
not 'toilet-trained'.

The playgroup movement is still in its first act and the next ten
years will show if it can make up some of the ground lost by inaction
or opposition to the claims of early childhood. Its practical progress
has been remarkable, and the assistance given it by several ministries
augurs well for future financial needs. The involvement of parents
could lead to a long-term change in attitudes by the public and has
already shown how educational ideas can be regenerated from outside
the system.[27]

In many places the playgroup movement is like the early rush of
assistance in a famine-relief project; it is enthusiastic, well-meaning,
and not terribly efficient. The concept of total care for a child's
well-being will require a degree of organization and co-operation
between local authorities and the community which is now non-
existent. But the playgroup movement is teeming with ideas, and
already expanding downwards. Thus in some areas, 'Toddlers' Clubs'
encourage mothers to begin meeting and learning by informal
discussion with their under-three and under-two-year-olds playing or
crawling around the rented hall or borrowed home floors. The
response was overwhelming in many places, and in a southern county
'hordes of women descended on an initial meeting with babies from a
month upwards. The Catholic priest, seeing the great need, offered
the use of his flat, the only possible place for a Pram Club'. Toddlers'
Clubs are not child-minding centres, because the mothers all remain
there with the group leader, learning the first principles of child care
in social units. Their value is undoubted in certain areas where children
under three are prohibited from attending regular playgroups on
health grounds. By the dissemination of information and group
observation they supplement the role of the Health Visitor, who is at
present almost the only protector a battered baby may expect to see
inside the home.

Despite these developments, doubts have been raised in Britain
as to the value of pre-school education. Widlake at the University of

Birmingham investigated whether improvement was measurable in terms of *social competence* between ex-nursery school attenders and a control group of non-attenders at a British infants' school (lower elementary) in a deprived area. The children were six- and seven-year-olds. Reviewing the available information on gain, he stated that 'even the most conscientious workers have been unable to establish conclusively that nursery education has measurable, statistically significant, long-term beneficial effects'. A comparative study between nursery and non-nursery children in an infant school in London had led O'Sullivan to conclude that 'the results of this study and of the many others on this topic lead one to believe that there is little difference between children who have been in a nursery and those who have not'.[28]

Puzzled, but apparently undaunted by these conclusions, the Birmingham team decided to investigate 'social competence' as measured by Doll's Vineland Social Maturity Scale. The groups were matched by using, firstly Southgate Group Reading Tests, taking twelve to fifteen children at a time out of eighty-nine to be tested; secondly, the Raven's Coloured Progressive Matrices which are, it is claimed, a culture-free test of non-verbal intelligence.

The Vineland Social Maturity Scale was combined with the English Picture Vocabulary Test (similar to the US Peabody Picture Vocabulary Test) for the final results. The items in the Vineland test are claimed to be independent of sex, personality, social status or special opportunities, and the Birmingham team used the child-subject as his own informant. The result given by the Vineland Scale was that the nursery children 'retained a significant advantage in social competence over a peer group which had not had any organised pre-school education'. The Picture Vocabulary Test, and a Listening and Remembering Test adapted from Miss D.E.M. Gardner yielded *no significant differences* between the experimental and control groups.

The Birmingham results led Widlake and his collaborators to conclude that one of the assumptions underlying British nursery-school organization is that linguistic development will accompany social development without any specific need for a programme to improve the latter; the presence of large proportions of deprived children in these schools in educational priority areas makes the criticism sharper, for no one doubts any longer that there is a close link between language skills and later school success.

The Birmingham report did not go on to specify the type of nursery-school which might be organized to benefit disadvantaged children in the educational priority areas. It rejected the idea of drill in syntax for little children. But there is additional light to be found for this dark corner in a study made in Israel. The Smilanskys knew how much the child-centred, play-oriented, laissez-faire type of nursery school or kindergarten is favoured today and set down in what deserves to be an essential passage for students their reasons for rejecting it in the interest of the child:

> Disadvantaged children have difficulty in learning by the self-discovery method. They are unable to benefit from trial and error in a non-regulated environment because they lack the internal motivation, abilities, habits and techniques necessary to learn under such circumstances. Active intervention is necessary. When there is something they do not know or cannot do, their natural curiosity does not lead them to ask questions; in their home environment, their curiosity has not been encouraged, but actively suppressed. Observations have shown that the disadvantaged child, instead of trying to understand new things and to persist in efforts to find out about them, reverts to what he already knows, and to the familiar routines from which he has learned to get security; he derives almost no profit from situations that may provide advantaged children valuable experience and significant new knowledge.[29]

Looked at from this point of view, many of the expensive ventures into compensatory education may have failed through faulty conceptual planning; the premises themselves on which programmes were based may have been dubious, at least for this kind of remedial exercise. When in England experiments were begun in the 1960s to introduce language instruction on the basis of the Peabody Language Development Kit in nursery education for downtown children it aroused, said an informed commentator, immediate hostility among those teachers 'committed to the Froebelian naturalist developmental tradition and a metaphysic of unfolding from within each child'.[30] Elsewhere the blame is laid at the door of Jean Piaget, for when teachers attempt to follow his developmental stages they surrender the urge to guide and direct the child in new perceptive experiences for fear that they are anticipating the stage at which he can cope with them. Montessori is also blamed or cited in support of alternating theories, for which she is liable because of her manifold, and at times rather vague, utterances. But Montessori's work in Rome was among

the earliest compensatory programmes, was undeniably successful, and
has a strong bias towards cognitive and sensory development; thus
she is returning more and more to the forefront of discussions of this
type. Yet Montessori, *sui generis* so frequently, would never be able
to go along with the strongly-directive approach of the Israeli team:
her 'method', directive by its equipment, is indirect in all other respects.
Child and task find their own pace and proceed or mark time at a
rhythm which is not dictated by the supervisor. A Montessori observer
can admire the same manœuvre or exercise repeated for an hour by a
small learner, or see one of the pupils play with the same piece of
apparatus for an entire morning.

Results of compensatory programmes when measured in terms of
IQ gain have therefore not always brought spectacular support to the
pre-school advocates and this has inevitably caused some disappointment among the converted. If one knows a thing to be right, it is
exceedingly inconvenient not to be able to prove your cause in the
modern way by fact, figure, logic and the voice of expert authority.
Some results did indicate gain, but the question has not yet degener-
ated into a tug of war between rival teams of psychological testers.
A balanced statement of the position was that 'Gains in IQ scores
and augmented language-cognitive ability have been found in several
follow-up studies – but this is not evenly true: some follow-up studies
have not found such effect'.

One exceptionally widely-based study, which does not limit itself
solely to gain or non-gain in intelligence factors but takes in the class
background of the child, health, family housing, type of school,
growth, behaviour and adjustment, is the fascinating report on the
British cohort of babies born in one week of March.[31]

The children originally numbered nearly 16,000; information was
gathered to study the working of British maternity services and to
investigate the causes of stillbirths and deaths in the first week of life.
Six years later, in 1964, the opportunity arose to trace these babies
of 1958 vintage and to gather materials for a study of their post-natal
fate in early years. The first report was interesting on reading ability,
arithmetic, special educational needs, medical and developmental sex
comparisons, environmental findings, behaviour and adjustment,
schooling and parental situations and attitudes with regard to school.
The second report was more detailed and dealt, for example, with
malformations, congenital defects, the effect of birth-weight, gestation
and other obstetric factors on disabilities at the age of seven, ability
and attainment. This random sample – if one could call such a large

collection of babies that — taken from all over the country is of particular interest because of the wide differences in parental background, social strata, and health. The effects of the seven years' existence in modern Britain as they are reproduced in the report are absorbing and deserve examination. We will try here to reproduce their main findings.

The editors of the report comprised medical practitioners, psychologists and educators; it was only reasonable that in the 1960s the issue of disadvantaged children and compensation should be foremost in their minds. That there was a strong association between social class and reading and arithmetic attainment at seven years of age was evident, and the chances of an unskilled manual worker's child being a poor reader were six times greater than those of a professional worker's child.

Not only were the children of this social class likely to be poor readers, but they included a large proportion who needed special educational help at school; this figure was very much in excess of the one for children of non-manual skilled workers. In an average infant school of two hundred children about forty were considered likely to need special help on account of backwardness. Could not these children have been helped by proper nursery schools with a programme balanced on the side of cognitive development? We leave the reader to supply his own answer, but there is no evidence of harm resulting from proper pre-school treatment, and of these children mentioned above, only fifteen per cent had been to nursery school! Nor has the situation in accommodation improved since then.

It is easy to find fault with provision in the United Kingdom if one concentrates attention on the youngest age-group and neglects what is being done for the five-year-olds. The so-called *infant school* traces a long and not always gloomy history back to the early nineteenth century, and had flourished, numerically, because of the 1870 law bringing children to school at five. Nursery classes in infant schools, moreover, could admit children wherever possible, from three years of age: only nursery schools are permitted to receive them at two. Thus a large number of under-fives have traditionally been sheltered, in varying conditions, inside the compulsory school organization.

School at five has attracted a great deal of attention because of the innovatory aspects of the English primary school and foreign observers have written enthusiastic accounts for their home audience. The 'open plan' classrooms and the 'discovery method' have been inspected and admired by visitors from the US and other countries, who have recommended adoption of the English ideas and adaptation of the learning environment to local conditions. Weber (1971) reported approvingly her impressions of *The English Infant School and Informal Education*;[32] on our desk as we write is a French report on the *Écoles Anglaises à Aire Ouverte*, visited in the Liverpool area in early 1973, and the plans for the first French school of this type, opened in Paris late in 1974.

Weber recorded her impression that the setting was informal, children were seeking their own answers and that human relationships in these infant schools seemed to be an extension of the child's way of learning through play. From American standpoints, the teacher-child relationship seemed informal (which seems remarkable when one reflects that British manners in society are usually more formal than their American counterpart); cleanliness was more marked than in schools at junior level in the United States; rich supplies of materials to use in learning were available; and what was even more admirable, this equipment was used in free ways rather than in sequential Montessori ways. Classrooms were re-arranged to create stimulating situations, there was a corner for 'what makes sound', a corner of blue objects, a table only for 'round things'. There was a freedom of adaptation and improvisation displayed by teachers apparently unknown in the United States in the 1960s, a search for 'definition and relevance' by the children themselves and, said this American visitor, 'learning was going on all the time'.

What is historically curious about this reaction is that American ideas were instrumental in rescuing the English infant school from the gallery, and the drudgery of the 1900s. A grisly description of an infant classroom in the pre-World War I period shows us fifty or more children in a gallery, learning to write with the right hand, the left firmly folded behind their backs. Publication of Dewey's essays in 1906 refreshed the memories of English educators with Froebel's emphasis on play and the child's instinctive urge towards knowledge; as in the French *maternelle*, the 'Winnetka Plan' and the 'Dalton Plan' were both adopted in English infant schools after 1918. The Froebel renaissance spread outwards from America when the battle for a new kindergarten had been won there by the progressives. After adaptation to the British scene it is now being re-exported across the Atlantic.

English expert opinion about the infant schools and lower elementary classes has been more cautious; Her Majesty's Inspectors warned about some of the difficulties encountered in the 'Open Plan' schools, whose innovations may conceal extra demands on teaching-staff for team-spirit or 'empathy' as it is now called. Webb[33] indicated that the interests of younger children were not always safeguarded: four-year-olds were in rooms without direct access to outdoor space, at some distance from lavatories and washing facilities, overcrowded with desks, cupboards and junk. Thirty-five or forty children could hardly move around 'freely' under such conditions, in the care of one teacher. There was, of course, no teacher's aide such as the *femme de service* in France, to be summoned when a crisis loomed, a child was sick on the floor, or wet his pants. Methods and ideology had made giant strides in the last few decades, but the teacher's over-exacting duties have not been brought within reasonable bounds.

One cannot fail to be disappointed at the fate reserved for the under-fives in Britain. A protagonist of their cause pointed out in 1971 that education costs the country about £2,500 m a year; that less than two per cent of this is given to little children, and that the kindest thing which could be said about policy in the pre-school field was that no government had possessed one. Wartime conditions had grudgingly exacted from the government of the day some recognition of the cause, as a by-product of the demand for female labour in the factories, and hopes were raised by 'what Lord Butler said in 1944'. The Welfare State did not, however, extend its welfare services as far as the children, who benefited indirectly from better housing and free medical treatment. The belated recognition of what were picturesquely termed 'Twilight Zones' in industrial towns, led to intervention on behalf of their denizens, who certainly deserved all they could obtain. In the few and fortunate places which do have a nursery school, the waiting lists are so long that the principal has to act the final arbiter and admit as many desperate cases as she can: that is to say that a child whose background is moderately deprived has little hope of entry. 'The desperate cases,' wrote one head teacher in reply to the NUT Survey, 'are so many that it is impossible to consider the children who would benefit by attending a nursery, e.g. only children, homes with elderly grandparents, etc.'[34]

When the Conservative Government issued Circular 5174 in December 1972, it appeared as if, at last, the needs of children under five were to be recognized. Stimulated partly by the approach of closer union with Western European countries, the official statement admitted that Britain's provision was low indeed compared with some EEC countries; Circular 8/60 which had been the bane of nursery school supporters for a decade was finally to be withdrawn, and an attempt to carry out the recommendations of Plowden (1967) for ninety per cent provision for four-year-olds, and fifty per cent for three-year-olds would be made. Ambitious teacher-training programmes would expand the number employed with this age-group from 10,000 to 25,000. The cost of all this would involve special building pro- grammes of £15m in each of two successive years to 1976, and expenditure would be increased overall from £42m in 1971-2 to £65m in 1976-7.

The government was not, however, thinking of nursery schools in the McMillan-Grace Owen sense. It was planning to extend provision inside the elementary schools by using places which the birth-rate led them to expect would become vacant and by building on to these schools. Most of all, probably, it was relying on the rapidly expanding playgroup movement, which it promised to support increasingly and, lest Circular 5174 be considered a landmark in our story, it commented dourly that 'Any significant expansion of nursery schools would slow down the rate at which the Government's objectives will be reached.' (Para. 26.) Thus the eventual goal was large-scale development of the infant, or sub-infant classes in elementary schools; this was, in other words, the exact opposite of France's policy to reduce the *classes enfantines* and create more *maternelles*.

Multiple economic and political crises in 1973-4 interrupted progress in the old familiar way. Doubt and gloom encircled the hopeful projects of Circular 5174, and the new government was soon occupied in 'writing off' a deficit of £100m incurred in the coal industry. Such a sum as this, it is ironic to reflect, would have constructed and staffed many hundreds of nursery schools in working- class areas, or even financed an institute of pre-school studies on the Soviet model. It is too soon for adult society to realize that a priceless asset for the future is being neglected. We can look back at the nineteenth century and comfort ourselves with the progress achieved since then in diet, housing, and medical care; the bad old days seem a long time ago when we see the pictures of infant galleries and East End slums. It takes an effort to remember that half a century has gone by since Margaret McMillan wrote of nursery schools for 'the masses' and garden cities of children which would become the schools of tomorrow. They are still the schools of tomorrow.

9 THE UNITED STATES

During one of those crises which beset Froebel in later years, when his material situation was almost desperate, he considered a move to North America. His brother-in-law was then in Philadelphia and Froebel despatched in advance a plan to establish a kindergarten and training college in that city; his life was nearing the end, however, and before a reply came across the Atlantic, he was dead. It is interesting to muse on what such a venture would have meant to education: there would have been something appropriate in another 'renewal of life' in the country which welcomed Edouard Séguin and so many other liberals after 1848. As it happened, immigrant sympathizers opened a kindergarten in Wisconsin for German-speaking children as early as 1855 and five years later the redoubtable Miss Elizabeth Palmer Peabody of Boston (1804-94) took up the cause.

Miss Peabody's enthusiasms were not of the sort which burn briefly but intensely and then vanish, leaving little trace of their existence. In the course of a long life, which spanned the century, her undertakings bore the mark of her intelligence and energy. As secretary to Dr Channing, one of the leading philosophers of his time, she shared his interests and later wrote a memoir of his life; as a co-founder of the 'Transcendentalist Club' she was in touch with the ideas of European thinkers like Baron de Gérando and she translated and published his works in English.

Elizabeth Peabody's sister had married Horace Mann, Secretary of the Massachusetts Board of Education, and the Manns brought back from a visit to Germany in 1843 news of the 'whole word' method of teaching reading. They may have spoken to Miss Peabody of the kindergarten idea which was then in its very early stage of acceptance; in any case, just as de Gérando had taken the news of London progress back to Paris, she was instrumental in carrying the kindergarten method to Boston. A conversation with a former Froebel pupil, Mrs Carl Schurz, led Miss Peabody to found the first American kindergarten, in Boston itself. A perfectionist, she soon became dissatisfied with her work, and abandoned the centre in 1867 after seven years' activity. Then she betook herself to Hamburg, to study the Master closer to the source and became quite converted to Froebel, whose thought she set out to explain to the United States in the pages of her new

magazine, the *Kindergarten Messenger*. She travelled about, lecturing
and persuading charitable persons to endow kindergarten foundations,
one of which became the first free kindergarten, in Florence,
Massachusetts. One hundred and fifteen local associations were
formed across the whole country, and by the 1880s the Golden Gate
Association in San Francisco was able to support forty-one kindergartens from endowments of half a million dollars.

Economic recession and opposition to the movement from various
quarters cut back this promising advance to a steady pace during the
last decades of the century. Boston closed the public kindergarten
on the grounds that the city could not afford it; private benefactors
all over the country closed their purses to the cause when times were
bad; Miss Peabody who had done so much for the cause, left it,
first for history teaching and subsequently for a scheme worked out
by a plausible Sioux woman for educating the Red Indian tribes in
the Far West.

Fortunately for the story of pre-school education in America,
a superintendent of schools in St Louis, Missouri, brought great
gifts of organization and insight to the cause during the 1870s.
William T. Harris, later US Commissioner of Education, was an
educator in the nineteenth-century tradition of philosophy and
linguistics; like Froebel himself, de Gérando and Miss Peabody, he had
been deeply interested in idealistic philosophy. He was also a man of
courage and persuasive powers: he managed to introduce the kindergartens (between four and six years of age) to the public school system
of St Louis. By 1880 seven thousand eight hundred children were
enrolled, and the system was well enough established to weather the
financial storms in which many kindergartens disappeared in the US.
In the history of North America, the experience was crucial; had it
failed, Harris's assistant, Miss Susan Blow, observed later, it would
have been difficult to prevail upon other cities to introduce the
kindergarten into their public schools. Conversions followed in
pleasing succession, and kindergartens became part of the public school
system in one hundred and eighty-nine cities during the last twenty-
five years of the century; it was no mean achievement to credit to the
American pioneers in three brief decades after Miss Peabody's
pilgrimage to Hamburg.[1] A visiting inspector from Toronto took
home the news of St Louis' experiments and saw the kindergarten
included within the state school system of Canada. These material
successes were accompanied by literary and publishing activity of
considerable significance, for it was Harris who edited the International

Education series which brought the writings of Froebel belatedly before the English-reading public on both sides of the Atlantic. By 1900 Froebel was at last available in English for students.

The interpretation of Froebel's method and his writings had previously been the rather exclusive province of training colleges and senior scholars who studied German or had visited German centres. A ripple of dissension spread through the movement when younger teachers came in contact with the new child-study centres where psychologists like Stanley Hall and William H. Burnham propounded the elements of hygiene on the Continental model. The radicals wanted more freedom from authority, less rigid adherence to the old way of using the gifts as they had been used by Froebel's disciples, Middendorf, Barop, and the rest.

That there had been some strange alterations to the original teaching of the master appears from John Dewey's brilliantly lucid essay in praise of Froebel's principles published in *The School and Society*:

> There has been a curious, almost unaccountable, tendency in the kindergarten to assume that because the value of the activity lies in what it stands for to the child, therefore the materials used must be as artificial as possible, and that one must keep carefully away from real things and real acts on the part of the child. Thus one hears of gardening activities which are carried on by sprinkling grains of sand for seeds; the child sweeps and dusts a make-believe room with make-believe brooms and cloths; he sets a table using only paper cut in the flat (and even then cut with reference to geometric design, rather than to dishes), instead of toy tea things with which the child outside of kindergarten plays. Dolls, toy locomotives and trains of cars etc (*sic*) are tabooed as altogether too grossly real — and hence not cultivating the child's imagination.

This was surely mere superstition, as Dewey remarked, and the progressives, grouped around Miss Anna Bryan and Miss Patty Hill in Louisville, Kentucky, felt, as did critics in Europe, that a 'religion may lose power by being transformed into a routine of rites and ceremonies' and from some Froebel routine it seemed as if all the spirit of the Master had fled.[2]

The dispute was bitter and lasted throughout the 1890s; on the one hand it was suggested — and probably with much justification — that there was too stringent an emphasis on fine work, efforts of

co-ordination in plaiting, pricking, and sewing, threading small beads
and so on. Neurologists gave their critical support to those educators
like the Louisville school who did away with all this, and wrote that
'chorea and nervous affections' were occasioned by finger-tip work by
children under six. The gifts were treated with less reverence than
before, and one began to see paper dolls made to fit the beds of the
third and fourth gifts: the 'Froebelized' rigidity which Pauline
Kergomard detested in Europe was broken to form a new sort of
kindergarten, American-style.

Let us enter an American kindergarten a little before 9 a.m. in those
faraway days: 'all the little chairs are placed round a circle boldly
painted on the floor'. (Note the progressive touch here: furniture
adapted to children's needs: the gallery system was still in use on the
other side of the Atlantic.) Opening the morning session a song, hymn,
or child's prayer is heard; then there follows the morning talk, given by
the teacher, which is 'Nature lesson, and story, verse and song all
combined'. The talk deals with nature study, an excursion, discussion
of objects and pictures, enriched, one would say today, with verse and
songs in the true Froebel manner. To wind all this into the skein
naturally required considerable skill and experience. After the talk the
pupils — numbering about thirty — move around to tend the plants and
pets and enjoy free play.

The remaining hour and a half consists of three periods of thirty
minutes, given to the gifts, occupations, songs or gymnastic exercises.

A quarter of a million under-sixes attended morning sessions like
this one at the turn of the century, and numbers in fact rose by 1910
to 360,000, about twelve per cent of the four-to-six year-olds and a
large proportion of public class attenders. Had the trend continued and
some public organization been set up for the under-fours, the United
States might have made a significant contribution to rival the steady
development of the *maternelles*, for example. But just as English early
education stagnated after the Elementary Education Act, the quarrel
between progressives and conservatives in kindergarten circles seems to
have exhausted American vigour in the field; the impressive increase in
psychology departments and their involvement in learning research
became oriented towards the adolescent and the problems which were
likely to beset him. The kindergartens were more and more absorbed
into the elementary school system, although their retention of free play
and what might be called vivacity did not always seem welcome in the
primary classroom. Alert and active, eager and questioning, the kindergarten children arrived in the primary classroom happy, self-confident,

and talkative. So one of their lifelong devotees described them, but went on to admit that 'on the other hand the discipline of such children is very hard, and it requires the greatest effort on the teacher's part to accustom them to the quiet, independent work of the primary room'.[3] Poor teacher! Poor kindergarten children with their eagerness and chatter, learning the ordered ways of the primary system! By 1918, between four and six was accepted in the kindergarten as 'the first rung of the American ladder system'.

To English visitors, indeed, the American kindergarten seemed to have been run on permissive lines unknown in the United Kingdom; children were allowed to cut up coloured paper as they wished and when they wished; they were even allowed to *run from the ring*. The laxity of discipline shocked Miss Grace Owen at the turn of the century (and the trend continued when the progressives won the day in Froebel societies), so that, although she perceived the psychological aim was to allow American children's personalities to develop spontaneously, she observed stiffly that 'this appeared to result in an excess of individuality'.[4]

Forty and fifty years later French *inspectrices* were making the same sort of observation, pointing out that the French way of life does not favour this degree of permissiveness. But by this time England had been converted to the cause, and in fact carried it further, through the nursery schools and infant schools.

The kindergarten movement was lively enough to enjoy its reformation, but this was really only for the five-to-six year-olds. Interest in the under-fives and under-fours was lacking in the heyday of measurement, learning theory, and the cult of the adolescent. The child from birth to four years of age was considered to belong within the province of his family, for good or ill. The assumption of high family capability in all areas in the United States appears to be basic; according to recent studies, the reluctance of governments to invade the privacy of the family extends even to providing information about child-rearing (Robinson and Robinson, 1973).[5]

Despite the truth of this, it is only federal government intervention which has advanced public provision of ECE in this century. The kindergarten movement was linked to the first grade of school-work, and did not diversify downwards to benefit the millions of under-fives in the USA; indeed historians often point proudly to the increases in numbers of five-year-olds at either kindergarten or elementary school (when kindergarten facilities are lacking.)[6] There is therefore, a striking parallel with the British tendency to provide for five-year-olds in the infant schools.

By 1933, when the Hadow Committee reported progress in pre-school education, there appear to have been 723,000 American children in public kindergartens and 54,000 in private centres. This represented more than double the 1910 figure, and probably comprised about half the five-year-old cohort on the eve of the depression. Both the depression and the war years benefited children by increasing investment in schools for the children of unemployed Americans or working mothers in wartime. Recent figures, which show the effect of large-scale support such as 'Head Start' provided, indicate not fewer than 3,263,000 children in kindergartens in the United States. Seventy-two per cent of five-year-olds and twelve per cent of the nation's four-year-olds, it was believed, attended for one year's kindergarten before elementary school entrance at six.

Public provision of a short preparation course before school age has therefore risen impressively in the last sixty years, but the content of courses and objectives of the administration has not really satisfied progressives. Innovation and adaptation to a changing world are absent from most kindergarten programmes, it is said, and 'indeed, most are not very different today from kindergartens a quarter of a century ago'.[7]

The nursery-school was the latecomer to pre-school provision in the United States but, with its broad approach to the needs of three-, four- and five-year-olds it was soon accepted on its merits by professional or intellectual communities. English and North American exponents of the nursery school method enjoyed a warm glow of mutual admiration in the 1920s, and when Hadow reported in England, it mentioned some 262 nursery schools in the US, which owed their inspiration to the McMillan venture in Deptford. The English showed interest in American theories of 'home economics' as a training for better motherhood, and home economics students used nursery schools for observation and practice. Americans, for their part, admired the planning in Britain centred about the Nursery Schools Association, and the 'technically trained nursery workers and fine provision for physical care and hygiene.'[8] Where the two countries differed sharply was on the question of research and the influence of psychology.

It was felt in the United States that all aspects of child development required examination under the authoritative guidance available from psychologists and paediatricians; nursery schools would be reception grounds for research results as well as providing the

control-situations for investigators. In this way, once standards had
been established from above, they could be passed on to set the
movement on a footing which was scientifically acceptable, not to
say respectable. Optimistically, American workers in the field
believed that the right standards could then be allowed to *spread
downwards* through the social scale, which was a viewpoint markedly
in contrast with the English faith founded in the disadvantaged
quarters of Bradford and the East End. Yet the process of vertical
descent towards the poorer orders of American society moved so
slowly that there were only a few hundred nursery schools in the
United States in the 1930s. Only emergency programmes for
unemployed teachers, coupled with 'educational and health
programs for the children of the unemployed', contributed to raise
this figure to fifteen hundred (federally supported) and one thousand
(private) nursery schools on the eve of World War II.

At the demonstration school run by the Connecticut State
Teachers' College the timetable was:

08.00–08.30:	Children arrived, were each given a glass of water, and played indoors.
08.30:	Picture books were taken out and an informal music period arranged for those who preferred.
09.15–09.30:	Fruit juice distributed. Toilet.
09.30–11.00:	Free play out of doors.
11.30–11.45:	Washing for dinner.
11.30–11.45:	Rest before dinner.
11.45:	Dinner.
12.15:	Toilet. Rest on cots.
12.30–14.30:	Nap.

At least the children were not overtaxed during the twenty-five
mornings this timetable was observed at Connecticut. Discussion among
nursery-school adepts in the thirties ranged over the problems of diet:
should the clean-plate theory be enforced? Should the nap take place
in the morning or afternoon? How many children should sleep in one
room? What material and pattern was preferable for the childrens'
blouses or overalls. An attempt at definition of nursery-school aims
on the eve of World War II emphasized protection of health; provision
of 'interesting, varied and stimulating play materials' for the
'unfolding of mental powers and the promotion of special interests';
and getting along with other people socially. The description does not

add very much to the British nursery-school programme of McMillan days, in spite of a decade of university research and experiment. Fifteen years later the *genetic aspects* of child development were mentioned as something the teacher must understand in order to adapt the appropriate play experiences to the child. Throughout, the goals have been the traditional British ones of health, motor development, social-emotional growth and, *to a lesser extent,* intellectual growth.(The phrase is that of Robinson and Robinson, Section VI, Programs.)

Federal Government assistance did benefit nursery-schools during depression years and there were said to be as many as 2,500 in both public and private sectors by the 1940s. Figures rose sharply as a result of compensatory education investment in the 1960s, which were once again endowed by Federal funds.

What nursery schools were like after 1930 is difficult to assess, for even now there seems to be a wide variety of programmes. Toys are offered in abundance, clay, paint, paper and other materials for self-expression are provided. There are group activities in dancing and singing, excursions, and entertainments. There is said to be little interference from the teacher who assumes that socialization will take place without direction from above.

Some sort of 'pecking order' will be established, staff believe, as the nursery process runs its course, and there is a wide variation in standards and surroundings. Backyard schools which are little better than day-care units may be contrasted with 'enrichment' programmes with lavish equipment and more helpers than children. In one university, cognitive development is a major goal in certain select establishments linked with university departments, and it is among the nursery schools that the so-called 'academic pre-schools' have been created recently. The movement is eclectic, however, and in one university town an observer came upon the 'Tic Toc Nursery and Kindergarten' which offered its services from 7 a.m. to 6 p.m. with creative and dramatic activities, science and reading concepts, coupled with muscular development. Could one ask for more?

The kindergarten movement, a German export, had launched early education on its way in North America, but the theory on which it was based seemed to be shaken by the comparatively new science of psychology. Likewise, the North American nursery school, which only appeared in this century, was indelibly marked by the authority of psychology and child-development studies. The American contribution to early childhood education, therefore, cannot be discussed without reference to the sudden, remarkable growth of experimental psychology in the 1890s and its consequences for education in general.

By 1894, incredible though it seems today, there were already no less than twenty-seven psychology laboratories in the United States; the impetus had come from Wundt in Leipzig and other German centres which attracted students like G. Stanley Hall in the years before 1900. Within a very few years appeared techniques of measurement and observation of behaviour which claimed the status of a science, and child-study based on a wide range of examples taken from kindergarten pupils. Although Hall's child-study research led him into embarrassing difficulties the subject was much discussed among mothers and was the predecessor of the strong American child-development studies of the 1920s.

The new psychology tended to discredit the older schools and deny the principles which Froebel's contemporaries had advocated. Many came to the conclusion that Froebel's whole method must be of dubious value as his psychology derived from an outdated epoch. The kindergarten at this time was a target for Ellen Key, the Swedish feminist, in her bestseller, *The Century of the Child;* where the authoress preached the cause of a scientific interest in child-psychology. 'The modern school,' she wrote, 'has succeeded in doing something which, according to the law of physics, is impossible: the annihilation of once existent matter. The desire for knowledge, the capacity for acting by oneself, the gift of observation, all qualities children bring with them to school, have, as a rule, at the close of the school period disappeared. They have not been transformed into actual knowledge or interests.'[9]

A general dissatisfaction with the prison-style schools and routine instruction of the time was more glibly expressed by a French humourist who snapped, 'You say that you have never been to school, and yet you are such an idiot.'

Psychology, with the prestige of men like Hall, Thorndike, Cattell and Dewey behind it, seemed to offer a child-centred way out of the impasse and non-learning situation blamed on the traditional schools. As a result, forward-thinking educators and experimental nursery schools (when they appeared) looked towards psychology and followed the lead given by Thorndike and his henchmen. In Europe too, psychologists like Binet had a considerable influence, but there was nothing like the authoritarian trend towards educational psychology as it flourished in the United States. Several features of this study concerned kindergarten and nursery school closely and need

to be mentioned here; by mentioning their errors and limitations
our aim is to show how unfounded were some of the pretentions
of this 'psychology of education' until quite recently; activity in the
laboratories was considerable but the long-term achievement of this
science was hardly scientific, if by that we mean that laws were
formulated which stood the test of time.

To begin with, the field of study was so limited by its founders that
it properly deserves to be called a period (approximately 1900 to 1940)
of *pre*-psychology rather than a proper study. Following the lead of
early research in Italy and other places it tended to examination of the
child in adolescence. Secondly, with the exception of a few neglected
students such as Meumann, who was interested in the classroom situation,
it did research on the single subject, the learner in isolation. Stimulus-
response techniques were ingenious and often attracted publicity: they
were new, advanced, and 'scientific'. Their contribution to the study
of learning in animals and humans dazzled laymen and teachers alike
in the twenties and thirties. Their limitations were glossed over, and it
became a matter of orthodoxy to express support for behaviourist
methodology.

American schools of pre-psychology therefore, diverged from the
biological and physiological views of education put forward by Edouard
Séguin and developed, for instance, by Claparède, Jean Piaget's
director in Geneva. When Madame Montessori appeared in the United
States, an influential section of the academic world classified her as
'unscientific', and of course, by their narrow standards, so she was. The
expansion of psychological research to include neuro-physiology, bio-
chemistry of the nervous system, and other key aspects of the science
of man was not to come for another thirty years or more. Ignoring,
or pretending to ignore, the child-mother, child-teacher relationship,
relatively unaffected by the arguments of psycho-analysis, educational
'psychology' concentrated on aspects of learning in rats, apes or
children. A widening gap of comprehension appeared between the
school and research so that the relationship between 'laboratory
learning', and 'school learning' became quite tenuous. Let us look at
the early leaders in this American movement and see how they viewed
the child.

G. Stanley Hall (1846-1924), although the acknowledged father
of American child psychology, was one of a generation which was
strongly influenced by the Froebel tradition. In addressing teachers,
he reminded them that 'childhood, as it comes fresh from the hand of
God, is not corrupt, but illustrates the survival of the most

consummate thing in the world – there is nothing else so worthy of
love, reverence and service as the body and soul of the growing child.'

Edward Thorndike (1874-1949), however, who came to the study
of psychology in the 1890s, moved in a different direction. Thorndike
turned like Karl Groos and others to see what light the study of
animals could throw on human beings, and began work on animal
intelligence in 1898. His work included experiments with the
problem-solving ability of animals inside the box and maze situation;
it led to a wealth of subsequent imitation and discussion.

Thorndike elaborated the famous 'stimulus-response' technique on
the basis that the recurrence of a stimulus recalls a response and so a
stimulus-response (S-R) band is strengthened and learning habits are
formed.

By making psychology experimentally testable, Thorndike had
apparently founded its claim to be a science; the IQ testers followed
soon afterwards and elaborated impressive batteries of questions
which were supposed to result in prediction of later intelligence and
capacities. More than this, Thorndike had managed to end 'the search
for mind by eliminating it as a separate entity' and discarding along
the way Biblical, Rousseauan, and Lockean views of human nature.[10]

It will be seen that by discarding these authorities, from which
Oberlin, Owen, Cochin and Froebel derived much of their inspiration,
Thorndike had eliminated the view of early childhood which sees
it as a form of intrinsically valuable existence. Many behaviourists
and others have followed in this path, which leads back to
instruction, preparation for school work, learning and the old 'three Rs'
under the new guise of cognitive development. The views of another
influential contemporary, John Dewey, were not quite so restricted.

John Dewey (1859-1952), was not only a psychologist and teacher,
but a philosopher whose influence extended far beyond his university.
Counting the work of teachers as a matter of real importance, he
maintained a lecture course at teacher-training college parallel with
his university work. Like Ovide Décroly, he was aghast at the barrier
which had been put up between school-experience and life-
experience, and attacked the isolation and unreality of schools in his
time. Dewey's ideas were discussed in Europe by a wide public
and the Swiss Institute at Geneva translated and published his
Interest and Effort with a first-class introduction by Edouard Claparède.
In England, Susan Isaacs admitted the effect of Dewey on her own
thinking and ranked him with Froebel.

Dewey was a native product of New England, owing little to the late nineteenth-century German schools of psychology where Hall had studied. Through his writings about education ran a thread of hope that democracy, in the American sense, could be brought into the life of the school community and that students could learn about their society by practising self government themselves. He therefore became an important figure for the progressive educators who were trying to cultivate a more permissive atmosphere for children.

His debt to Froebel was acknowledged in *The School and Society* where he set down the principles on which the Chicago University Elementary School was based. Urging students to look for the real intention behind Froebel's method, rather than the conventional aids and occupations, he quoted Froebel as the originator of education based on the 'instinctive, impulsive attitudes and activities of the child.' Teaching throughout the school, not only for the kindergarten age-group (four to six) should be linked with the child's mode of growth, and governed by Froebel's real principles, not by artificial external factors or impositions. There was a freshness about Dewey's style,[11] and his ideas of a free Froebel school were novel in 1900, heralding the application of ECE principles to later education; Dewey-Froebel principles affected more than one generation of American teachers. He treasured his connection with the elementary school, despite his growing international repute as philosopher, and when the university president at Chicago moved to eliminate the school's 'laboratory' character and turn it into a teacher-training school pure and simple, Dewey thought the issue important enough to fight. He resigned his chair in protest and departed.

After Dewey, and before educational psychology threw its shadow over Froebel's aura, a leading authority at Columbia Teachers' College, W.H. Kilpatrick, took up the giant-killer's axe and hewed away with devastating effect on both Maria Montessori and Friedrich Froebel. After *The Montessori System Examined* (1914) Kilpatrick wrote *Froebel's Kindergarten Principles Critically Examined,* published in 1916. His 'critical examination' is curious because while it contains scathing criticism of Froebel's excess of symbolism, faulty psychology (as seen from the heights of 1914) and curious philosophy, it remains for all that a laudatory study. The critic had apparently come to scoff and stayed to pray, for Kilpatrick's summary of Froebel's innovations leaves us even further in wonder at the originality of the kindergarten. For Kilpatrick even Froebel's psychology, confused though it was by contemporary German teaching, derived strength from his natural sympathy for childhood; his love and

sympathy for childhood was intense, and more than any other man of
his time Froebel respected the child's individuality.

Froebel's symbolism was baseless, intoned Kilpatrick, and his
'fundamental laws of the universe' unknown to science today, yet the
Thuringian gave to play for the first time in history its practical
standing in education; the consequence was to open the way to
manual and constructive activities. 'Ignorance, and error' explained
much of Froebel's reputation, warned the Columbia Professor of
Education, and his belief in innate ideas was not supported by modern
psychology. His doctrine of self-activity nevertheless came 'wonderfully
close' to the best modern doctrine of interest and Froebel's insistence
on social relationships and their importance to the growing child was far
superior to any ideas of Rousseau or Pestalozzi on the subject. Finally,
Froebel had, in the kindergarten programme, expressed his concern for
the aesthetic element in life, long before the ordinary primary school
had dreamed of such a thing.

Kilpatrick's 'criticism', which virtually established Froebel in his
rightful position as the founder of modern education, was given in
an age when schools and philosophers enjoyed a mutually rewarding
interchange of views. Now laboratories and campus began to hum
with activity in research on child development, directed by leaders
like Arnold Gesell (1880-1961), pupil of the prestigious G. Stanley
Hall, and the age of the educational psychologists began. While
the problems of teenagers were debated in the new light of psycho-
analysis and the cult of what one French author called 'adolescentism'
gathered way, the early years faded into the background of
educational study. Behaviour was the focus of research, upon which
massive charts of child development were constructed: Watson
himself had received a small grant in 1916 to study newborn infants,
and Gesell in the early twenties began his ambitious account of
The Mental Growth of the Pre-School Child. With the co-operation of
Pathé Films it was possible to illustrate the book with what were
called 'action photographs' of the children. The later *Atlas of Infant
Behaviour,* published in 1934, contained no less than 3,200 photographs
of the infant.[12]

Gesell had qualified in medicine before turning to child
development, which he called 'a branch of biology or of anthropology
concerned with human growth'; although he became the leader in the
development field he was, therefore, fully aware of the importance
of other specialist studies in discussions about child education. He was
much concerned with the matter of maturation, and with other

psychologists examined the concept of 'readiness' which led to a long
debate of which we still hear murmurs. Froebel had talked about
budding points in the learning process, and warned that if these were
missed, 'every later attempt arbitrarily to introduce the subject lacks
interest. . . .' If and when the right point was found, however, the
subject develops in its own way, teaching the teacher himself. It was
still early for Piaget's influence to be diffused in translation, but
Madame Montessori had talked about stages in growth and development.
Arnold Gesell also felt that maturation came mainly from inside the
personality, but with the contemporary behaviourist interest in
conditioning, the question was raised as to whether we cannot
accelerate the child's development by providing the appropriate
stimuli? In Austria, Charlotte Bühler, too, worked on research about
maturation, experimenting with Albanian children who had been bound
down to small wooden cradles during their first twelve months, and
finding that, upon release, they caught up with the movements of
freely reared children in only _two hours_. The capacity, but not the use,
it was decided, had been maturing in idleness during that first year.[13]

After Thorndike's feat in abolishing mind, the psychologists of the
twenties were almost inevitably ready to disprove the effectiveness of
moral training. The core subject in infant school practice in the
nineteenth century, moral training retained its place in the more
modern and secular _maternelles_ and kindergarten. But Hartshorne and
May, after extensive investigations into moral training followed up by
testing on standards of honesty and service, sketched a gloomy picture:
such training, whether given in Sunday School, Boy Scouts, classes
in 'character training' at school or simply in the home was found to be
quite ineffective. Not only was this proven in the heyday of testing,
but Kohlberg, writing in 1964, stated that 'recent research provides
little reason to revise their conclusions.' Regretfully, he pointed to
Russia, where the entire classroom process is defined as character
education.

Kohlberg might also have directed his attention to kindergarten both
in the United States and Western Europe, where teachers obstinately
continue to see their duty lie in preparing the child for society _(la vie
collective)_ and in developing firmness of character and truthfulness. In
other words, nursery-school and kindergarten teachers in most
countries follow the practical lead of Kergomard and Froebel; the
latter, while admitting the negative aspects of childhood, believed that
they could disappear with the right training. Are then, French, Russian,
British and American teachers quite misguided, or were psychologists

misapplying their tools of inquiry? Like some of the other results established by an embryo science, the abolition of moral training and indeed, the mind, must be received with some scepticism by readers mindful of the historical tradition to say the least.[14]

During the 1920s and 30s, debate about development and maturation became highly specialised in the United States, as part of the growing obsession with psychological processes, as distinct from a study of the whole child. For the layman, or practising teacher, the difficulty of catching up with one's reading was intensified by the rivalry between schools: leaders like Watson, Wertheimer (Gestalt) and Abraham (Freudian psycho-analysis) gathered their disciples about them and research results appeared to contradict the conclusions of other theorists.[15] Moreover, comparative studies, when they were considered at all, were sometimes in rebuttal of locally acceptable findings. On one occasion, for instance, English children were said to be learning arithmetic at an age when for American experts this seemed hardly acceptable. The work of anthropologists revealed societies whose child-rearing practice was very different from basic patterns described in Western European and North American studies. It was difficult for anyone to discern what implications there were in all this for the teacher.

Much of American activity concentrated on the learning process, and the effects of conditioning on behaviour. The star of B.F. Skinner (born 1904) was rising, offering to a generation the possibilities of experimental research into variants of the Thorndike Law of Effect, and modifications of Pavlov's famous experiment with the dog, saliva, and buzzer. Animals, especially rats and the higher order of primates, were very much in vogue for experimental work on learning. Two American academics, man and wife, even adopted a baby female chimpanzee for a period to keep company in the nursery with their own child, Donald, who was less than one year old.[16]

The story of Gua, the baby ape, and Donald together in cot, and play-pen, was told by Kellogg in their *The Ape and the Child* as a report on parallel development released for scientific purposes. Gua became very attached to her human scientist foster-parents, clinging to the father for security in her very first days out of the cage. Donald was equally attached to his companion. After some time Gua ran to her 'Mummy' and 'Daddy' when their names were mentioned, and responded to a number of language stimuli, especially connected with food. Donald seemed retarded in speech development by comparison with the Gesell scales, and only had three real words at eleven-and-a-half months.

In view of the increase in experiment and controversy about language-learning of higher orders of primate, it may be worth mentioning that Gua could form several vowels 'and seemed to be able to manipulate her lips and tongue with greater facility than the boy (but) no additional sounds were ever observed beyond those which she already possessed when we first made her acquaintance — there were no "random" noises to compare with the baby's prattle or . . . the chatter of birds . . .' Gua's language stage was, therefore, identical with that of Itard's Victor.

After the period of experiment was over, Gua was disposed of, and the little boy lost his friend. We have been unable as yet to discover whether any follow-up observations were recorded on the effect of deprivation of companionship on chimp and child in later years. Nor do we know the extent of suffering involved in being returned to the cage after 'living free' in a middle-class American home during nine critical months of infancy. The observations of behaviourist psychologists in the thirties and forties did not result in evolving a test-scale of emotional rises or falls, and we are left even now very much in the position of Itard when he realised that the curtain of non-communication and non-memory would never be broken between 'Victor' and our world.[17]

As experimental reports multiplied even special abstracting services and selective review-articles were unable to bridge the gap between laboratory and teacher-layman. The problem of the research-practice fissure became a serious one, and not only in the United States: reviewing the content of one thousand reports in two psychology journals over a twelve-year period, Underwood[18] estimated that several thousand reports in North American psychology journals over the same period of time had been devoted to learning studies. Teachers and parents were obliged to rely on magazine review-articles and await publication of the encyclopaedias of research, a branch of learning in which America excelled.

The practice of testing children for health and particular disabilities (eyesight, hearing, etc.) was begun in Germany during the 1880s and was later applied in France and other countires. Testing of 'intelligence' however, came to overshadow these useful tools for assessing the all-round capacity of the school child, and eventually became a quasi-religion in the United States. For early childhood studies the paradox lay in the rapid growth and change in individuals both mentally and physically during the first four years. Testing norms at a

particular time was feasible, but predicting change or capacity much
less so.

The essential characteristic of early childhood, most would agree,
is its extraordinary creativity. Vast sums have been expended to little
avail in order to find out if our children are learning or not; there is
no doubt that in kindergarten, nursery school or Russian *detskii sad*
they are growing, building, and creating. And yet all the effort
invested in discovering – even with recent and improved techniques –
a predictor for creativity has produced scarcely any result at all.

Institutes of Child Welfare, which multiplied on university
campuses, became oriented towards the behavioural school of
psychology and endowed with generous research budgets. A newcomer,
'Gestalt' psychology, came to inflate the aura of what it called
'cognitive development', and before long an artificial debate arose
between the 'cognitive' school and those who believed in the
tradition of the whole child. Why, one hundred years after Owen
and Froebel, the all-round development of the child had to be
defended against critics whose authority came from a transitory
intellectual fashion is yet another mystery.

While testing and what was called "The Learning Process"
dominated research, the IQ tool (whose invention is credited to
Wilhelm Stern in 1912) enjoyed wider and wider prestige. Its use in
industry, wartime recruitment and selection was assured when big
corporations and the armed forces staffed their psychology
sections with experts trained in the testing tradition. It was soon
forgotten that Binet himself had expressed dismay at the use
his questionnaires were being put to in other languages than
French, and without his supervision. In 1909 he complained that
'Some recent philosophers appear to have given their moral support
to the deplorable verdict that the intelligence of an individual is a
fixed quantity . . . we must protest and act against this brutal
pessimism . . . (for) one increases that which constitutes the
intelligence of a school child, namely, the capacity to learn, to
improve with instruction.'

Faith in fixed intelligence and the wonders of testing in a
technological age deafened teachers and experts alike to the real truth
about intelligence and education: that a deadening environment and
lack of opportunity could maim children like hereditary defects.[19]
Yet, as early as the 1920s Woolley reported on rapid increases even
in the 'IQ' scores after certain children were given help which seemed
to ease their emotional blockages or their feelings of deprivation. In

the general climate of subservience to intelligence-testing, fixed intelligence, and the other dogma of the Schools with a capital 'S', there was little publicity for research in support of a contrary view.

Interest in small children was rare until the twenties, after Freud and other psycho-analysts had stressed the importance of early experience in forming later attitudes, and Piaget, Descoeudres, and the Genevan School published conclusions about the language and thought processes of children. The respect for testing in the USA ensured that little children, too, would have their intelligence estimated and related to future development. Rachel Stutsman published *Mental Measurement of Pre-School Children* in 1931,[20] and the book is well worth examining to see how children's intelligence could be measured before their speech develops properly. It is interesting to see the debt to Séguin and Décroly, so largely ignored by the fashionable American schools of psychology: emphasis is on visual stimuli; classification and observation.

Only converted believers in intelligence testing could accept a correlation between picture cards and child intelligence, and the doubts about this sort of thing grew with the years, as early childhood acquired expert interest. Writing after many years of investigation, Nancy Bayley was obliged to admit that 'we cannot predict later intelligence from scores of tests made in infancy.'[21] One is reminded of Séguin's comment after visiting the Vienna Exhibition as US Delegate in 1873: he remarked drily that it was unfortunately still popular to extol, and alas, to excite what is called the intelligence of infants.

The age of dissection, therefore, after discarding mind, diverged from the tradition of all-round development. Even nutrition and physical health received little public attention compared with 'learning' and 'behavioural science'. But the majority of teachers found it difficult to adapt learning theory and other revelations to their daily task; there was thus a distinct difference between schools and the college-university atmosphere where staff members came under the spell of learning-testing and were of course examined in it before graduation. Research studied the child (when it did concentrate on the child rather than on the rats and apes) in isolation, and even Gesell, whose normative studies had more relevance than the work of other noted psychologists, proceeded as if the maturation of behaviour went on in an environmental vacuum.[22] There was little communication between different schools of thought and much internecine warfare, so that even now, for example, the gulf between Jean Piaget's exposition and the views of leading United States learning theorists is wide. It was not until after the Second World War that American psychology broadened its outlook to include environmental factors and so re-discovered the motive forces of love and empathy. In this way an enlightened section of the learned also came to reconsider Montessori and examine Piaget more carefully.

In the late 1930s, when Piaget's research was almost unknown in North America and early childhood was still eclipsed by adolescence as an attractive stage for university research, a report appeared which moved the trend in investigation away from sterile experiments directed at a single subject. Two orphans had been moved for a time, to an institution for mentally retarded girls, who were allowed in certain cases to look after the two-and three-year-olds. Skeels and Dye reported an increase in the children's IQ figure after six months had passed, and suggested this had been due to stimulation received from the handicapped girls. Later, thirteen other infants were similarly transferred, and showed gains on the inevitable IQ score. In the psychological climate of the day, the report was received with comparative indifference, and there was little publicity to show that this report marked a turning point in educational psychology.[23] Part of the significance of the report lay in the fact that it dealt with the other partner in the growth or learning processs, and raised the half-forgotten question: what part does love or affection play in a child's reaction to the environment? We have seen how Bowlby took up the challenge in the 1950s, but meanwhile exciting things continued to happen in American research.

René Spitz, whose study dealt with baby rearing from three months old in a home and a penal institution aroused public concern at the possible negative effects of early years in an institution, and follow-up studies suggested that such effects were still to be seen at the adolescent stage.[24] Children in an Iranian orphanage provided further evidence of arrested development for Dennis (1960), and Hebb worked on the effect of isolation from stimuli in the cases of humans as well as animals. Volunteers in the experiment situation were placed in cubicles, eyes covered and limbs gloved and cuffed, to test the resulting inhibited perception and coordination. Riesen had already placed two newborn chimps in completely darkened rooms for a period of sixteen months, and found visual incompetence and a drop of acuity of vision; in 1951, however, the surprising fact emerged from opthalmoscopic examination that the chimps' retina and optic disc, especially the latter, did not reflect as much light as did those of chimps in the usual cages.

The transformation or damage to biological features resulting from inhibited use, or disuse, received confirmation from Brattgård, who found similar atrophy in the retinal ganglion cells of rabbits reared in darkness. Researchers began to discuss deficiency in 'RNA' and other effects which were, of course, unheard of when fixed intelligence theory held undisputed sway. Examining the result of 'enrichment programmes' in enlarged cages, on animals, the astonishing fact emerged that improved maze-learning was accompanied by increased thickness of the cerebral cortex. It seemed that Jean Piaget's dictum that 'use is the aliment of a schema' and the theories of functional education put forward by his compatriot Claparède might have unsuspected significance. J. McV. Hunt, who collected all the research evidence of this type for his book, *Intelligence and Experience* (1961) threw down the gauntlet to the traditional inherited-intelligence school of thought and also adduced evidence which seemed to indicate the severe limitations of the behaviourist 'telephone switchboard' portrayal of the brain. Thereafter, a variety of reports on stimuli applied to the vision and touch of newborn infants appeared in different research journals and changed ideas about the child's rate of psychological development. 'Fisted swiping', and 'top level grasping with hand shaped in anticipation for grasping' were baby performances which, after twenty minutes handling each day, turning on stomachs, and viewing and feeling a stabile, appeared weeks earlier than expected. (White, 1967).

The human brain-computer, wrote Hunt in his later work, *The Challenge of Incompetence and Poverty,* is programmed by experience, and investigations such as those conducted with infants showed how right Sigmund Freud had been in stressing the importance of that experience which comes before the use of language.[25] A hierarchical arrangement of the brain was suggested by experts who had programmed computers in problem-solving, and in 1965 Bronson identified three critical (sensitive) periods in brain development from birth to seven months and beyond. Bronson's levels, which represent stages of functional maturity for the central nervous system, are:

I.   birth to one month: formation of the brain-stem,
II. two months to six months: sub-cortical forebrain,
III. seven months onwards: the neocortex formed.

Anatomical and physiological research is now breaking new ground and may confirm that 'not merely what an organism learns at a particular age, but how it learns, is limited by what neural networks are mature.'[26]

Once the importance of early childhood was accepted by psychological science, the social implications of the environment began to be seriously examined in the United States. The challenge of ignorance and poverty was freely mooted as a negation of the American principle of equal, democratic opportunity in elementary education. The child from ghetto areas, minority groups, or low income homes had passed several years in a deadening environment without proper stimuli; how could he hope to compete in elementary school with those who had come from affectionate, stimulating and varied backgrounds? The challenging of the forty-year old tradition of inherited intelligence capacity set up a chain reaction, a sort of seismic disturbance in almost every level of education. What became of the millions of dollars invested in elementary and secondary education if the front-runners in school results had nearly all come from favourable backgrounds before they entered the school learning environment?

In a bustle of activity comparable perhaps with the stir in scientific education after the launching of Soviet Sputnik I in 1957, the Federal Government decided to act on the challenge presented by disadvantaged children. Their 'strategies' were to a large extent controlled by the educational scientists brought up in the psychological traditions of the forties, but there was a great deal of public interest and lay involvement in 'Head Start' activity; the theme of pre-school education rose to the headlines and made more than an occasional appearance on the science pages of the national press. The 1960s, in which terms like 'compensatory techniques' and 'acceleration' came into common usage among teachers and parents, might be called the decade of pre-school education.

Once the importance of compensatory early education for disadvantaged socio-cultural groups was admitted, the United States began an enormous campaign to help little children in urban communities. Generous funds were allotted to the scheme, and panels of experts advised the Government through the United States Office of Education as to where they should be spent; a special Office for Research and Evaluation was set up to report on the progress of the enterprise, which was strikingly labelled 'Project Head Start'. In addition, independent firms of educational consultants were called in

from time to time to carry out field work and assist in developing the
overall strategy of the scheme.

Head Start began during the summer of 1965. In order to provide
teaching care, forty-hour 'orientation' courses were given to 56,000
teachers and what were termed teacher-aides. (In the United States
another name, 'para-professionals', has also been coined for off-duty
mothers and other interested adults who work in schools but are not
trained teachers. Teacher-aides seems a more appropriate term for the
under-sixes.) An additional 2,500 teachers a year enrolled in five to
eight week training courses during the first three years of Head Start.

The goal of Head Start, as proposed by President Lyndon B.
Johnson, was to break the poverty cycle which trapped an estimated
six million children whose parent or parents earned three thousand
dollars a year or less and were living on the 'subsistence' level. Classes
of fifteen pupils aged three to six under the care of one trained
teacher and a number of aides were selected from these tragically-
deprived households, which were as badly in need of medical
attention as any slum-dwellers in the East End during the Margaret
McMillan period.

The educational results of Head Start have given rise to some heart
searching; the results in terms of hygiene and child health were as
striking as anything done by the reformers of the *maternelle*-nursery
school epoch in the early part of the century. Sixty-two per cent of
these children had never been tested for tuberculosis; twenty-one
per cent had 'major' medical problems, and fifty-eight per cent had
never seen a dentist. The last is significant in a country where the
middle-class and the affluent have always been concerned about dental
care. The results of providing medical and dental inspection, basic
hygiene and nutrition were as rewarding as they are in emergency
relief programmes for India or the Philippines: some millions of
children below the poverty-line received basic attention in the first
campaign.

The point at which one can distinguish between physical benefits
and 'cognitive' benefits is one of the most elusive in the slowly-
forming outline of ECE. In the United States, moreover, the type of
programme undertaken as a part of Head Start varied considerably
between different communities; most of the work was aimed at social
improvement and what one observer called 'personal-social development,
enrichment experiences, and creative play in a "teacher initiates while
the child responds, atmosphere" '. Follow-up studies were positive
in assuring the taxpayer that children became more sociable and not

so introverted. A multi-million dollar investment in improving the start in life of poor white children, Navajo Indians, Puerto Ricans and urban ghetto Negroes could hardly be expected to do more, perhaps, and yet the search for an observable improvement in cognitive achievement has gone on in a mixture of hope and despair. Coleman, reporting on the effects of the 1965 programme, said that Head Start had in fact reached those children who needed it, for 'the highest degree of participation was in regions characterized by low socio-economic status and low test scores.' Achievement scores were comfortingly higher for the Head Start attenders than for non-participants from the same racial, regional, and socio-economic backgrounds. A broad evaluation by teams from Ohio University more recently found no difference in cognitive ability between Head Start participants and a matched group of non-attenders. The researchers went further and suggested that the reasons for this might lie in inadequacies of the programme – Head Start may not have caught the children early enough; its methods may have been ineffective, and so on. In proposing these explanations, it is clear that the Ohio team was working from a premise that cognitive results *could* be improved by an appropriate course of ECE. Yet they were prepared to admit that, in the biggest enterprise of this sort (since the kindergartens spread throughout the US, at least) nothing had happened.

Reports such as this have failed to deter adherents of ECE – and of Head Start; in fact, they frequently say just the opposite. Writing in the widely-read British journal *Child Education* in December 1972, a correspondent discussed Head Start's manifold advantages, and wrote that 'Head Start, like many other centre-based pre-school programmes, repeatedly has been found to stimulate cognitive, language, and personal-social development in children'.

One of the many difficulties in the way of assessing results of this sort concerns the type of school to which the child is sent after what might be called 'treatment' at the pre-school centre. In an inferior school setting any gains which have been made in the wake of enthusiasm and stimulation from the care of extra staff will be lost in an elementary (primary) school where these advantages do not pertain. Longitudinal studies were, of course, lacking when Coleman and the other experts made their early reports; it is now suggested that in 'typical, tax-supported' (i.e. public) schools children who have had the benefit of the Head Start enrichment retain their places in the grade or form which is proper to their age while those who have bypassed pre-school assistance are held back, repeat their grades, or are the

occupants of special, remedial, classes. That the good effects do not
persist if the child moves from Head Start to an inferior primary school
is certain; thus a large financial investment is lost if the nation does not
turn its attention to the improvement of primary education in order
to make it prove worthy of Head Start.

It would be invidious to charge Head Start with failures in a
programme which it had not claimed to accomplish, and the objectives
laid down by the panel of experts chaired by Dr Robert Cooke in
February, 1965 placed cognitive improvement as only third on a list of
seven major goals. First came the need to improve the child's physical
health and physical abilities. Second came the need to help emotional
and social development 'by encouraging self-confidence, spontaneity,
curiosity, and self-discipline.' The remaining four were as follows:

> Establishing patterns and expectations of success for the child which
> will create a climate of confidence for his future learning efforts.
> Increasing the child's capacity to relate positively to family members
> and others while at the same time strengthening the family's
> ability to relate positively to the child and his problems.
> Developing in the child and his family a responsible attitude
> toward society, and fostering constructive opportunities for society
> to work together with the poor in solving their problems.
> Increasing the sense of dignity and self-worth within the child and
> his family.

From Head Start sprang an experimental departure from the
pattern of pre-school centres called 'Home Start'. This bases activities
inside the home, an obvious advantage in remote areas where climate
or distance would involve small children in discomfort if they were
transported to Head Start centres. The additional advantage of
involving the parent in ECE hardly needs to be pointed out, for this
has been a preoccupation of nursery schools, *maternelles,* kindergarten
everywhere. Another concomitant venture was termed 'Health Start',
which aimed at taking health services to siblings of Head Start
children who would not otherwise have seen a doctor or a dentist. Ten
thousand children were put in contact with health services in the first
year, 1971, doing something to relieve the situation which arises in the
United States where babies and their mothers may not see a doctor
after leaving hospital; no one in the community, in fact, may know
that the baby exists.[27]

Some American follow-up studies on Head Start found fault with the subsequent treatment of pupils in reception classes of primary schools, and other experts saw lapses in the kindergarten preparation year, when, they thought, too much time had been wasted in providing an indirect atmosphere for learning and a rather vague 'enriching environment'. The criticism could of course be levelled at the whole tradition of ECE through Froebel, the nursery schools, to most present-day environments in the British tradition of play-learning. In their fascinating recent digest of child care in the United States Robinson and Robinson speak of certain 'tacit assumptions' in the nursery schools (three- to five-year-olds) such as the belief that some sort of 'pecking order' will be established among the children, and that the oppressed will learn to stick up for their rights. When there are group activities such as singing or dancing the disinterested child is rarely asked to participate; and 'the only essential rules communicated to the child are that he must "play fair" by sharing toys with others, taking turns, etc.' And this in spite of the fact that one of the very admitted aims of such schools is what is called 'socialization'.[28]

If the reproach levelled against the first school is usually lack of direction and structured curriculum, what are the criticisms made of the elementary school which (as in the case of the Head Start evaluations) was frequently found to be wanting *after*wards? Usually evaluations have been made on a basis of IQ improvement, real or supposed, and it was necessary for the protagonists of compensatory education to show that under good conditions, the IQ improvement lasted or was even further advanced.

In assessing the results of Head Start it was found that effects on educational *motivation* were larger than effects on ability test performance, and that participants from the lowest socio-economic backgrounds, especially Negro pupils from poor families, had a higher educational motivation than non-participants. 'For whites, participants from lowest socio-economic backgrounds seemed more motivated than non-participants in some regions, while no effects of Head Start participation could be found for higher SES white pupils.' This, then, would appear to be a positive result from the programme and subsequent assessment, although not in terms of IQ gains, or not as yet.

Other investigation in the US examined the impact of the campaign on local communities to see whether for instance, there had been increased involvement of the poor with institutions and greater educational emphasis on the particular needs of minorities and the poor.

Education and health had traditionally been the provinces of
professionals in the US. These estimable persons had a long time
protected, taught, and disseminated middle-class values for the benefit
of middle-class families.[29] There were signs that changes which occurred
after Head Start in many communities tended to modify institutions
drastically. Some examples will illustrate the sort of thing that has been
happening:

> In a northern community an 'Extended Kindergarten' programme
> was developed for operation in two low-income area schools. The
> school official responsible said she had seen the need for it long
> before, but had been unable to act until federal funds became
> available.
> A black southern community now operates, through its school
> system, a comprehensive health clinic, and the school system has
> altered its traditional role of educator to include that of health-care
> provider as well. 'The idea for a health-care facility was generated by
> a Head Start nurse who realized the need for such a program
> after examining the Head Start enrollees, most of whom exhibited
> symptoms of chronic disease and malnutrition. Many had never
> been examined by a doctor.'

Hundreds of such examples of change tending towards greater help
to the poor and minorities were listed in the report, which in the
examples quoted above, brings irresistibly to mind the labours of the
McMillan sisters in London fifty years before. The side-effects of
compensation one would assume, then, are not inconsiderable, and
their eventual impact may be even stronger.

Leaving the United States for a digression which the academic reader
can ignore as being based on no statistical evidence whatsoever, the
writer describes, in another chapter, visits to the pre-school centres in
France. In one border area where there has traditionally been a great
deal of immigration from the neighbour country the *directrices*
(headmistresses) were emphatic about one thing: the small children
(two to four) who came to them from migrant families — and these are
usually manual labour groups — were under no disadvantage by the
time they reached elementary school. In other words, the linguistic
compensations of two to three years attendance at the *école maternelle*
were thoroughly effective in the majority of cases. After talking with
other *directrices* and observing neighbourhood children and migrant
families I believe that this happens to be true. Pre-school work in a

second language *while living in the environment of the second language*
is successful. This probably has something to do with the interest taken
by parents, who have something to gain by assimilating their children
to the governing society-structure.

Follow-through studies on a large-scale are sadly lacking when we
look at the information available to any student eager to resolve the
question of gain and compensation, at least for his own peace of mind.
Many small-scale reports, some positive, some negative have been done
on groups of children in the United States by psychology and
education departments, working along the well-trodden, but often
devious tracks of IQ tests, before and after pre-school work.

The decade of excitement and interest seemed to be brought to
an end when Arthur R. Jensen made his attack on compensatory
education in 1969, writing that compensatory education had been tried
and it apparently had failed.[30] Jensen's view was that the achievement
gap between 'minority' and 'majority' pupils had not been bridged by
the programmes 'evaluated' to that date, and his views lent force to the
arguments of sceptics who wished to see a reduction in government
expenditure on pre-school education.

In the course of his argument Professor Jensen did, however, become
quite optimistic about the work being done by Bereiter and Engelmann
(1966) at the University of Illinois pre-school,[31] which was
academically oriented, and gave to small groups instructions in twenty
minute bursts, on reading, language, and arithmetic. Attention,
motivation, and participation were maintained, he said, at a high level,
and as a result, the 'pre-post gains . . . in Stanford-Binet over an 18-
month period are about 8 to 10 points. . . .' Moreover, the scholastic
performance of the children showed gains commensurate to that of
children of higher IQ, ten or even twenty points higher, in fact.

Jensen's main complaints were competently dealt with by J. McV.
Hunt and David Elkind and there is no need to spend more time
than is necessary on the prophets of doom, of whom there is no
shortage at the present time. He was writing one year after Bank and
Solomon had reported on a tutorial language programme to develop
abstract thinking in socially disadvantaged children as follows: 'The
most striking gains in the program were the apparent joy in learning and
the feeling of mastery which the children displayed as the tutoring
progressed. The untutored children, even those who received individual
attention, showed none of these attitudes'.

In the same year (1969) as Jensen's report appeared, spreading
gloom abroad as far as Germany, where interested parties were waiting

for a clear optimistic result and prognosis before embarking on American-style programmes, Merle B. Karnes described her work. After engaging the interest of mothers from financially-poor homes, she had involved them in making instructional materials and using them at home. She found that over twelve weeks the children of these mothers gained an average of approximately eight points in IQ, insignificantly less than the average gain made by a comparable sample of children taught in a nursery school by professional teachers. At about the same time, Rosenthal and Jacobson produced a fascinating account of work which had led them to believe that it was the teacher and his expectations of the pupils in his care which fostered or inhibited growth of these pupils' IQ. We seem to have returned again to Froebel's original attempt to involve and interest the mothers of Germany, and Séguin's emphasis on the love factor in advancing achievement in severely retarded children.

But to return to Professor Jensen and the Illinois programme which seemed to win his approval by 'academic' methods. One of the authors of the Illinois project, Carl Bereiter, wrote later that his programme 'had more impact on IQ and achievement than the traditional, child-centred approach, but not necessarily more impact than other programs with a strong instructional emphasis'.

The Karnes programme and the DARCEE programme were cited as similar in general method, and these had shown gains in reading readiness and the Peabody Picture Vocabulary. The traditional nursery school and kindergarten, said Bereiter, could not be considered a serious contender as an educational programme! Montessori work had also been inferior to classes exposed to the 'instructional approach', he wrote, but then it had to be admitted that the Montessori method was unusual and likely to make *a strange bedfellow* no matter what category of programme it was put into.

The grounds of Bereiter's criticism are extremely significant, because they reveal the cul-de-sac into which psychological fashions have led the pre-school investment. Traditional nursery schools are a lower order of education, (if they are educative at all) where teachers do little teaching, and seldom intervene in these wholesome, middle-class surroundings which often involve parental expenditure and moderate affluence. The 'non-teachers' in these centres do not and cannot (as they have no learning programme) produce results; these are therefore custodial institutions, rather than centres for education, and depend for their existence on loose talk about 'the magic years' and similar fine sentiments which have circulated during the heyday of pre-school investment.

On the other hand, the few directive programmes such as Karnes and Bereiter-Engelmann begin with definite objectives: to develop learning capacity in useful areas such as reading and writing. They have managed to bring children of six years (the end of kindergarten year in the USA) up to the level of second graders in elementary school. They have achieved as Jensen admiringly recorded, 'pre-post gains in Stanford-Binet,' which are higher than in nearly all other programmes, including Montessori. These gains do disappear as the years go by, and there has accordingly been disillusionment among even the successful programmers of the directive schools. Yet this may mean, not so much a criticism of the pre-schools which are succeeding, but of the elementary school programmes which have not, to date, been examined in this merciless scientific light. Dr Bereiter has two criteria: the first appears to be the IQ and the second utility. We should teach these four- and five-year-olds the things which will be of use to them later.

This disillusionment with the results of the gallant US venture into pre-school education for the disadvantaged seems to be based on some of Pauline Kergomard's bogies. One recalls her striking condemnation of 'ignorant and ambitious parents' who wanted to assess the *maternelle* on their childrens' powers to read and write and do things which the inspectors and inspectresses of the French schools thought, not only inessential, but probably harmful. But that was before the IQ tests, which can only assess the very skills which Madame Kergomard, Froebel, Décroly, the McMillans, wished to defer. The vast circle of argument has run around from literacy as a goal, to testing literacy by the IQ tool and finding one school good when it shows high tests, and the others (thousands of them in the US) bad because the children show little gain.

This technique had all the attractions of the 'scientific' age, and when it was applied in Britain led to the famous eleven-plus years, when differential tests were applied on the eve of secondary education. As the test was similar in form to the school examinations it led to subsequent high average success which favoured, as the eleven-plus had done, the children from literate homes. 'Neither test nor school examination,' pointed out Professor Liam Hudson recently, 'represents more than a fraction of the qualities that any sane teacher or psychologist would wish to foster.'[32]

It is possible that programmes with a strong instructional emphasis do benefit a child's general development and improve his self-image in ways as yet undefined. There is a great deal we do not yet know about the factors which make for success in child-handling, and cognitive development — rather neglected in many centres and several countries — holds an important place. But we cannot anchor the movement from Froebel onwards to an adult-constructed assessment called the IQ test. By inflating the cult of the IQ, its partisans have stifled criticism from a public which is awed by the claims of scientific procedures. The fact that these procedures are often founded on intuition (like Itard's first teaching experiment with Victor) or hit-and-miss techniques does not always appear to general view. What we have termed the existential aspects of childhood, have been ignored or discarded as part of the myth of the 'magic years'; the place of music, the folk tale is passed over in silence or rejected as part of the time-table in the 'traditional' (i.e. unsuccessful) kindergarten. What nonsense it all is!

One of the fundamental frustrations the teacher always experiences in his work is that he has no objective way of knowing when some of his class is learning, yet often knows instinctively that this is happening. Those who found a positive value in much of Head Start spoke of the 'apparent joy in learning' revealed by pupils, and the increased effect on both children and parents when the latter were involved. When extravagant criticism of methods which stress the other aspects of personality have been moderated by experience, the growing United States contribution to child welfare and education may be seen in proper perspective. There was certainly little need for the feelings of despair which infected inquiry in West Germany, for example, when it was shown that expensive experimental programmes were having meagre results on IQ scores.

One would scarcely hold up performances of Beethoven symphonies until the right way of playing the *Eroica* was discovered. No one would suspend the secondary school system until research and debate had ascertained what, if anything, it was achieving apart from the preparation of students for tests. Pleas for putting the system into reverse and 'de-schooling' society are studied with the patient respect given to extreme intellectual views which smack of harmless anarchy. But for many years there has been this unreal debate about whether, just possibly, care before five can help an individual to improve a thing called the IQ and, if not, why should the government bother?

Maturation, among the more popular laboratory research topics and one on which Gesell and the generation of Susan Isaacs spent much time, has now lost its place. In other areas, what became of eidetic images, of chronaxie, or tropisms, asked an American psychologist in 1964.

Some leading theories have almost disappeared from discussion; others which have been successfully attacked and rejected by the majority show astonishing survival powers, such as Tolman's theory of latent learning. Having failed to die, latent learning persisted within the systems systems of Tolman's critics as a "domesticated" theory.[33] There seem to be indications that the dominant position of the IQ may now be shaken after fifty years of almost undisputed prestige.

If this happens, educators in the future will perhaps be able to call on several different disciplines to agree about a measurement tool which will assess the child's broad response to pre-school environment. A 'pre-post gain' in IQ, alertness and judgment, high spirits and physical well being will then indicate the successful schools rather than a single factor which has claimed some of the prestige of the philosopher's stone in pre-Baconian science.

PART 3: PERSONAL EXPERIENCES

10 A VISIT TO A NURSERY SCHOOL: BRITAIN AND FRANCE

Britain

The centres we describe here are not 'show' places, but actual schools which represent fairly well the average type of provision in Britain today. It so happens that they belong to semi-rural areas in the South of England, which is less well provided with maintained nursery education than Yorkshire, the North-West, Wales or the Midlands.

The market town and two nearby villages are separated by farmland and the highway; their population is a mixture of industrial workers who commute to factories, and local shop or farm employees. Old houses and cottages contain the remnants of the *rentier* classes and a few professional families – doctor, dentist and solicitor, while further outwards near the fields are two or three estates of council-built houses which contain the bulk of the youth population.

Each village has a small primary school, well-built and fairly well staffed. These contain six classes of as many as thirty-four children each, aged from seven to eleven; the 'infants' (five-year-olds) number more than a hundred in a purpose-built classroom unit built away from the main blocks. They are grouped in family units of about thirty pupils each, and are looked after by four hard-worked teachers and a few helpers.

In one village there is a struggling playgroup (about twenty children under five) which meets in the church hall four mornings a week. In the second village there is a playgroup which meets in makeshift surroundings under the supervision of a capable woman, and another which meets in someone's house and is barely legal. Neither village has proper accommodation for the under-fives, no adventure playgrounds or council-built equipment for physical exercise. Only private initiative has begun the playgroups, and many mothers in this rural area refuse to pay the fee of fifty pence per week required for expenses. Mothers take it in turns to help in the playgroup on a roster system, which pleases the children who get excited when they know 'Mummy is coming to help the teachers tomorrow.' Participation and idea-sharing helps a lot in these small rural communities, isolated by the long English winters from the main stream of PPA organization. Children play in the church hall, help to put out the chairs and toys, listen to a noisy record on a makeshift player, pause for a story in mid-morning, and play outside when the weather permits. There is little organization or 'pre-school theory' about it all, and it is doubtful if many of the mother-helpers have heard of Froebel or even read about Montessori. The children do much as they like. For our little girl this was her first school, and she loved it in spite of a few awkward days of 'school refusal' shown in tears and screams of rage. It compared more than favourably with the playgroup in London later, where the helpers seemed to be about the same, but several children were rather disturbed, very noisy, and occasionally violent.

In the nursery-school across the river, an old wartime building, there are no casual mother-helpers. About sixty-four children have been admitted and there is a long waiting list of under-fives. Parents are advised to 'put the child down at birth' and hope for the best at age two.

Probably only one in five of the local child cadre is fortunate enough to be admitted to the solitary nursery school, supported by the local authorities and offering care by trained personnel. Twenty children stay all day, and two groups of twenty alternate morning and afternoon half days, so there are about forty children inside the building morning and afternoon.

The building is inadequate, but it is inside a quiet park, which may explain the absence of garden plants and growing things. It is only necessary to open the doors and the children have access to a 'jungle' and wired-in playground. The park is their school garden, reserved hundreds of years ago from the rush of 'enclosures' which threatened the Englishman's common land.

The lady principal was a pleasant, rather serious, young woman, who told me that nearly one-third of her children were admitted because of serious problems in the home environment. A severe selection procedure was necessary because of the shortage of places, and she was continually refusing children who definitely would have benefited from nursery school in the McMillan-Isaacs tradition. There was nothing to be done about this, unless local authorities took up the challenge and built some more centres, which they showed no sign of doing. She had two trained assistants, a part-time trained teacher (secondary), and three students-in-training, who were completing their two-year 'NNEB course' at a nearby town. There were thus about six to eight children for each grown-up assistant. I was put in a corner seat and began to watch.

Almost at my knees six children were standing and sitting around a small table, watched by a pleasant young woman with a slight Scots accent whom they called by her Christian name, Morag. They were drawing and painting. Another lady teacher was occupied in tidying and putting away a multitude of coloured blocks in cupboards. The room was fairly large, large enough anyway to contain a mass of material: there were five or six small white deal tables and many small chairs; a big Christmas tree in a corner, a tank with water in it and objects floating about, a two-sided Wendy House shutting off a far corner for home-games, a small cage with two little creatures like hamsters which I was told were gerbils, jig-saw puzzles, mobile objects floating, big pictures in colour pinned to the walls for display. The impression was one of confusion, which was added to by children walking through the room either alone or in twos, and disappearing into the next room where the washtubs and coat hangers were. Only the six near me seemed to be intent on their work, and I began to wonder if they had been trained for the part.

Fifteen minutes had passed and I had begun to wonder how four-year-olds could concentrate for so long when, almost imperceptibly, the group began to dissolve. A small boy came round the table to me and put in front of me a black scribble faintly resembling a horse: 'Black Beauty,' he said. A little girl with a lot of personality and smiles came up to tell me she was Amantha. A third produced a black drawing which was faintly terrifying and said 'That's my Mummy — she's got long teeth.' A fourth came to tell me she 'had done the Christmas tree' which seemed rather miraculous as she was pale and thin and the tree was six feet high, decorated with bells and parcels, and planted in a pot. Then I noticed Lissa, for that was her name, was pointing elsewhere, looking up at the high windows; stuck along the windows were cut-out pictures from coloured paper stuck on white paper to make designs. The second small picture paper was of a red tree on green paper.

Near the gerbil cage was a tank with a few inches of water in it and Lissa drifted over to it, followed by me. She put her hands in and began picking out cylinders, watching the water pour out — much of it poured over me. Quietly and deftly, Morag the teacher came over to roll up sleeves, and the pouring went on, watched intently by Lissa as she tried out different shapes; I said one of them wasn't floating, a heavy shell, and she agreed, pensively, picking it up and seeming to weigh it. We had been joined by strangers from the next room, one or two burly little boys, who hit me and then smiled. 'I'm a doggy.' one told me. 'I'm a monkey,' countered another and they chased each other

into the next room. A smaller, quiet, lonely-seeming boy with fair
hair was standing next to me by now and told me that he had two
fishes but one was dead. This little boy did not seem involved in anything; he watched Lissa with the water and the burly boys who had
begun on jig-saw puzzles at a table next to me. I saw that Amantha had
gone back to the first table and resumed drawing, Sheila had gone over
to an easel where there was a large piece of paper and long brushes.
Quickly a helper followed her and arranged a smock over her dress. By
this time, I had had a discussion about the jig-saw with one boy, another
had come up with a piece of brown plasticine on a yellow plastic
saucer and told me 'that's bread and butter' only to be outsmarted by
another with a bigger blob of the stuff who said 'and that's cake'. Peter,
the small loner boy, was sitting on my knee and one of the little girls
told me 'He is new'. Someone had gone into the Wendy House and was
arranging furniture. Everyone, except little Peter, was busy in different
places, and I began to adjust to the strange and unusual pattern of it
all, there was order, but also full freedom inside the order. One of the
helpers came by and answered some of my questions: 'you will notice
that although they play or work sometimes in a group one of them may
be there but not really *of* the group, alone rather inside the group.' 'How
do you tell that?' I asked. 'Well, you can see when they aren't sharing
or passing things, for instance.' From the next room where Peter had
gone came the sound of uncontrollable sobbing; one of the helpers had
him on her knee and was comforting him and rocking him. He had only
been at the school two weeks, and had come from a home which had
broken up; now his mother had to go to work to keep him and his
father had left the area.

At eleven-thirty all the other children ran off to hear a story in
another room, and it was possible to have a short conversation in the
office, with Peter the newcomer within watching distance. Even he,
the principal pointed out, was making progress, for he had come up to
me voluntarily and this would have been unthinkable a few weeks
earlier. The other children, too, would have been shy with a stranger
in the first weeks of term. Their sociability revealed their adjustment
to the group, and at first there were a few, like Peter, who sat alone, or
wept for days on end. Unfortunately, we were close to the Christmas
break, and Peter like some others, would be sent to his grandmother or
a child-minder's house.

We began to talk about the equipment of the school, and the
principal became involved in what was clearly part of her pride in the
centre. Makeshift without — for this was the local authority's

responsibility — she and the helpers made it as efficient and friendly as possible inside. Everything on tables and floors seemed scattered at random to my ignorant eye, but she explained how false was this impression. In a nursery school every piece of equipment, including the toys, is there for a purpose, psychological or didactic — as little as possible is left to chance.

There was no reading taught, as such, in the nursery school, or writing, but in the course of the nursery year, or two years, teachers could see the development of a child's interest and muscular control. Moreover, many of the class came — even in 1973 and in a prosperous (and rather smug) little community — from homes which could not provide a variety of enrichment experiences for their children. Many mothers were ignorant of what should be offered, and others were in cramped accommodation.

In this nursery school individual records of the psychological sort are not kept;[*] the principal, watching, guiding and helping the children all the time prepares a full report which she sends on to the infant school which the child is to enter at five. When they do enter school, many of them, she thought, were still not ready for it, as the nursery school teachers could see. Some, but only a few, were ready earlier. When I asked how learning was measured at this early stage, I was told that the teachers could tell, by observation, just what was happening and they knew learning was going on, by play and through play, which was the only possible way of learning. I asked if she had considered the need for more guidance, more directed activity and met with opposition; each child was learning at his or her own speed and his own way. Although older ones did help the younger ones, because of 'family' grouping, they could not help them really until the younger ones were ready for it.

The writer had previously spent two terms teaching at a boys' secondary school in the district, where he had been surprised at the number of disturbed boys in classes picked at random, and at one or two boys whose reading stage seemed to be almost that of a five-year-old. Her answer was prompt: these were children who had not found places in a nursery school.

So here was one principal convinced of the rightness of the present method, which she had learnt in a two-year course of infant teaching at an education college. There was no Montessori equipment in the school 'because there are special schools which teach Montessori.' The

---

[*]   A standardized record sheet is now being planned for British nursery schools.

other interesting thing was that she considered there had been a slackening of interest in hygiene during the last five years; showing me the individual basins, and towels, in the entrance room where the coats hung on individual pegs, she explained that the children usually washed when they arrived, and she liked them to wash before meals. But they just did it — it was not a compulsory routine.

As I left, a file of urgent little figures was pushing from the story-room towards the end classroom, where some low tables had been set with twenty knives, forks, and spoons. A lady had come in to cook the midday meal, which was eagerly awaited on this winter's day, and the children would have their food at four or five tables, each with a staff member to sit with them. The entrance hall was empty and quiet; I unlocked the railing gate which had a bolt about four feet up on the far side, and left, looking back. There was nothing to be seen of the entrance to the rooms where Peter was learning to overcome his separation fears and the others were training eye, ear, touch, and feeling for the rapidly approaching day when they would be 'rising five' and sent off to spend all day in an infant school. Outside, in the parks, streets, or flats were the majority of under-fives in the district, under the care of minders, relatives, or the playgroup leaders. The fortunate few I had left behind me inside a specialized institution run on principles slowly but surely evolved from Froebel to the present-day.

France

My visit to a *maternelle* in the South was in winter, and rain fell in bursts over the olives and vines, heavy clouds masking what, for the children along the Mediterranean, is usually a clear blue sky. One has to be received at a *maternelle* by appointment; a *'femme de service'* came out to unlock the outer doors and tell me that the *directrice* was ready to receive me in her office. Like every other room in the building, it was spotlessly clean and had very little furniture. It opened on one side into the room where the older children *(les grands)* had their classroom; on the other side, where we began our tour, it adjoined the big hall where, by regulation, rhythm, music, and exercises can be enjoyed on rainy days.

The building was light, built of stone painted cream, with tiled floors. There was not only no dust anywhere, it was as if while the lessons were going on, the assistants were walking around dusting and polishing continuously. There was no unnecessary furniture; in the big hall where we began by meeting the *petits* at their first activity of the day — rhythm and music — there were four thick columns supporting the roof, a bench on one side where the record-player stood and a low bench on the corridor side. The children moved around or sat on the tiled floor. The teacher was perpetually on the move, demonstrating a way to walk, or sway to the music, guiding the slower ones, leading a slow dance, picking one up or moving one to another place. The *directrice* said to me: 'You can see why we often cannot keep the teachers who take the little ones: it is so tiring. They are always working, and nearly always leaning over or stooping down.'

A broad corridor ran right around the classrooms, forming an L-shaped enclosure. There were solid walls each side at child-height except where, outside each classroom, a row of hooks was fixed, above each one a picture drawn by the owner, and a name: Mario, Louise, Justin. One of the assistants had a table and chair in mid-corridor where she was sewing blouses, and could see any happenings at either end, and where a child who had strayed would see a reassuring figure. Large painted pictures taken from the classwork hung at intervals along the corridor.

The corridor was the outside limit of activity during the school day from 8.20 a.m. to 11.20 a.m. and from 1.20 p.m. to 4.20 p.m. The inside area was the playground and garden and all the rooms opened out on to this precious region so that each class disgorged its fill of noisy excitement directly into freedom. When they returned, however, they came in the main doors and filed around the corridor to their room, and this was done in silence, with much timid looking towards the figure of the teacher waiting for them. 'They are absolutely quiet,' I remarked with the naivety of an ex-secondary teacher. 'But *of course*,' said the *directrice*. The same atmosphere was to be found inside the classrooms. Noise is for outside; silence and concentration are for within the maternelle.

The playground was asphalted and there was no sand-pit. As the school was a large one (seven classes) the scene at recreation time was one of barely intelligible bedlam. The little ones had their own playground joined to a garden, and this was walled-off from the older children. Four fine young eucalyptus trees grew inside the playground and around the outside was a border of colourful flowers. Inside the garden for the *petits* was a merry-go-round, with wooden horses. I noticed some paving stones, brightly painted white against the green lawn, and missed their significance until the *directrice* pointed out to me that they were spaced for hopping from one to another; attention to detail, once again. Beyond the garden was a small building where a cook and several assistants were preparing a midday meal for those children who stayed behind. Above was the blue sky of Provence with some winter clouds and a glimpse of rocky hills. Anything less like the prison buildings of conventional schools could not be imagined, and the atmosphere of serenity was completed by the presence of complete sound-proofing throughout the building.

The teacher in the middle class (three- and four-year-olds) was dynamic and very much in charge of her task: I asked her to show me some teaching aids she had made up herself, because foreign visitors have usually remarked on the laudable inventiveness of the French teachers. She pulled out large folio albums and showed me, explaining rapidly as she went, the pictures and symbols inside them and what they were supposed to teach the children. Then there were boxes containing sets of pictures the size of table mats, drawn, coloured, varnished and fixed on stiff cards or light boards, boxes containing shapes, boxes containing pictures cut out of magazines, pasted on to cards for class use. They were all drawn with what one can only term *élan;* light, not boring or intimidating, attractive and even witty.

Exercises in observation which Pauline Kergomard had recommended to teachers in preference to learning abound in the modern *maternelle.* Sets of pictures to be matched are carefully prepared, and require both observation and concentration for the required result; working at different speeds the pupils in the course of a year are introduced to recognising sets of common qualities. Much of this sort of work prepares them for concepts in the 'new maths', which were introduced into French schools only a few years ago. [*]

One exercise the teacher of the middle class had prepared was a series on stiff varnished cards which featured a tall and handsome mouse, or several mice, for the mouse altered in important details. Shuffling through the pack of cards one found that what seemed to be the same mouse, bewhiskered and standing, now had four feet instead of two. Then it acquired a pink ribbon tied in a bow around its long tail. Several mice shared the pink ribbon and other characteristics, but were looking backwards towards their tails. Four- and five-year-olds who were 'playing' with these cards were exercising a high degree of concentration.

---

[*] An English teacher who worked on exchange in Bordeaux reported that she found the most striking thing in the *maternelles* was the importance given to development of mathematical concepts. There was a wealth of pre-mathematical experience: children were introduced to the idea of sets, learned 'greater than', 'smaller than' and mapping all through simple games. (See *Child Education,* June, 1973.)

Sorting and distinguishing qualities was going on a lot at this level: another album displayed a whole series of little sailing-boats with round hulls, which began very simply indeed, drawn large on a folio page with only one sail, a square one, and labelled *'une voile'*. It was joined on the next sheet by another similar sailing-boat. On the third sheet one of the yachts had acquired a second sail. On the fourth sheet they both had two sails. On the fifth one had changed to a red instead of a blue hull. Then they both acquire red hulls and one decided to have a green sail instead of a white one. The hulls changed colour, the sails changed colour, the boats acquired little tricolour flags, and so there were six or seven different sets of detail on the big sheets, which hinged out to be quite easily visible to the class. Another exercise in making sets and grouping things was shared in by the children, who were put to cut out of old magazines large numbers of pictures of toys. These were pasted on to cards and then sorted over a period of several weeks into: toys for girls (label *'filles'* attached to example pinned on wall); toys for boys *(garçons);* and for babies *(bébés)*. There were dozens of these, and the mistress told me that the complete sorting takes the average child at least fifteen days.

In the centre of the room hung a brightly-coloured group of strange-looking objects, tall party hats and coloured masks; a project built around the idea of Carnival, which was just about to start in the district. On the walls were coloured drawings and paintings of people, and animals and animal designs whose outlines had been set out with brightly glittering beads, or seed such as yellow corn. Painted red or blue the beads alternated in more complex designs, but each different colour was in its exact place, and I noticed how frequently the younger children were occupied with muscular control and co-ordination: roneoed sheets were issued with a simple landscape over which raindrops shown by rather large strokes were falling. The children drew or coloured in these strokes with great care and precision. The result after some months was the gorgeous display of beads and paint on the walls, added to and developed by chance encounters or the teachers with new materials. One fascinating animal with a furry glistening shape on the wall drew my curiosity until I ran my finger over it: the *directrice* on her journeys round the town had come on a carpenter's shop and appropriated a heap of new shining wood-shavings for the 'middles' and their teacher.

The pupils' albums are carefully kept in the classrooms during the year: they do not take work home although the parents are invited to come and see it. The pages are numbered, labelled from September

onwards and the development of pictorial control and confidence can
be seen through the year (the French speak of a child's 'progression',
rather than development). Record-keeping is attempted in spite of the
large classes: in the little ones' classroom the teacher had placed among
all the other bright posters on the wall a log-book of experiences, like
this:

WE HAVE	Sept.-Oct.	Nov.	Dec.
tasted	chestnuts	bananas	
looked at	giraffe (tall)	roses	
smelt	roses	gum-leaves	pine-needles
	mimosa		
touched	walnuts		
heard			

The gaps were partly in the original and partly due to my speed of
note-taking falling behind the 'happenings', for by this time I was back
with the original class of little ones rapt in observation of the teacher
practising group-work with a tape-recorder and microphone. Ten or
fifteen children were taking it in turns to say a few lines of a poem
about a fish into the microphone and then hear their enunciation from
the box in the corner. They were quite unselfconscious about it, an
extraordinary thing to anyone who has tried to overcome teenage
embarrassment during this sort of activity. The rest of the class was
very seriously and quietly occupied at easels in the corner near the door
wielding long brushes and choosing their colours from a palette. This
would go on for about twenty minutes, and then there would be play
or an entirely different sort of activity. It was laid down in
regulations early in the century that the children must not be kept
at any activity to the point of fatigue and that manual work and
physical activity must alternate with exercises requiring concentration.
The average activity lasts for twenty minutes and up to a half-hour
for the bigger ones, several of whom by the way, had turned six.
   Here is an example of a time-table for the older pupils taken from
a *maternelle* in the 1970s. It provides interesting material for
comparison with the earlier time-tables quoted:

EMPLOI DU TEMPS: SECTION DES GRANDS

	Monday	Tuesday	Wednesday	Friday	Saturday
0750 to 0810	Arrival and welcome: exercise and dances: songs and rounds				
0815 to 0900	Beginning reading (every morning for 20 minutes)				
0900 to 0930	First steps in writing, following reading practice				
0900 to 0930	Beginning exercises in rhythm in the hall, using aids				
RECESS TIME	PLAYTIME	PLAYTIME			
1000 to 1030	Story	Speech	Observation	Story	Speech
1035	Painting or Drawing		Drawing from painting or drawing		
1120	either free or to illustrate story		object to illustrate story or subject discussed		
NOON BREAK	FOR LUNCHTIME	NOON BREAK			
1320 to 1340	Arrival and welcome: exercises and games together				
1340 to 1400	Reciting verse and singing songs				
1400 to 1430	First steps in mathematics: reasoning games: individual and collective exercises				
FIVE MINUTES FOR RELAXATION					
1435 to 1500	Manual work	painting	cutting out	sticking and collage linked with a theme in daily life	
PLAYTIME	RECESS	PLAYTIME			
1530	Continuation of hand work, collectively or in small groups				
1600 1620	Music	Puppets	Stories (not linked with theme)	Films	
1620 1630	Getting ready to go home HOMEWARD BOUND				

Remembering that the object of the *maternelle* is to supply all the care traditionally given by a mother in the home, one reflects after a first visit to the school scene that the care is strongly directive.

Children seldom seem to be left alone for very long, and much is expected of them. Thus the situation is that, instead of being inside the home walls where he or she can 'do their own thing', they are really continuously on show among the other children and to the other children and the teacher. This gives an Anglo-Saxon visitor a feeling of unreality, of a non-childhood situation created by adults in the interests of adults.

These impressions, however, fail to take into account the French way of child rearing. It is impossible to assess the *maternelle* without considering the home matrix from which the toddlers emerge at two or two and a half, and this in turn is only part of the national way of life. There is mutual interaction between the home and the *maternelle,* with perhaps a tendency for the *maternelle* to set higher standards (certainly in the learning process) and hope to see them communicated to the parents. Now the French place importance on appearances and on a child's deportment; when a French mother takes her small child down the street or boulevard, not only is he or she prettily dressed and neatly brushed, but is under continual surveillance to stay that way. A French woman herself is on show, she is part of the spectacle of life in a country where 'the visible world exists'. Her child is not to dawdle along, but to stay *sage* (good), not to drop toys on the pavement, not to put fingers in mouth, and so on. I remember a small child being carried in one of the poorer *arrondissements* of Paris – the eleventh. It all happened very quickly indeed. The mother passed me, carrying the child at her shoulder: the child dropped his teddybear: I stooped and picked it up: while I was doing so the toddler was being told that he would get a good smack on the bottom for this, was given it, silenced, and the teddybear was taken from me with a radiant smile and *Merci bien, monsieur,* as the lady stepped onwards on her high heels along the boulevard. Junior must not step out of line. In the *maternelle* it is the same: *pas de pagaille,* said the efficient and charming mistress of the middle class in Provence, pulling a small rosy-cheeked three year old out of the file.

The French language is stronger in negatives than in affirmatives and one continually notices the preference for negative statements and questions constructions in conversation. The upbringing of the small child in the home is a succession of don'ts, not only in France but in many countries where toddlers get in the way and do untidy things. But the French insist on standards which the British are inclined to let slip, one suspects. The French child is always expected to behave as if he were being watched by courtiers; the dignity of the *Grand Siècle* has been considerably diluted, but traces of it still are evident in the middle-class home. One thing is sacred and must be the focus of positive thinking: the business of eating. Every scrap must be removed from the plate; no distractions or messing about are permitted; Marie must eat her bread and drink her soup.

A French clinical psychologist probably went too far when she said that even in the most liberal French families childhood consists of duties and no rights; or rather, the child has the right to obey, to work in school, and to help at home — 'even his rights are duties.' Yet it pays to keep this view in mind before making too harsh a judgment on the strictness of the *maternelle*.

Another factor which inhibits the quest for greater freedom is a physical one. In conversation with a young *directrice* (who had not shown me her pupils at work that day) she explained that she had forty-five children in her class, which was the older group — *les grands*. The building in which we were talking was solidly built late in the last century: yet there was no free space where children could play, and a classroom only just accommodated the forty-five *when they were in their places*. She showed me a diminutive concrete garden area where she had planted flowerbeds with bright colours, and a box in which sat a large and nervous-looking rabbit, a male. ('He is feeling lonely; we will have to find him a mate soon.') Madame told me she had heard of Summerhill in England and seen a film about a permissive school in Switzerland; she wished she could be less rigid, and tried not to be, but with forty-five children. . . . The next day, although I was not allowed to visit her classes, which was understandable under those conditions, I met two of the younger teachers, the assistants. They both showed signs of strain, which was inevitable given the size of class and their cramped working quarters.

The *directrice* in that school was a thoughtful and frank woman and it was especially interesting to me to find that a person in another country, another system of education, and working at an entirely different level, shared some of the crucial problems I had felt when teaching in England. When I told her how interested I had become in Pauline Kergomard her face lit up and she told me she had been trying for some time to obtain more information about her. The *directrice* showed me her class work based on the 'centre of interest' method. They had followed for three months in great detail a study of life in a Red Indian settlement in the Far West, and the packed album of drawings bore witness to their response. Half-apologetically, she said that there was a move to let children choose their activity and abandon the strict principle of the common centre of interest but she had not had the courage or the training to do this. 'In an *école maternelle* I think probably the most important thing is the personality of the *directrice;* I feel that my training was not really adequate in putting me in touch with progressive theories, and the assistants are influenced of course by my views. I obtained the *Baccalauréat* and training but I don't have a university degree, and am attending courses part-time at night to obtain more education.'

We passed through a classroom where I counted thirty-six small tables — each with its built-in drawer, both neat and comfortable. Three brightly shining saucepans hung on wall-hooks not for cooking, but for playing kitchens. There was one basin and a single tap at the end of the room, presumably for washing paints and hands. Mobiles hanging from the ceiling, bright friezes, flowers and models of animals provided the usual cheeriness and interest I had begun to associate with the *maternelles.* The last room, opening on to the outside courtyard was the kitchen, which was, of course, spotless and light. There I was introduced to the dietician *(économe),* the cook, the cook's helper, and a general assistant who works between 10 a.m. and 4 p.m. For the benefit of parents a small menu was hanging outside the front door, just like any attractive restaurant in France; the parents now have to pay nearly four francs for each meal taken at the school, so they are entitled, said the *directrice,* to see what their offspring are given. Part of the cost is taken up by the local council (the *commune)* which is also responsible for the staff wages bill for the kitchen. Sixty children eat their midday meal in that school, and as we walked back to the office we went through a room where twenty or more little ones were sitting around tables, even though it was after school time. These are the children who are minded until a much later hour because their parents are unable to pick them up at four-thirty. They were about to be given another light meal by the kitchen staff; the social as distinct from the educational role of the school had begun, and I was reminded of a story told by a visitor in the fifties who came upon a similar group on a winter's day afternoon in Paris, holding hands and singing together to pass the time, 'we are the little caretakers, busy taking care . . . .' while a watchful assistant swept and cleaned around them. It is the moment when the modern *maternelle* seems closest to the plain realities of Madame de Pastoret's *asile* for neglected children.

The previous year, Madame — told me, she had taken into her *grands* class a difficult boy, aged five, who seemed to have turned against his parents and the world at large. It had been a particular problem because of the lack of space and the directive methods this imposes for much of the day. The boy had withdrawn from normal speech and only communicated in grunts, giving no sign that he had learned to speak. With the other children it was a continual story of aggression: he spat, kicked, or punched (some of which is *'normal'* at this age, but not when it excludes any acceptable social behaviour). She decided to take the boy on as a particular challenge, after talking to the mother, who obviously did not know what to do with him at home. 'I think they need to feel loved by someone — one must always keep the smile on one's lips in a *maternelle,* whatever is happening — but also feel that there is someone who expects a lot from them.' The social security people had been contacted, and arrangements were made for speech therapy at a private clinic, paid for by social security funds. The *directrice* kept him as close as possible during school hours; towards the end of the year he had begun to co-operate in class, very slowly and timidly as the disturbed ones always do, to answer when spoken to, and occupy himself with the activities recommended in the school. What was even more interesting was that he made the transition after that to primary school, where he came under a *male* teacher, without difficulty, and reports from the teacher and from the mother continued to be satisfactory. The real work of early education is being done here, and that despite overcrowded rooms.

Many children find the transition to more formal teaching situations almost traumatic, to use the fashionable term. Madame — and others told me of children crying and refusing to take part in the lessons for a long time after entering the elementary school. One, she recalled recently was deeply upset and frightened for five long months, during which the mother and the child came to visit the *maternelle* and recounted their tale of woe. The comparative freedom of the *maternelle* is now having some effect on the classes above, repeating the process of reform which penetrated upward in Britain from the progressive nursery school theorists, but there is still a long way to go in France, before there is a genuine reform of a learning situation which remains tense. *The école maternelle is considered already reformed,* and so is in marked contrast with the unchanging methods of France's primary schools since the last century. It is the pride of the *maternelle* and the shame, one might almost say, of the primary level, that the authors of a recent French study could admit that *'les écoles maternelles sont en France la seule expérience généralisée d'éducation nouvelle.'*

Visitors from abroad are often surprised that we do not leave the children alone to take up some activity, carry on with it and then drop it when the spirit moves them; they are surprised that the teacher does not hold back like an observer, a silent supervisor, as she is told to be in many foreign schools. In France the freedom of the child is calculated by the staff because we think that if it is precisely measured, this is what will ensure their freedom as men, later. Alain called this the real freedom, which is 'at the centre of obedience' and is a willing submission to reason, necessity or pure feeling. The place assigned to freedom and free activity varies according to the age of the children and the exercises which have been put before them or chosen by them. From two to four, for example, their play and their exercises are free; but as the child grows and his ego displays aggressive traits we feel that it has to be restrained; are we not right in thinking that he has to become a social being?

'Happiness for us is not altogether dependent on bright sunshine and a clear day of spring,' went on the inspector of *maternelles*. 'Nor is it only a matter of comfort, material possessions, or the hunt for a new amusement: it is based on our very being, our humour, our thoughts. . . and our habit of conquering ourselves in order to maintain — whatever happens — the best of our nature on the surface.' Thus the claim is made that a nursery-school upbringing should be, in some measure, an expression of a nation's best habits and traditions. The children's happiness is sought within a well-regulated life and self-control is considered equal with submission to the laws of their peer-group among the ideals of an *école maternelle*. Philosophically the French view regards the pursuit of happiness as a simplistic concept, which disregards the happiness consequent upon strenuous effort, upon the urge to discovery, and the striving to bring under control our anti-social urges and selfish outbursts. Teachers themselves have been through a gruelling preparation in public competitive examinations, inspection, training and probation. They well know what awaits the little children when they have to enter primary school in France, for it is only very recently that health and education authorities have realised that primary children in France have been over-burdened in work and under-nourished with fresh air. Not for them, as yet, the 'open-plan' classroom of the English junior experimental schools, free activity periods, multiple options and fluid time-tables. Greatly as Pauline Kergomard desired French *maternelles not* to be influenced by the standards of the first grades in primary level, any teacher knows that standards and examination systems loom over one's progressive enterprises like a threatening ogre.

France has never suffered from waves of anti-intellectualism such as Anglo-Saxon countries have known in this century. The working-class Frenchman has a respect for learning and academic qualifications which is unknown in Britain or America. He certainly knows, also, that the only avenues to high places are held open through the *lycées, écoles normales,* institutions such as the *Polytechnique* and the universities. There is always the danger that 'acceleration' may be applied to the detriment of freedom.

That there were dangers in hurrying little children along too fast were apparent to the people who founded the modern *école maternelle* between 1889 and 1921. They issued a warning, in the form of a decree, to remind parents and teachers that a committee had inquired into the disastrous effects of premature intellectual education on the physical development of the child and on its health. Because of this, the committee recommended that 'all work requiring immobility be abolished in the *écoles maternelles;* that, at least, no two intellectual courses be given consecutively and that an intellectual course should be separated from a manual course by 15 minutes of physical activity.'

Moreover (and one seems to detect the voice of Pauline Kergomard speaking),

'Parents and teachers are greatly responsible for the errors committed in the *École Maternelle:* ignorant and unduly ambitious parents demand that their children learn to read and write long before being able to speak or understand what is said to them; teachers of Primary Education, misjudging the danger of the initial intellectual effort, blame the Principal of the *Maternelle* if their children do not know how to read, write, and count before entering Primary School. Neither parents nor teachers seem to be aware that the subsequent progress of intelligence is assured if the child has made a habit of personal observation and if it has been methodically acquainted by vision with the objects of its surroundings.

It has been from the time of Pauline Kergomard a central credo that the *école maternelle* is a happy place. Writing in 1886, she appealed for little children to have 'freedom and happiness, so that they may expand like vigorous and healthy plants. In their own homes they had frequently been witness to sad and ugly occurrences and consumed a sort of poison: let the *école maternelle* be the antidote.' It has to offer, said a leading authority in our time 'space, air and light, toys . . . sand and water' to children from the most disadvantaged areas. Other French writers with experience of the schools went even further, saying the *maternelle* was to be 'a paradise for children, where they will find air, light, tenderness, calm and beauty.'

This wonderland of childhood was remote from the grim walls of the older *salle d'asile-maternelle* tradition. Farringdon observed sadly in 1906 that the spirit of real enjoyment which seemed to underlie the play of kindergarten children in his country was quite unknown to the *école maternelle.* There is certainly in England and America even now a bias towards emotional and social development and balance which critics feel may neglect the cognitive aspect of growth. We need to remember that there is a wider margin of liberty left to teachers at this level than elsewhere in the rigid French system; all sorts of approaches and methods are used under the same roof. And so it is that centres exist where the unreal atmosphere of 'early one morning', as the poet Walter de la Mare called it, is created and endures for a time. 'Some teachers believe,' wrote Jeanne Bandet recently, 'that childhood is, in itself, a precious possession which should be preserved in its perfection. In their classes one senses the construction of a world of faery and a conscious or more or less conscious preservation of the past through the magic of images and words. They separate, in order to defend it, a poetic style of living from the harsh reality, which in their opinion is not made for children.'

The existential view of childhood still lives therefore inside some schools of our industrialised 'new' society, and these are schools where cognitive advancement is given due weight. Something has remained of the late eighteenth-century esteem for a divine element in childhood which is worth preserving; looking upwards at the next grades in primary school and the demands of an unsympathetic world scientific educators may deplore the fact. Readiness for the next level, and the next, is not achieved by creation of a world of faery, they would say. But without it, we might as well admit that we are not talking about childhood, we are talking about the ladder of book-learning and ambition. Nursery schools have to achieve a very delicate balance; in the French conclusion to a hundred years of practice and reflection, 'all the infant teachers are convinced that *their first task is to ensure the happiness of their charges . . . their other task is to help them grow up and become themselves.*'

NOTES

Chapter 1

1. Anon., *Memoirs of John Frederic Oberlin*, William Bell, London, 1835.
2. The best account is in Parisot's biography (Paris, 1905), which quotes from Oberlin's letters and contemporary documents.
3. See, for instance, Prost, *L'Histoire de l'Enseignement en France 1800-1967*, Armand Colin, Paris, 1968.
4. *Manuel des Salles d'Asile*, 1833.
5. It is worth recording that the *crèche* movement, which looked after infants between fifteen days and three years, began in 1841, following Madame de Pastoret's isolated early venture. *Crèches* were described as a reward for women's industry, and were not to be considered a right for women, whether they worked or not. They were launched by private enterprise under the slogan, 'while we look after the children, industry looks after the mothers' and received State aid after 1862. By the end of the century they had appeared all over France and been copied in other European countries. There were then 320 *crèches* outside Paris, which may be compared with the figure for England, where there were 19 outside the London area.
6. Hunt, *Parents and Children in History*, Harper Torchbooks, 1970, p.194.
7. After 1876, the school lunch movement spread through Germany also, and the idea of feeding children's bodies as well as their minds finally caught on in New York City (1898) and England (1902).
8. Jules Ferry (1832-93) was variously Education Minister, Fine Arts Minister Foreign Minister and Prime Minister during the crucial years of reform.
9. See John E. Talbott, *The Politics of Educational Reform in France*, Princeton University Press, 1969.
10. This revealing passage is quoted in John W. Padberg's *Colleges in Controversy, The Jesuit Schools in France from Revival to Suppression, 1815-1880*, Harvard University Press, 1969.

Chapter 2

1. Thanks to Robert R. Rusk, who obtained a copy from Jena before the Second World War. Rusk concluded that Princess Pauline, rather than Robert Owen, should be given credit for the first nursery school, but the inspiration came from Paris and Madame de Pastoret's circle. R. R. Rusk, *A History of Infant Education*, University of London Press, 1933.
2. A Leipzig professor called Schwarz apparently wrote a book on education in 1832 which set down exact plans for the care and 'meaning-ful occupation' of children between 3 and 6. We have not been able to find a copy to date. *Die Schulen in Nürnberg*, Fränkische Verlagsanstalt, Nürnberg, 1966.
3. *Die Menschenerziehung*, 1826. It appeared in English as translated by Josephine Jarvis, New York, 1885. W. N. Hailmann's translation followed, offering the work in abridged form, 1887.
4. During Froebel's formative years the Romantics had welcomed Brentano's publication, *Des Knaben Wunderhorn*, which collected three centuries of German poetry and lore; in *Youth's Magic Horn* the German Romantics breathed the 'fresh morning breeze of Old Germany' and its traditions.

Des Knaben Wunderhorn appeared in 1806-1808, and the brothers Grimm were working on their collection of tales at the same period. Grimm's *Märchen* appeared in 1822.

5. The meeting was recorded by Krause's son-in-law, von Leonhardi. It is worth repeating that this door into the early stage of life opened for Froebel *after* writing The Education of Man.

6. Jan Amos Komensky, 1592-1670. The *School of Infancy* was translated by E. M. Eller in 1956. There is a good summary of this influential thinker's works in John E. Sadler's *Comenius,* Collier Macmillan, 1969.

7. Burgdorf, 1835-1836. At Burgdorf Froebel encouraged yet another remarkable innovation: an open-air gymnasium for the boys, run by young Adolf Spiess, leading exponent of 'Pappa' Jahn's campaign for physical exercise and founder of gymnastics. It may give some indication of the originality of all this to note that gymnastics were recommended in Britain's Parliament by Lord Elcho thirty years later (1862), but rejected as 'a Continental practice of little value.' The Clarendon Commission compared physical exercise systems unfavourably with games as practised in the English public schools! They had missed the point somewhat: Lord Elcho was trying to benefit pauper children in industrial cities, not the sons of the landed gentry!

8. It was called simply the *Anstalt für Kleinkinderpflege* at first.

9. Usually referred to by her full title, which is rather cumbersome, Bertha, Freiin von Marenholtz-Bülow.

10. Adolph Diesterweg, 1790-1866. Diesterweg wrote about Froebel's work in journals published both in Berlin and Frankfurt.

11. *'Wholeness'*. Both the dominating concepts of nature and of wholeness, so important to Froebel, united in Goethe's response as a young man to the sight of Strasbourg cathedral, *'ganz, gross . . . wie Bäume Gottes'* ('whole and growing like the Lord's trees, living and undivided, not patched and pieced together').

12. Almost precisely the same view was expressed recently by Jean Chateau in France. See Chapter 6.

13. See Fletcher, *Froebel's Chief Writings on Education,* Edward Arnold, London.

14. Irene Lilley, *Friedrich Froebel: A Selection from His Writings,* Cambridge University Press, 1967.

15. See *Pedagogics of the Kindergarten,* trans. Jarvis, 1907, p. 144 *et seq.*

16. *Household Words,* 1855, reprinted in James L. Hughes' *Dickens as an Educator,* D. Appleton and Company, New York, 1906.

17. See Hanschmann's *Life of Froebel,* adapted by Fanny Franks under the title, *The Kindergarten System,* George Allen, London, 1897. Maria Montessori also claimed that the inspiration of her material came from observing children.

18. The implied castration threat has, of course, been pointed out by psycho-analysts. Hoffmann wrote these choice pieces as a Christmas entertainment for his three-year-old son!

19. Compare Tolstoy's observation in his essays on education (1862) 'The Spirit of Man,' say the Germans, 'must be broken in as the body is broken in by gymnastics' *('Der Geist muss gezüchtigt werden').*

20. See Morton Schatzmann, *Soul Murder: Persecution in the Family,* Allen Lane, London, 1973.

21. Jacob's *Manuel Pratique,* 1859.

Chapter 3

1. Robert Owen (1771-1858). The passage is from his Third Essay of *A New View of Society*, printed in 1814. It was not until 1816 that he opened the infant school in the Institution.

2. The school Owen visited was probably a school for the poor run by a Catholic priest called Father Girard.

3. R. Owen, *A New View of Society*, Third Essay, *passim*, London, 1814.

4. *Life of Robert Owen by Himself*, quoted Rusk, *A History of Infant Education*, University of London Press, 1933, pp. 133-4.

5. *Life of Robert Owen*, quoted Rusk, p.134.

6. A young village woman called Molly Young helped at first, according to Owen. It is unfortunate that more thorough records have not survived, although family records by the Buchanan family, unearthed by Rusk, help to give to James Buchanan more of the credit than Owen bestowed.

7. *An Outline of the System of Education at New Lanark*, Glasgow, 1824.

8. S. Wilderspin, *Early Discipline Illustrated*, Westley and Davis, London, 1832, pp.3-4.

9. There is a fascinating account of all this in Marion Lochhead's *Their First Ten Years*, John Murray, London, 1956.

10. See Lochhead, *Their First Ten Years*, pp.33-35. The little boy was Augustus Hare. He had neither toys nor playmates, but only a kitten. When an aunt who was 'kind' to him discovered his love for the animal it was taken away from him and hanged.

11. The *Swiss Family Robinson* by Wyss was an earlier island fantasy for children and marked a halfway point between Crusoe and Stevenson's masterpiece, having appeared in English in 1813. It lacked the genius of either Defoe or Stevenson, but still provided escape for Victorian children from morning prayer, Latin and Greek.

12. Publication of J. Gathorne-Hardy's fascinating book about the *Rise and Fall of the English Nanny* fills out our picture of Victorian childhood in much detail, seen from the point of view of upper middle-class families. One item of technological advance is too important to pass over in silence: in 1883, the Army and Navy Stores brought out a pram where 'for the first time, baby and Nanny face each other.' Here, indeed, is material for psychological research about stimulation! In our time, when mothers do their own pushing, the hardy new-style collapsible push-buggy represents a similar advance of great importance; since it can be slung quite easily over the parent's arm it is acceptable in car, bus, or tube-train, and so adds greatly to the freedom of movement allowed to mothers today. 'The Sociable Vis-à-Vis' pram was, after allowing for changes in currency value, also almost twice the price.

13. G. L. and Barbara Hammond, *The Town Labourer*, quoted Walter de la Mare: *Early One Morning in the Spring*, Faber and Faber, London, 1935.

14. We have drawn on de la Mare and Ariès, *Centuries of Childhood*, for some of these details.

15. On Public Health see especially G. M. Howe's *Man, Environment and Disease in Britain*, David and Charles, Newton Abbot, 1972.

16. Minutes of the Committee of Council on Education for 1853-4, pages 1088-9, quoted Rusk, *A History of Infant Education*, pp. 171-2.

17. See R. Sellmann, *Devon Village Schools in the 19th Century*, David and Charles, Newton Abbot, 1967.

18. Szreter, *The Origins of Full-Time Compulsory Education at Five* (B.J. Ed. St. Nov. 1964).

19.   From F.O. Mann's *Albert Grope*, quoted Raymont, *History of the Education of Young Children*, Longman, London, 1937, p. 242.
20.   Tessa Blackstone, *A Fair Start*, Allen Lane, London, 1971.
21.   G.A.N. Lowndes, *The Silent Social Revolution*, quoting Education Department Reports, 1894, 1895. In a few cases it is possible to pin-point the actual appearance of new attitudes: in 1882 a Nottingham inspector urged teachers to stress play and develop curiosity; kindergarten classes opened in the following year.

Chapter 4

1.   We owe a debt of gratitude to Monsieur Pierre Kergomard, great-grandson of the true founder of the *maternelles,* who lent a copy of the rare memoir of Pauline Kergomard written by her sons. As there is no biography at present available, we give here some of the childhood details in the life of this remarkable Frenchwoman.
2.   This later became the Cours Normal d'Institutrices de la Gironde.
3.   In her periodical, *L'Ami de l'Enfance*, 15 June 1883.
4.   *L'Éducation maternelle dans l'École*, Hachette, 1901, Vol. 1, p. 67.
5.   M. Lapie, speaking at the funeral ceremony for Pauline Kergomard in 1925. (Before she was appointed to the inspectorate, Fanny and Charles Delon had published their book on the Pestalozzi-Froebel method *(méthode intuitive)* which she certainly knew.
6.   This interesting letter was written in 1879. See Rambaldi, *L'École Publique Française.*
7.   From the instructions of 1887, which included in part the regulations of 1881 and 1882, and which were themselves modified in certain respects in 1895, 1905, and 1921.
8.   Gymnastics were also part of the *méthode intuitive* of Fanny and Charles Delon.

Chapter 5

1.   Jean Itard, 1775-1838. Itard also published the first scientific treatise on diseases of the ear and puncture of the eardrum.
2.   From Itard's first report, 1799.
3.   *Idiocy, and its Treatment by the Physiological Method*, New York, 1866, p.91.
4.   Ibid., pp.169-170.
5.   Ibid., pp.170-171. Compare the experience of Miss Janetta Bowie in a Glasgow Infant class during the Depression: 'All the failings are caused by lack of love. I used to think it was lack of leathering.' (Penny Buff, *A Clydeside School during the 'Thirties,* Constable, London, 1975).
6.   Décroly was writing in the *Revue Scientifique,* 1906.
7.   *The Montessori Method,* Heinemann, London 1915, p.87.
8.   *Early Childhood Education,* NSSE, Chicago, 1972, p.45. Marvin Lazerson's comment.
9.   'The importance of this period . . . has been largely lost sight of during the past 15 years, a fact due to the widespread influence of President Hall and his followers.' This was the opinion of an infant-education authority in 1912: it remained true of the state of affairs in America for many years thereafter.
10.   Giovanni Calo, in Jean Chateau, *Les Grands Pédagogues*, PUF, Paris, 1956.

Chapter 6

1. Johan Huizinga, *Homo Ludens*, Temple Smith, London, 1970.
2. Later psychologists like Stern and Bühler reclassified play in various patterns, as individual or social play, functional games, make-believe games and passive or constructive play. One is reminded of Richter's preliminary organization of the subject.
3. *Intellectual Growth in Young Children*, Routledge & Kegan Paul, London, 10th impression, 1970.
4. Ibid., p.33.
5. M. Klein, *The Psycho-analysis of Children*, trans. A. Strachey, Hogarth Press, 1932, 1969.
6. Mélanie Klein and Joan Rivière, Hogarth Press, London, 1967.
7. From Chateau's *École et Éducation*, VRIN, Paris, 1957.
8. See *Early Child Development*, Gordon and Breach, Vol. 1, no. 2.
9. The reminder of Froebel's insight is well put by Barbara Priestman, in *Froebel Education Today*.
10. Such books as Eva Noble's *Play and the Sick Child* (London, 1967) and Anne Marie Smith's *Play for Convalescent Children* (New York, 1961) deserve attention.
11. J. Alvin, *Music for the Handicapped Child*, Oxford University Press, 1965, 1973 and Philip Bailey, *They Can Make Music*, Oxford University Press, 1973.
12. Taken from Piaget's article on ECE which appeared in the *Encyclopédie Française*, Vol. XV :'Éducation et Instruction'.
13. As, for instance, the case described in Margaret Mead of a sixteen-year-old girl whipped and isolated for four hours until she agreed to say 'dear mama' at her father's behest. (*Childhood in Contemporary Cultures*, University of Chicago Press, 1955).
14. Miss Bärbel Inhelder wrote a valuable summary of Piagetian theory for publication in English in 1962. It is reproduced in Hans G. Furth's *Piaget and Knowledge*, Prentice Hall, 1969, which we recommend to the reader.
15. Henry W. Maier, *Three Theories of Child Development* (Erikson, Piaget, Sears), Harper International, 1969, p.140.
16. *Play, Dreams, and Imitation in Childhood*, quoted in Maier.
17. John L. Phillips, *The Origins of Intellect: Piaget's Theory*, W. H. Freeman and Co., San Francisco, p.61.
18. Piaget recently reported with naive pleasure Albert Einstein's reaction to the child's response: ' . . . he was quite delighted by the reactions of nonconservation, of children 4 to 6 years (they deny that a liquid conserves its quantity when it is poured from one glass into another of a different shape: "There is more to drink than before" etc.) and was greatly astonished that the elementary concepts of conservation were only constructed towards seven or eight years.'
19. See *Psychology and Epistemology*, trans. P. A. Wells, Penguin University Books, 1972.
20. Piaget is unmoved by the criticism that his conservation-stage is set too high (8 to 10 years) and appears much earlier in some other groups in, for instance, America. 'The important point in Piaget's position is that *order* tends to be invariant.' Hilgard and Bower, 1975, p.328.
21. See 'Bryant Replies on Piaget', *Times Educational Supplement*, 2 February 1972. Also *Nature*, August 1971, with T. Trabasso.
22. *Times Educational Supplement*, 11 February 1972. Professor Lunzer is Professor of Educational Psychology at the University of Nottingham.
23. 'Piaget, est-il dépassé?', *L'Éducation*, 25 April 1974.

Chapter 7

1. Near the original McMillan school in London's East End today are large blocks of 1935 vintage workers' flats, structurally sound, but scheduled for replacement because they lack central heating and hot water for the tenants.
2. M.B. Synge, Parl. Paper, Great Britain, 1909, Vol. xviii, pp. 40, 41, 42 and 106, 107. The observation shows how difficult was Madame Kergomard's task in recommending fresh methods to schools, for she explicitly recommended care for plants and animals as part of the moral training of the older pupil. (See *L'enfant de 2 à 6 ans*.)
3. Cf. Mme Naud-Ithurbide (*Les Écoles Maternelles*, PUF, Paris, 1964, p. 11). The *maternelle* 'sauf rares exceptions, s'infusa beaucoup moins qu'on ne le dit communément les idées nouvelles.'
4. Rénée Mouflard on the *Maternelles: Encyclopédie Francaise*, Vol. XV, 15-30 *et seq.*
5. Chukovsky, *From 2 to 5*, Moscow, 1956.
6. See *Enfance*, 1969, 1-2: 'Quelques remarques sur le contenu litteraire de l'enseignement préscolaire français.' A. Mareuil. Van Gennep, the folklorist, wrote in the *Revue Bleue* an estimate of the educational value of fairy-tales. (1921, no. 19.) Alain's remarks appear in Pléiade collection, p. 287.
7. Changes in modern France have been very well decribed by John Ardagh in his book *The New French Revolution*, Harper & Row, N.Y., 1969, from which this quotation was taken.
8. The private sector, although relatively small, had also increased, from 19,615 children in 1958 to 30,485 in 1969. It includes kindergarten *(jardins d'enfants)* and twenty Montessori schools, one of which takes pupils over five years of age.
9. For a report on the exhausting effect of expanding enrolments on overworked *Assistants* see Ida Berger's *Les Maternelles*, CNRS, Paris, 1959.
10. Mme Naud-Ithurbide, *op. cit.*, found that there was an almost static population of working women in France between 1921 and 1954 — between six and eight million according to sources.

Chapter 8

1. Quoted in *Margaret McMillan, The Children's Champion*, G.A.N. Lowndes, Museum Press, London, 1960, from a conversation with Cyril Burt.
2. D'Arcy Cresswell, *Margaret McMillan, A Memoir*, Hutchinson, London, 1948, p.141.
3. See 'The Open-Air Nursery School.' *The New Era*, 1930.
4. D'Arcy Cresswell, *Margaret McMillan, A Memoir*, p.140.
5. See Daiken's *Children's Toys Throughout the Ages*, B.T. Batsford, London, 1953.
6. See Selleck, *English Primary Education and the Progressives*, p. 41 *et seq.*
7. The Hadow Report has been republished by Cedric Chivers Ltd.
8. Secretary of State for Scotland, quoted by Margaret Drummond in her plea for the educational value of nursery schools. (*Contemporary Review*, April, 1919.)
9. In spite of the enlightenment spread by the progressives, it was still stated by the Board of Education in 1936 that 'Nursery schools have as their primary object the physical and medical nurture of the debilitated

child'. It is a fair justification for restricting nursery schools to a minority.

10. *The New Era*, July 1928.
11. Published by Routledge & Kegan Paul in 1930.
12. Routledge & Kegan Paul, 1933.
13. See Susan Isaacs, *Childhood and After, Some Essays and Clinical Studies*, 1937.
14. Evelyn Lawrence, quoted by D.E.M. Gardner, *Susan Isaacs*, Methuen Educational, London.
15. Taken from Susan Isaacs' pamphlet, *The Educational Value of the Nursery School*, 1937. Reprinted in *Childhood and After, Some Essays and Clinical Studies*. pp.47-73.
16. Blackstone, *A Fair Start*, p.149.
17. Lowndes, *Margaret McMillan*, p.94.
18. *Child Care and the Growth of Love* appeared originally in 1951 as *Maternal Care and Mental Health*, WHO, Geneva, Vol. 1, *Attachment*, and Vol. 2, *Separation, Anxiety and Anger* of a further study entitled *Attachment and Loss* followed in 1969 and 1973. A third volume – *Loss* – is in preparation. *Child Care and the Growth of Love*, Pelican Books, 1953, *Attachment and Loss*, Vol. 1, Pelican Books, 1969 *Attachment and Loss*, Vol. 2, Hogarth Press and the Institute of Psycho-analysis, London, 1973.
19. *Child Care and the Growth of Love*, Additional chapter 17.
20. See Bruno Bettelheim, *The Children of the Dream*, passim.
21. Maintained schools increased in number from 374 in 1946 to 480 in 1952. Thirteen years afterwards, there were still only 477. Over a similar period the number of *maternelles* in France rose from about 4,000 to 8,000.
22. See *Two to Five in High Flats*, Joan Maizels for the Housing Centre Trust, London, 1961.
23. Anthea Holme and Peter Massie, *Children's Play: A Study of Needs and Opportunities*, Michael Joseph, London, 1970.
24. See *The State of Nursery Education*, NUT, London, 1964.
25. See *The Importance of Playgroups in Education and the Social Services*, PPA, 1972.
26. DES, Circular 5174, December 1972.
27. As Edmund King pointed out in 1973. (*Comparative Education*, June 1973).
28. By the 1960s, however, Widlake reported that some positive results had begun to appear from the work of M.V. Harrold and N.H. Temple (no reference given) and J.W.B. Douglas and J.M. Rose ('Subsequent progress of nursery school children,' *Educational Research*, 7, pp.83-94).
29. Smilansky, Int. Rev. Ed. XVI, 1970, pp. 56-9.
30. Nanette Whitbread, *The Evolution of the Nursery-Infant School*, Routledge and Kegan Paul, London, 1972.
31. *11,000 Seven-Year-Olds*, (1966) and the more recent follow-up *From Birth to Seven* (1972) sponsored by the National Children's Bureau.
32. Prentice Hall, New York.
33. Lesley Webb, *Purpose and Practice in Nursery Education*, Basil Blackwell, Oxford, 1974.
34. Quoted in a Conservative party policy pamphlet in 1966.

Chapter 9

1. Taking public and private kindergartens together, there were in 1873, forty-two; in 1882, three hundred and forty-eight; in 1892, one thousand three hundred and eleven, and in 1898, four thousand three hundred and sixty-three. Of these, one thousand three hundred and sixty-five were public.

2. See, for instance, M.E. Findlay's article in *Child Life*, 1900.

3. Susan Blow, op. cit., p. 15.

4. Miss Owen returned in 1921 to lecture on the new nursery schools at Columbia University Teachers' College.

5. Pamphlets on child care have been made available by some government agencies, the editors point out. But these are the joint work of specialists, and contain combined views of professionals, not governmental attitudes. See Sections II, III: 'Conceptions of the Child and the Upbringing Process and 'The Compact Between the Family and Society.'

6. Yet the trend towards a kindergarten year for all five-year-olds falters in regions like the South-East where only half the total cohort was enrolled in the 1960s. See R.C. Nehrt and G.C. Hurd. Also Unicef *Carnets*.

7. Halbert B. Robinson and Nancy M. Robinson, *Early Child Care in the USA*, Gordon and Breach, 1973.

8. Cf. Ilse Forest, *The School for the Child from 2 to 8*, Boston, 1935.

9. Ellen Key, 1902, trans. 1909, G.P. Putnam & Sons, New York and London.

10. Cremin, *The Transformation of the School*, p.103 *et passim*.

11. He liked to tell the story of the visitor who said she had come to see the kindergarten; when told that they had not yet provided one, 'she asked if there were not singing, drawing, manual training, plays and dramatizations, and attention to the children's social relations. When her questions were answered in the affirmative, she remarked, both triumphantly and indignantly, that that was what she understood by a kindergarten, and that she did not know what was meant by saying that the school had no kindergarten.' *(School and Society,* 1899, Chapter V, Froebel's *Educational Principles.)* The Macmillan Co., New York, 1916.

12. There is an extensive literature on child development or all aspects of 'ECE'. A standard introduction to early childhood education cites some two hundred and fifty works for general reading, nearly all of them American in origin. If one turns to Mussen's *Handbook of Research Methods in Child Development* one can find a review of the situation as at 1960 in one thousand pages of selected readings from *General Research Methodology* to *The Study of the Child's Social Behaviour & Environment.* The same team has produced a revised *Manual of Child Psychology* in two volumes, the first of 1500 and the second of 830 pages, N.Y. and London, John Wiley, 1960. N.Y. and London, John Wiley, Revised, 1970. A more practical guide to *The Years Before School* supplies almost everything a parent or teacher might wish to know about pre-school matters: understanding the pre-school child, the curriculum in pre-school centres, parent participation and parent education are all treated helpfully with fine illustrations and excellent bibliographies for each topic (by Todd and Heffernan, The Macmillan Co., New York, 1964). Whatever is lacking in American pre-school education, it is certainly not adequate documentation and background reading for teachers and group leaders.

13. After reviewing the evidence, Hadfield wrote: 'there is therefore an optimum in maturation which, if we could discover it, is the best time

for giving such training and practice as we deem necessary.' The parallel with Froebel is obvious. (*Childhood and Adolescence*, 1962, p. 52.)

14. Kohlberg's essay appeared in Hoffman and Hoffman (ed.), *Review of Child Development Research*, New York, Russell Sage Foundation, 1964. For the contrary view see, for example, Madeleine Faure: *Le Jardin d'Enfants*, PUF, 1957, esp. chap. VI. Also, USSR *Program of Innovation*, p. 2. Present traits should be developed in the children.

15. In Western Europe there was nothing like this burst of research activity. In France, for example, although the universities admitted degree courses in psychology, there were still only two laboratories devoted to research in educational psychology by the late 1950s, and even non-specialist laboratories were few and far between. (Cf. Jean Chateau, op. cit.)

16. The ape was 7½ months, the boy 10 months when the experiment began. See W.N. and L.A. Kellogg, *The Ape and the Child*. Hafner Publishing Co., New York and London, 1933, 1967.

17. K. & C. Hayes succeeded in teaching their chimp, Vicki, to mouth 'mama', 'papa', and 'cup' in the 1940s. Allen and Beatrice Gardner taught 'Washoe' how to use American Sign Language; and Ann and David Premack at California University have furnished 'Sarah' with about 130 terms by using plastic shapes which each represent a word. Very little work, however, on the sounds chimps make in their natural environment.

18. Benton J. Underwood, 'Laboratory Studies in Verbal Learning,' in *Theories of Learning and Instruction*, Illinois, 1964.

19. See J. McV. Hunt (1961) *passim,* and Boyd's *History of Western Education,* p.409. Binet's *purpose,* it is now seldom recalled, was to locate retarded children in Paris schools in order to give them special education. 'Anyone's intelligence,' he had insisted, 'is susceptible to development.' See Theta H. Wolf, *Alfred Binet,* Chicago University Press, p.207 *et passim.*

20. World Book Co., New York.

21. N. Bayley: 'On the growth of Intelligence,' *American Psychologist,* 10, 1955.

22. See the interesting comments of Levine, in Miller (ed.) *Foundations of Child Psychiatry*. Pergamon, 1968.

23. Skeels published a follow-up report on the later lives of the orphans in 1966, indicating a higher adjustment to the demands of adult life by the control group. Both reports are, of course, criticized by psychologists on methodological grounds.

24. R.A. Spitz, 'Hospitalism, an inquiry into the genesis of psychiatric conditions in early childhood', cited Hunt, 1961, p.33. Technical defects were found in Spitz's study as they were in John Bowlby's argument published in England. The impression left on the lay public by Spitz, Skeels & Dye, and other research findings was probably unaffected by such criticism.

25. Hunt, *The Challenge of Incompetence and Poverty* 1969, p.47.

26. Hutt and Hutt, *Early Human Development,* Oxford University Press 1973. Bronson's report appears pp.85-109. Russian research has for a long time emphasised the importance of neurological investigation.

27. Cf Robinson and Robinson, *Health care, American style.* p.70.

28. *Early Child Care in the United States of America*, Gordon and Breach, 1973, pp. 130, 131.

29. See US Department of Health, Education, and Welfare, Summary Report, May 1970, *A national survey of the impacts of Head Start Centers on Community Institutions.* It is interesting to compare the UK Report, *From Birth to Seven,* 1972, 'Quite apart from their

education ethos, schools are middle-class institutions.'

30. 'How much can we boost IQ and scholastic achievement?', *Harvard Educational Review*, 39, i., 1969.

31. See 'Pre-School Programs for the Disadvantaged' (1974). Bereiter, C. and Engelmann, S., *Teaching Disadvantaged Children in the Pre-School*, Prentice Hall, 1966.

32. *The Cult of the Fact*, p. 133.

33. Ernest R. Hilgard, *The Place of Gestalt Psychology and Field Theories in Contemporary Learning Theory*, NSSE Yearbook, 1964. Hilgard observes justly that science, reviewed from this point, is not an unidirectional forward march.

INDEX